A Dictionary of Old English Music

Also from Westphalia Press

westphaliapress.org

The Idea of the Digital University

Criminology Confronts Cultural Change

Eight Decades in Syria

Avant-Garde Politician

Socrates: An Oration

Strategies for Online Education

Conflicts in Health Policy

Material History and Ritual Objects

Jiu-Jitsu Combat Tricks

Opportunity and Horatio Alger

Careers in the Face of Challenge

Bookplates of the Kings

Collecting American Presidential Autographs

Misunderstood Children

Original Cables from the Pearl Harbor Attack

Social Satire and the Modern Novel

The Amenities of Book Collecting

Trademark Power

A Definitive Commentary on Bookplates

James Martineau and Rebuilding Theology

Royalty in All Ages

A Short History of Medicine

The Man Who Killed President Garfield

Chinese Nights Entertainments: Stories from Old China

Understanding Art

Homeopathy

The Signpost of Learning

Collecting Old Books

The Boy Chums Cruising in Florida Waters

The Thomas Starr King Dispute

Salt Water Game Fishing

Lariats and Lassos

Mr. Garfield of Ohio

The Wisdom of Thomas Starr King

The French Foreign Legion

War in Syria

Naturism Comes to the United States

Water Resources: Iniatives and Agendas

Designing, Adapting, Strategizing in Online Education

Feeding the Global South

The Design of Life: Development from a Human Perspective

A Dictionary of Old English Music & Musical Instruments

by Jeffrey Pulver

WESTPHALIA PRESS
An imprint of Policy Studies Organization

A Dictionary of Old English Music & Musical Instruments

Westphalia Press
An imprint of Policy Studies Organization
1527 New Hampshire Ave., NW
Washington, D.C. 20036
info@ipsonet.org

ISBN-13: 978-1-63391-544-2
ISBN-10: 1-63391-544-1

Cover design by Jeffrey Barnes:
jbarnesbook.design

Daniel Gutierrez-Sandoval, Executive Director
PSO and Westphalia Press

Updated material and comments on this edition
can be found at the Westphalia Press website:
www.westphaliapress.org

A DICTIONARY OF OLD ENGLISH MUSIC

To those who planted an acorn and to her who tended the oak and had the courage to wait, this book in gratitude is dedicated.

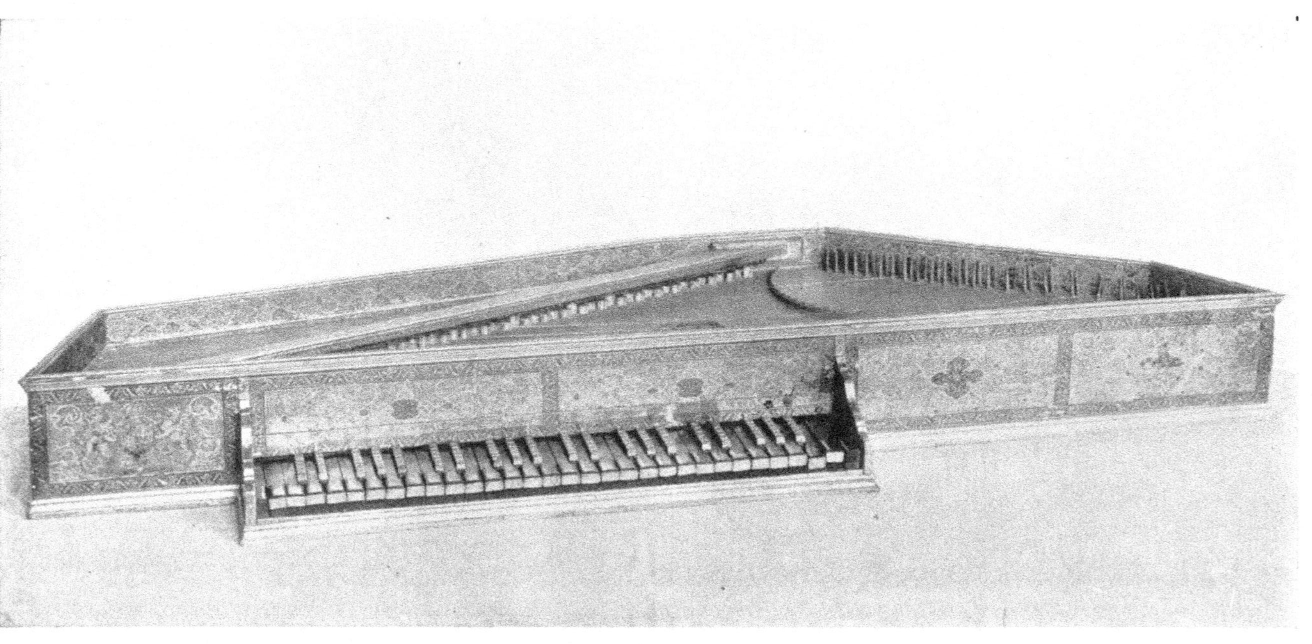

QUEEN ELIZABETH'S VIRGINAL
(*Victoria and Albert Museum*)

[*front.*

A DICTIONARY OF OLD ENGLISH MUSIC & MUSICAL INSTRUMENTS

BY

JEFFREY PULVER

"*Qui Satyros Musis praefert et Apollinis artes*
Spernit, is humanae nil rationis habet."

LONDON

KEGAN PAUL, TRENCH, TRUBNER & CO., LTD.

NEW YORK: E. P. DUTTON & CO.

1923

PREFACE

THE present revival of interest in our later Tudor and early Stuart music is the healthiest sign that English musicians could hope for. It is a revival of interest rather than a continuance only because Charles II, with his French tastes in music, commenced a cult of foreign art that was still more actively followed by the Hanoverians. Alien influence need not always be harmful; Elizabethan music would probably have been different, though not necessarily lower in quality, had the Netherlandish and Italian ingredients been wanting. What caused the break in the continuity of our national music was the intrusion of styles and manners alien to the British character and temperament, and hostile to the development of the native genius. We have outgrown the artificialities of the late Seventeenth and the Eighteenth Centuries, and most of us fear the possibly greater artificialities that may be called into being by the demand for something new in the coming generation. To save us from a return of the former, and to rescue our children from the latter, there is an antidote in the honesty of purpose, the plain directness of speech, the cleanliness of workmanship of the early Tudors; and the artistry, the poetry, the imagination, and the healthy, clean, but never weak, character of the writers active during the reign of the last sovereign of that virile house.

The revival of our ancient music has brought with it a vocabulary that needs some explanation; and while supplying the present-day musician with an account of the forms, instruments, and terms used by his forbears, a book of reference on this subject would also give to the student of literature contemporary with their music a source of information not always afforded in the glossaries attached to the modern reprints of our early writers' works.

There must be a great many readers of Chaucer's

> And pleyen songes on a small rubible;
> Ther-to he song som-tyme a loud quinible,

who have had to ask themselves, What is a Rubible, and what a Quinible? Perhaps an even greater number of present-day students of Shakespeare have been puzzled by such lines as, "Gamut I am, the ground of all accord," or "Then he's a rogue, and a passy-measures pavin." So also the music-student who has read the works of John Playford, Christopher Simpson, Thomas Mace, etc., must have encountered many expressions like Alteration, Hocket, Lyraway, Mutation, Naker, Organum, Prolation, Relish, and many others that have brought him to a standstill and cost him many a fruitless enquiry. It is to help such students of music and of our older literature that this book has been written.

While feeling the need for an apology on account of the unavoidable shortcomings of the present work, I also feel comforted by the thought that only the most unreasonable would expect a book of this magnitude to be all-embracing. After much consideration I decided that to include every word present in the vocabulary of the ancient musician would render the work a mere list of bare definitions. It has not been altogether easy to know which terms to omit, and to which the space thereby gained should be allotted. I am conscious of the fact that it would have been impossible to please everybody; for what one reader can afford to ignore, another finds most necessary to know. The plan I have followed was that of omitting such articles as have been adequately treated in the existing dictionaries, or in the standard text-books on harmony, counterpoint, form, etc. On this account such headings as Fugue, Counterpoint, and many others, find no place in the following pages, while many subjects not even mentioned in our most generally accepted Dictionary of Music have been included here. It is possible that musicians will think the inclusion of some of the terms unnecessary; these I would ask to be generous enough to allow space for the sake of the students of Tudor literature. A few subjects have been included that are neither specifically English nor obsolete. These have been added to assist in explaining other articles without the help of a further book of reference.

JEFFREY PULVER.

LIST OF ILLUSTRATIONS

A DICTIONARY OF
OLD ENGLISH MUSIC

ACCENT: In Plain-Song, the raising of the voice at a comma and its descent at a full stop, from the monotone on which the Lessons, Collects, Apostles, *etc.*, are read. The rules governing the proper accents for the comma, semicolon, colon, interrogation, and full stop having been learned, these parts of the divine service can be correctly rendered without the aid of books containing the music. The accents must be as old as the reading of the Scriptures and were doubtlessly suggested by, if not actually derived from, the practice of the Jews in their cantillation. Originating in the natural elocutionary desire to suggest finality at the end of a sentence and to give point to the sense of the text in other places, the accent was developed until the elements of true melody were evolved, and it was certainly varied until true recitative was arrived at. The accents used in Plain Song will be sufficiently familiar not to need illustration. Furthermore, accents varied and vary considerably in different churches and at different times, and thus a really full account of them cannot be given in a work of this magnitude. The so-called accents of the Jews, too, although handed down according to what is supposed to be unaltered tradition, vary in different countries and rites. Moreover, they differ from the Plain-Song accents in so far that they combine the whole of the Scripture-reading into a sort of chant to the general exclusion of monotone recitation.

A study of the accents used in Plain-Song is of the utmost importance, since they form a vital part in the history of notation in general; the signs used to express them having suggested the notes used later—first to determine pitch and later, after further development, value.

ACCORD: A term used in Elizabethan England to convey the sense of "harmony." The verb from which it was derived (Late Latin *accordare*, to agree) gave the Middle English *accorden*. Shakespeare, in *Taming of the Shrew* (iii. 1), has: "Gamut (*q.v.*) I am, the ground of all accord."

ACCORDANCE: An early name for a Tuning derived from the same source as Accord.

ACT-TUNE: A piece of entr'acte music in the Seventeenth Century was called an "Act-Tune" or "Curtain Tune," its function being to fill the interval during which the curtain obscured the stage. Before the end of the century such pieces were expressly written to suit each play, and a large number of very short airs labelled "Act-Tune" or "Curtain Tune" may be seen in the publications of John and Henry Playford.

ALMAIN: A dance-form originating, as its name implies, in Germany and coming to England *via* France where it was known as the Allemande. A good deal of uncertainty exists concerning its history, due, no doubt, to the confusion of different forms which, at various periods, were given the same name. This circumstance also must account for some authorities even asserting that the Allemande was not a true dance-form, and that it was never actually danced. In order, therefore, to understand fully the specimens written in England, it will be necessary to consider first the history of the various forms of the Almain abroad.

The original Allemande was in duple time, and in this measure it remained for the rest of its artistic career—until it ended as the opening movement of the Suite or Partita. Another form, which still survives in some parts of Germany (notably Suabia) and Switzerland, in the nature of a national dance, was in triple time. The two forms may have had nothing to do with one another; they may, on the other hand, have been both derived from a common source which had a duple and a triple form, as was the case with so many of the early dances. If the latter supposition is correct, the triple form followed the duple; and when the Courante rose in favour it usurped the place of the triple Allemande, leaving the duple form to continue alone. The Allemande and Courante (Almain and Coranto) were then used as a contrasting pair of forms which at first followed the Pavane and

Galliard (*q.v.*). When the latter pair became antiquated and the Saraband and Jig acquired popularity, the Allemande and Courante remained as the opening pair of forms in the Suite.

The typical Allemande was fairly simple in its harmonies, the melody (often highly ornamented) being kept to a single part. The semiquaver was the commonest time-value, and the dance commenced on the up-beat. The movement was generally moderate, but varied considerably in different countries. In common with the other dances of that era, the Allemande was sung as well as danced, and many examples with singing text are available in contemporary publications. Many specimens show much imagination and power of invention, but when the form ceased to be danced and became purely a piece of instrumental music, it lost many of its terpsichorean characteristics and became more sedate. Johann Mattheson said it reflected "a picture of a contented mind that delights in order and calm"; it was neither grave nor gay, neither slow nor quick. But "Allemandes to dance and Allemandes to play," said Mattheson, "are as different as Heaven and Earth." This must be borne in mind when we try to reconcile the Allemande of the Bach suite with the Almain of Shakespeare's England.

Exactly when the form originated on the Continent is not easy to decide; many specimens are to be found almost as soon as music-printing became common. And even at that early period some writers said that the form was already old and going out of fashion. Judging from Mattheson's remarks we must take it that the Allemande was still used as a dance in Germany while in France it had ceased to be danced, and was used only as an instrumental piece, before the middle of the Seventeenth Century (Mersenne, *Harmonie Universelle*, 1636). This statement is supported by the circumstance that the operas of Lully, Destouches, and Colasse, usually so rich in contemporary dance-forms, contain no Allemandes. The Suites of Marais, being purely instrumental music, provide several examples. Italy seems to have borrowed the form from France, and produced some specimens that are of a very high musical standard. Walther (*Lexicon*, 1732), as a truly patriotic German, asserted that the Germans excelled in the form, though Hawkins thought "this assertion rather too bold." The Allemandes of Corelli, Albinoni, and Geminiani, were "inferior to none we know." A glance at the Allemandes of Ariosti, Corelli, Vitali, Pergolesi, *etc.*, will prove the justice of Hawkins' claim. These Eighteenth-century writers, however, soon lost sight of the form's dance origin and wrote specimens that varied very much in treatment; Corelli, for example, composing Allemandes *Presto* as well as *Adagio*, and G. B. Vitali writing examples *Largo* and *Allegro.*

In England the dance, as such, enjoyed a very great vogue during the reign of Elizabeth. The music-books of the time contain a considerable number of specimens, and so popular did it become that its name is often mentioned in contemporary works. Shakespeare has it in *Hamlet*, and Ben Jonson in *The Devil is an Ass* (I. 1): "And take his almain leap into a custard." The Fitzwilliam Virginal Book contains Almains by such writers as William Byrd, Robert Johnson, and Thomas Morley. Elizabeth Roger's Virginal Book also includes it. The interesting set of books containing Anthony Holborne's "Pavanes, Galliards, Almains, *etc.*" (1599), gives two specimens. Further examples may be seen in Thomas Ford's *Musicke of Sundrie Kindes* (1607), in William Corkine's *Ayres to Sing and Play to the Lute and Basse Violl* (1610), in the second part of the same (1612), and in *Melothesia* issued by Matthew Locke (1673, Part II). These, of course, do not exhaust the enormous stock of pieces written in this form, but sufficient has been said to give the locality of examples should they be needed. In the English "Sets" or suites, the Almain became almost as popular as it did abroad, and J. Eccles, Jeremiah Clarke, William Richardson, D. Purcell, and Henry Purcell, to mention only a few of the better-known composers, contributed specimens of the Almain to the already rich literature of the form.

It is curious that a dance called "the German dance" should first be met with in France. I do not think that the Allemande had anything in common with the so-called *Deutscher Tanz.* The latter was generally in a triple measure, and was a favourite form with German composers. It was descended, in my opinion, from the Suabian (triple) form already mentioned, and the same source, no doubt, supplied the triple *Alemanas* of Merula and other non-German composers.

ALMAND. *v.* ALMAIN.

ALMOND. *v.* ALMAIN.

ALTERATION : In Mensurable Music (*q.v.*) a device employed to ensure the rhythm intended by the composer being retained. It occurred in the Perfect Mood and Time—*i.e.* in triple measures, and consisted of doubling the value of the second of two notes equal in themselves, but which do not total the contents of a perfect measure. For example :

would be performed :

Remembering that the Long in Perfect Mood (or triple measure) must contain three Breves, it is obvious that no music in a triple rhythm could be made out of the first example unless some such practice were resorted to. It is equally obvious that the longs in the quoted passage must all completely fill a bar (as we understand this term to-day), and thus nothing else could be done but alter the value of one of the breves ; and the canon of the early writers made it the second one. This breve was called an "altered breve." Supposing Alteration were not resorted to, the example above would have to be translated :

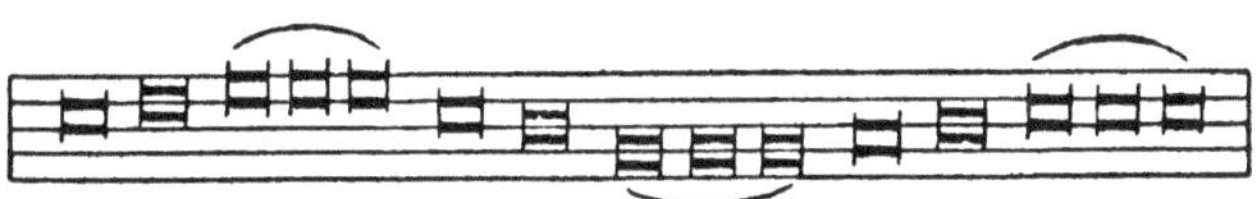

which does not give the rhythm indicated in the signature. In such a passage as the following :

the second of the two semibreves in the Ligature (*q.v.*) marked with the arrow would be altered to make :

The reason for interpreting the first ligature as marked at (x) will be found *s.v.* LIGATURES. It will be observed that despite the apparent complexity of the Alteration, it is really very simple, and resolves itself into nothing more formidable than this: If two notes which appear to be equal have to be made to fit a measure in triple time, one of them is doubled in value to secure this object. Naturally, if the note following the two equal ones is a similar note, no alteration will be needed, for the three together will equal the measure required:

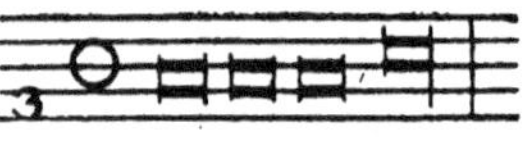

would be simply:

If a pair of semibreves were followed and preceded by longer notes there might have been a risk of misreading: and to avoid this a dot or a sign like a direct (√) was placed before them to indicate that the second of the semibreves was to undergo alteration, or, which is the same thing, that the breve before the dot comprised a complete measure in triple time:

was read:

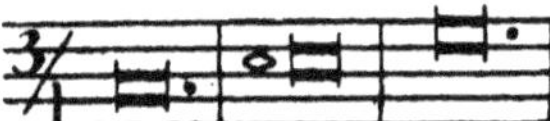

and not:

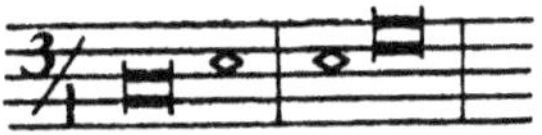

This dot or sign was called the *Punctum alterationis*, or "Point of Alteration" (*v. also* MOOD, TIME (*Tempus*), LIGATURES, *and* MENSURABLE MUSIC).

ALTUS: In old part-music, at a period when Latin designations were largely used, the term for the Alto voice or part.

AMBROSIAN CHANT: A modal system of chanting the divine service, organised and introduced, first in the Cathedral of Milan, by St. Ambrose (333–397). How far he himself based his chant on four of the older Greek modes (since called Authentic Modes), or how far he evolved his system directly from the tetrachords, cannot be determined. On his own evidence he appears only to have brought some existing manner of chanting into regular order. But the important and far-reaching effects produced by this organising of the hitherto vague and fluctuating methods of conducting the musical parts of the service, cannot be overlooked. Furthermore, Ambrose introduced many forms from the East and popularised antiphonal singing in the Western Church. Beyond this, to which a good deal of legendary matter is often added, very little is known of his work. It should be noted, however, that certain Ambrosian features were preserved in some districts even after the Gregorian system had become largely used, and the differences between the two methods may explain some otherwise puzzling remarks made by old writers. Whether we regard Ambrose as the inventor of a well-ordered, rhythmical, and dignified method of chanting, or merely as the organiser of existing traditions, he must certainly be considered the first great figure in the history of music in general, and in that of church-music in particular. Additional MS. 34,209 (British Museum) is a valuable Ambrosian antiphonary of the Twelfth Century, worthy of very careful study.

ANTHEM: Originally, as its name implies, the Anthem was a composition set to words taken from some part of the Scriptures (most commonly from the Psalms) and set in antiphonal manner. This latter characteristic was, however, soon overlooked, and the anthem as used in the Anglican Church became more in the nature of a motet or simply a sung form without any such distinguishing feature. The " Full Anthem " is entirely choral in treatment, while the " Verse Anthem " has as its chief feature soli, or maybe duets, trios, quartets, *etc.*, the choir frequently playing no greater part than that of supplying an overture and a coda. Other anthems contain both forms blended. Great freedom of treatment gradually entered, and by the time the great English musicians of the

Sixteenth and Seventeenth Centuries worked, the anthem had risen to a most important place in the church service of this country.

The anthem served another and highly important function in requiring the assistance of an instrumental accompaniment, especially in the " verses." Thus the flimsy support of a small organ (portative, positive, or regal) was gradually magnified by the addition of other instruments until the result was a very satisfying one musically. Wind music was added, and eventually the new violins, all-conquering, ousted both viols and cornets. Evelyn (*Diary*, December 21, 1662) says : " One of his Majesty's chaplains preached ; after which, instead of the ancient, grave, and solemn wind music accompanying the organ, was introduced a concert of twenty-four violins between every pause, after the French fantastical light way, better suiting a tavern or playhouse, than a church. This was the first time of change, and now we no more heard the cornet which gave life to the organ. . . ." By the time Handel was composing, the instrumentation of the accompaniment to the anthem had been expanded to include wood-wind and brass. This, of course, already foreshadowed the full orchestral support that later anthems were given.

The word *antym*, defined as *antiphona*, already appears in the *Promptorium Parvulorum* (1440), and is to be derived from the earlier *antefn* (*cf.* " biginneth thesne antefne," *Ancren Riwle*, *c.* 1230, *ed.* James Morton, Camden Soc.), its ultimate source being the Latin *antiphona*. Anthem is thus a doublet of Antiphon (*q.v.*), and, as we have seen, its earliest form was antiphonal. At the middle of the Sixteenth Century the service was concluded at the third Collect, and when the Anthem came to be adopted as an integral part of English divine worship, it took its place after this. Some of the greatest of native composers have left work in this form, and perhaps one of the best methods of studying the vocal writing of Tudor and Stuart England is in a careful analysis of the anthems of Tallis, Tye, William Byrd, and Orlando Gibbons among the earlier writers ; of John Blow, Jeremiah Clarke, Henry Purcell, Pelham Humphreys, Wise, *etc.*, in the middle period ; and of Boyce, Attwood, Battishill, and others too recent and too well-known to need naming. The earliest specimens are generally " Full " ; choral work was excellent in that age, and the talents of the writers of the period lay in that direction. The "Verse" anthem became more popular as the solo voice was developed and written for in a more virtuose manner; the increased instrumental support, also, made the solo anthem more acceptable. Men like Humphreys cannot but have been influenced by French customs, and this circumstance, added to the predilection of the second Charles for all things French, may have had a good deal to do with the later tendency.

ANTIPHON: One of the earliest forms used in rendering the Psalms, in which two half-choirs sang alternately as in response to one another; a form probably introduced into Europe from the Eastern Church by Ambrose, Bishop of Milan. Another class of antiphonal singing consisted of a solo voice alternating with choral responses. Later the two uses were kept less distinctly apart, and gradually they merged into one. The Antiphon, without doubt, had its origin in the psalmody of the Jews.

ANTIPHONAL: The book containing the antiphonary music of the Mass. Another collection bearing the name was the one containing the service of the Hours (*Antiphonale Officii*). Later the two terms became hopelessly mixed. After a period of careless nomenclature, the last-named book came to be called the Antiphonal, while the Mass music was given in what became known as the Gradual (*q.v.*). An alternative name in England was *Antiphoner*, and thus it is to be found in the correspondence between Cardinal Wolsey and the sixth Earl of Northumberland when the former requisitioned the books belonging to the fifth Earl. One of Northumberland's letters contains the passage: "I do perceaff my Lorde Cardinall's pleasour ys to have such Boks as was in the Chapell of my lat Lord and ffayther. . . . I am conformable, notwithstandinge I trust to be able ons to set up a Chapell off myne owne. I shall with all sped send up the Boks unto my Lords Grace, as to say iiij Antiffoners, such as I think wher not seen a great wyll, v. Gralls (Graduals), *etc.*"

Chaucer already uses the word Antiphoner in the Canterbury Tales:

> He *Alma redemptoris* herde singe,
> As children lerned hir antiphoner. (*Prioresses Tale, l.* 1708).

And in the *Promptorium Parvulorum* (1440) we find the form *Antyfenere* defined as *Antiphonarius.*

ANTIPHONER. *v.* ANTIPHONAL.

ARCH. *v.* HOLD.

ARCH-LUTE : A bass-lute of large size (some specimens being over six feet in height), rendered rather cumbersome by its great length. As in the Theorbo, the Arch-lute had the ordinary fingered strings running over the fingerboard and the extra bass strings (plucked open) at the side, and operated from a second peg-box situated at the end of a long extension of the first peg-box. This arrangement gave the bass strings a tremendous length, and consequently gravity of tone. It was used as the bass of the consort, and as an accompanying instrument we find it made and used after the middle of the Eighteenth Century. Its tone and effect were distinctive and no keyboard instrument could really replace it ; but the difficulties inherent to strings of such length and such great numbers, were responsible for the eclipse of this member of the lute family by the mechanically-plucked instruments—the spinet and the harpsichord. The arch-lute was the *Chitarrone* of the Italians, and it was often elaborately ornamented, some specimens having three sound-holes grouped in the form of a triangle.

ARE, or A-RE. *v.* GAMUT.

ARETINIAN SYLLABLES : The initial syllables of the lines of a stanza to St. John used by Guido d'Arezzo (Guido Aretinus) as a help to the memory in learning the notes and intervals in Solmisation (*q.v.*). The ascription of this verse to Guido has been alternately granted and denied ; but on the evidence contained in a letter of this great musical reformer, it is clear that he used it ; and there is no reason for denying him the honour of this invention. The hymn reads :

> *Ut* queant laxis *re*sonare fibris,
> *Mi*ra gestorum *fa*muli tuorum,
> *Sol*ve polluti *la*bii reatum,
> Sante Johannes.

It was used for the purpose indicated in the early years of the Eleventh Century. The music to which this text was set, was so arranged that the notes falling to the syllables *Ut*, *Re*,

ARCHLUTE

By Rauche, Chandos Street, London

(Victoria and Albert Museum)

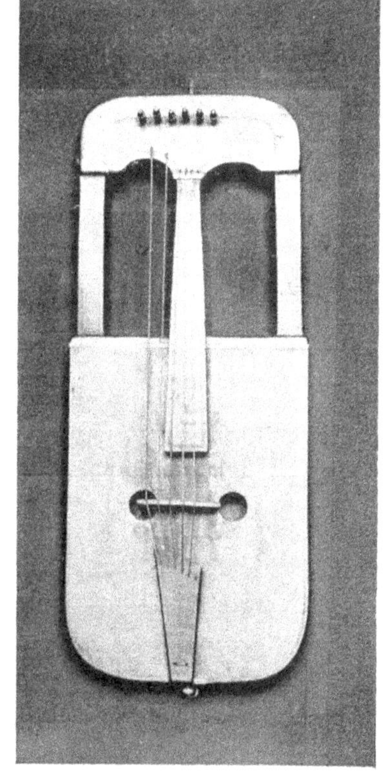

CRWTH

18th Century Welsh

(Victoria and Albert Museum)

[*face p.* 10

Mi, etc., were those which received these names (*v. also* GAMUT *and* SOLMISATION).

ASPIRATION : An obsolete ornament consisting of the written note preceded by the notes below and above it in rapid succession. It is not included in Playford's or Christopher Simpson's list of "graces," and was used only in music imported from the Continent of Europe.

AUGMENTATION : 1. In Mensurable Music, the reverse of Diminution, and most commonly used to restore a composition, halved in note-value by the latter, to its original state (*v.* DIMINUTION, 1).

2. In contrapuntal music the reintroduction of a subject in notes that are double the value of those in the original version (*cf.* DIMINUTION, 2).

AUTHENTIC MODES. *v.* CHURCH MODES.

AYRES : Melodies for which the composers of the Sixteenth and Seventeenth Centuries could not easily find suitable titles, were often simply dubbed Airs or Ayres. A large number of publications appeared in Seventeenth-Century England with no other title than "Book of Songs and Ayres," or "Ayres and Dialogues," and often the word was employed as a synonym for Canzonet. In purist quarters the term was more narrowly applied, and there the Ayre was supposed to have the melody confined to one part or voice. The Ayre, to live up to the requirements of the academics, had to be a tune for any voice or instrument provided with a simple accompaniment. The chief interest in the composition was to lie in the solo-part, and not in the way the composer could reintroduce the melody in the other parts of the harmony. The accompaniment to the Ayre was thus comparatively unimportant; and in this form the composition can be looked upon as the beginning of the modern "ballad," where the melody, such as it often is, counts for everything not covered by the stupidly sentimental words, while the accompaniment is valued at next to nothing.

BACKFALL : An obsolete ornament of a very simple nature. John Playford (*Introduction to the Skill of Musick*) gives it as follows :

A Double Backfall was a variation of this :

A Backfall Shaked was a frequentative of the ordinary Backfall :

The sign for this ornament (as given by Playford) was the same as that for the ordinary Backfall, and the choice of interpretation was probably left to the taste of the performer.

BAGPIPE : An exceedingly ancient wind-instrument, having been used as early as the classic days of Greece and Rome. In principle the Bagpipe is fairly simple. It consists of a leather bag, or air-container, which is filled from the mouth of the performer by means of a tube. A second tube, termed the Chanter (or Chaunter), emerges from the bag and is in principle nothing but a sort of Shalm with finger-holes and double-reed. Two or three additional pipes (with single reeds) provide a persistent drone bass, and are called *drones* or *bourdons.*

The Scotch Bagpipe has three drones which sound continuously, tuned in various ways, but nearly always containing a fifth between two of them. Some Scottish publications give the tuning as two G's (an octave apart) for the highest and lowest of the drones, with a D between them ; while others mention the tuning D and its octave with an intermediate A. The chanter has eight holes, seven in front stopped with the fingers, and one at the back of the pipe for the thumb. The series of notes produced are contained within a compass of an octave and a note, but they are tuned to no particular scale, nor is their intonation perfect. The Irish bagpipe is of very great antiquity, there being references to it in manuscripts dating from the Fifth Century.

The French form of the instrument was known as the *Cornemuse*, a word frequently used early in the history of English literature. The Encyclopedia of De Felice (1772) says that the *Chalumeau* (Shalm or chanter) had eight holes, one being underneath for the thumb; that the *gros bourdon* was an octave below the *petit bourdon*, and the small drone an octave below the chanter when all the holes were closed, and a fifth below when all the holes were open. The *Musette* was of similar construction and effect, but had the bag (which in the Eighteenth Century was often covered with silk and elaborately embroidered) filled from small bellows under the arm of the player instead of through a mouthpiece.

Many references to the bagpipe are to be found in the works of our early writers, but one or two examples will suffice to illustrate the use of the word. Chaucer has it in the *Canterbury Tales:*

> A baggepipe wel couthe he blowe and soun,
> And therwithal he brought us out of toun. (*Miller's Tale.*)

The household expense-book of a Fifteenth-Century nobleman contains the entry: "To him that played upon the bagpipe . . . xd."

BALLAD: A form of vocal composition that was developed from the song accompanying the dance in ancient times. Derived from the Late Latin (and Italian) *ballare*, to dance, through Provençal (Fourteenth Century) *balada*, a dancing-song, and Old French *balade*, the word was used by Chaucer (*Legende of Goode Women*, 1385) in the last-mentioned spelling:

> This balade may ful wel y-songen be. (*l.* 270),

and by Gower in *Confessio Amantis* (1393):

> And ek he can carolles make,
> Rondeal, balade and virelai. (*l.* 2708/9, *Lib.* I.)

The spelling *ballet* is from the Italian form *ballata* (from the same source), Milton having Ballats and Ballatry in *Areopagitica.*

It will be seen from the articles dealing with most of the ancient dance-forms that the earliest dances had vocal accompaniments, and these rhythmic pieces, when sung alone, were the first ballads. The Troubadours and Minstrels of the Middle Ages, singing of romantic and historical events, were clearly influenced by this form, and their generally improvised music followed the same lines. Later on the same class of text was used, wedded to music written with greater freedom, and the ballad which became so popular in England was evolved.

Indeed, it is not too much said if we assert that the minstrels who composed these early ballads saved from oblivion many romantic legends and preserved many an historical fact. The state of music in England from the Eleventh Century to the Sixteenth, although varying with the period, was always of a comparatively high standard, and there is no reason for doubting that the more modern ballad owes its existence to the further development of the work of these early musicians. The term was applied to compositions of very varied character, and Coverdale (1535) even calls the Song of Songs " Salomon's Balettes."

From the Eighteenth Century onwards, the ballad gradually degenerated, until it bore no resemblance whatever to the fine work of earlier times. Some excellent examples of the form were written on the Continent during the Nineteenth Century, but in England any maudlin text and any childish music, especially to-day, seems to be sufficient to qualify the joint production to use the term " Ballad." This decadence is to be deplored, since a really good romantic or historical text could give composers a splendid opportunity for vocal work of the highest class.

BALLAD OPERA : An essentially English production consisting of spoken dialogue interspersed with songs having a bearing upon the action. The peculiarity of these songs, and the feature which differentiates the Ballad Opera from the ordinary English Opera, lay in the fact that no special music was composed for them, and that they were adapted to existing tunes of a popular, and often traditional, character. They belong exclusively to the first half of the Eighteenth Century, and although a long succession of similar works followed the successful performance of the first—*The Beggar's Opera*—a success that probably caused the creation of the others—none made the same appeal to the public taste. Pope tells us how the idea of such an opera grew. Swift once remarked to Gay what a quaint notion a play in a Newgate setting would be. The latter thought the matter over for some time, and eventually decided to use the plan for a comedy, a procedure that did not win Swift's approval. Gay, however, persisted ; and when the finished work was shown to Swift and Pope, they both thought sufficiently well of it to offer slight hints for its betterment, although neither thought that it had much chance of success. It was laid before Congreve, who said it "would either take greatly or be damned confoundedly." Dr. Pepusch supplied an overture and accompaniments to the tunes. What Eighteenth-century Burney thought of the melodies need not be gone into here; but he considered Pepusch's "basses so excellent that no sound contrapuntist will ever attempt to alter them." Later producers, however, did alter them. The songs were set to such tunes as: "An Old Woman Cloathed in Gray," "Why is Your Faithful Slave Disdained?" "O, London is a Fine Town," "Thomas, I Cannot," "Pretty Polly Say," "Over the Hills and Far Away," "Fill Every Glass," "Lilliburlero," "Bonnie Dundee," "Old Simon the King," "Greensleeves," "Lumps of Pudding," and many others familiar to all who have looked through Elizabethan and Stuart music-books.

The opera was first performed on January 29th, 1728, and the Gay, Swift, and Pope coterie watched its fortunes with much trepidation. When the Duke of Argyll, who occupied the neighbouring box, was heard to say, "It will do—it must do! I see it in the eyes of them," the success of the *Beggar's Opera* was assured. Pope says that the "good nature of the audience appeared stronger in every act, and ended in a clamour of applause." It had an unprecedented run for those days, and did as well in the Provinces and Colonies. Soon the craze for the *Beggar's Opera* amounted to a mania, and at every turn allusions to it were to be met with. The heroine of the period was Lavinia Fenton, who played the part of Polly; she was fêted and petted; written about; talked about; and rose from the position of an actress with fifteen shillings a week to the dubious celebrity of being the mistress of the Duke of Bolton and eventually, on the death of the Duchess twenty-three years later, his wife.

The success of this work was due in some measure to the love of burlesque and satire that marked this era, and many political allusions were made. An excellent account of the whole story of the Ballad Opera is given by George Hogarth in his *Memoirs of the Musical Drama* (1838), a writer to whom I am indebted for much information on this subject. The opera was first offered to Cibber of Drury Lane and refused, a circumstance that made of Rich (Covent Garden) a richer man.

Puritanical minds thought that the glorification of a highwayman and his escape unpunished at the end, would damage public morals, and an attempt was made in 1777 to produce the *Beggar's Opera* with an ending that shows Macheath undergoing hard labour in a contrite spirit. The public, however, did not approve of the change, and as Hogarth says: "the piece was damned accordingly."

The fortunes of the *Beggar's Opera* encouraged Gay to write a sequel called *Polly;* but its success was not nearly so great, nor was the work so good. A long list of subsequent works of this kind can be seen in Hogarth's book already mentioned, and in a note of Rimbault's to North's *Memoires of Musick.*

BANDORA, BANDORE. *v.* PANDORA.

BARBER'S MUSIC. *v.* CITTERN.

BARRING: Before the introduction of the bar, or the line which crosses the stave to divide a composition into periods of equal length, music was measured according to the rules which governed the relative values of the notes (*v.* MENSURABLE MUSIC). In order to facilitate the reading of such music, the *punctum divisionis*, or "Point of Division," was evolved and used to indicate in doubtful cases the point at which the rhythmic figure of what we should to-day call a measure was completed (*v.* POINT OF DIVISION). With the laws relating to Alteration (*q.v.*) in force, some such device as the Point of Division was necessary to prevent a rhythm being given to the music that was not intended by the composer. And it was in all probability this point of Division that first suggested the bar.

The first attempt at a bar appears to have been a v-shaped mark, or one or more oblique lines to show the end of a strain of music; but no attempt seems to have been made to subdivide these sentences into smaller measures all equal to each other. Butler (*Principles of Musick,* 1636) called this "single" or "lesser" bar, an "imperfect close." When dealing with counterpoint Butler says that the composer should "divide each strain with a dubble cros-bar drawn straight through all the four lines; and subdivide them in the middle with a single bar." In Tablatures, it should be mentioned, bars were used very early, and may have been transferred thence to ordinary notation. The use of bars was very irregular for more than a century. We meet with the line printed in for each measure very early in some works, and absent in others a hundred years later. Generally speaking, the early examples are in score, the common use of the bar for single voice-parts being of much later date. Scores were barred irregularly at the commencement of the Sixteenth Century (*v.* Rastell's Interlude of the *Four Elements*, 1519). It was not until the middle of the Seventeenth Century that we meet with publications properly barred throughout, and Henry Lawes enjoys the honour of producing a work thus distinguished. His *Ayres and Dialogues* of 1653 is fully barred, while the *Choice Psalms*, in which he collaborated with his brother William five years earlier, is still unbarred. Morley, using bars in his scores (1597), left the single parts unbarred. There were English music-books printed as late as 1652 which were still innocent of bars. The 1697 edition of Playford's *Introduction to the Skill of Musick* mentions " a bar containing six crotchets," showing the wrong use of the word " bar " where " measure " is meant, to be very ancient.

BARS, *or* *BARRS :* In addition to the usual application of this term—to the lines which divide a piece of music into equal measures—it was used in the Seventeenth Century to name the strips of wood employed to support the belly of the lute, and to keep it taut and straight.

BARYTONE : A bass-viol strung with six or seven strings played with the bow, and a variable number of metal strings which passed under the others and through a double neck. The last-mentioned strings vibrated sympathetically with the bowed strings, and they were also sometimes plucked with the left thumb. The barytone enjoyed considerable popularity, and was to the bass-viol players what the *viola d'amore* was to the tenor violists.

BASE : 1. The Old English spelling for " Bass," or lowest part of the harmony.

2. The word Base was frequently used as a colloquialism for Bass-Viol or Viola da Gamba. In the Lord Chamberlain's Records, for example, we read of a payment of " £12 for a base " (*Vol.* 738, *p.* 174, February 20, 1629–30).

BASE VIOL. *v.* VIOLS.

BASE VIOLIN: A term often applied in the Seventeenth Century to the violoncello, and not to be confounded with Bass-Viol.

BASS STRING: The lowest string on the viols and the unfingered strings of the lutes. From the circumstance that the bass string produced the lowest note that was obtainable on a viol, Shakespeare took the metaphor: "I have sounded the very base-string of humility" (*I Henry IV*, II, 4).

BASSUS: The bass-part in old polyphonic music was often given the Latin form of the name, *bassus*.

BASS VIOL. *v.* VIOLS.

BEAR A PART: A common expression in Elizabethan and Stuart England meaning "to play an instrument in a consort," or "take part in a polyphonic vocal-composition." It was a figure of speech in everyday use in an age when playing and singing correctly at sight were two of the indispensable virtues of the cultured members of society. That celebrated pamphlet of Roger L'Estrange (enthusiastic amateur gambist and Licenser of the Press), *Truth and Loyalty Vindicated*, 1662, contains a typical example of the use to which the phrase was put: "I . . . found a Private company of some five or six Persons. They desired me to take up a Viole, and bear a Part."

BEAT: An ornament like a reversed Backfall. John Playford (*Introduction to the Skill of Musick*) explains it thus:

Christopher Simpson (*Division-Violist,* 1659) gives "Plain-Beat" and "Rise" as synonymous terms.

A more elaborate variety of the Beat was the Shaked Beat, given by the same two authorities as follows:

BEGGAR'S OPERA. *v.* BALLAD OPERA.

BERGOMASK: Why Shakespeare should make Bottom offer

the Duke " a Bergomask dance between two of our Company " (*Midsummer Night's Dream*, V, 1) would be difficult to explain did we not know something of its early history. It was a dance-form of a rustic nature, and originated among the peasants of that part of Lombardy which had Bergamo for centre. These peasants had the reputation—whether deserved or not, I cannot say—for being the most unsophisticated people known; and this probably explains Shakespeare's direction in the scene already mentioned: " Here a dance of Clowns."

The form seems to have had its inception in a song peculiar to the district, and which was used to accompany the dance it named. Two specimens of such airs are contained in the *Villote del Fiore* (*Bk.* III, 1569) of Filippo Azzajuoli, words and music being given. Uccellini's Two and Three-Part Sonatas (1642) give the Bergomask as an instrumental piece. Here it appears that the tune has been taken as a Ground, labelled " Aria sopra la Bergamasca," and supplied with a number of variations over a *basso ostinato.*

As a dance the Bergomask consisted of an even number of measures, generally multiples of four, and, according to most authorities, in 2/4 time. Variations in the time-signature may have existed, but two beats to the measure seems to have been the commonest indication. The example written by Piatti, the celebrated violoncellist, himself a native of Bergamo, is usually accepted as being typical of the orthodox form, though its time-signature is 6/8. Mendelssohn, writing the music for the " dance of clowns " in *Midsummer Night's Dream*, gives it a different form and treats it with poetic freedom.

The circumstance that the Bergomask was not used at Court in any country may account for the paucity of examples printed; but as absolute music for the lutes and viols, it enjoyed a certain vogue for a time. Used in the country of its origin it was most probably danced to traditional tunes that may never have been written down. A specimen " Bergamasco " in lute tablature is given in J. B. Besarde's *Thesaurus Harmonicus* (1603), and reprinted in modern notation by Dr. O. Chilesotti (Ricordi, 1886).

B-FA.
B-MI. } *v.* CLIFF, FLAT, *and* SHARP.

BOMBARD, BOMBARDE: A wood-wind instrument of conical bore, played with a double reed, and the bass of the shalm, or early oboe, family. This instrument was identical with the Continental *bass-pommer*, but should be kept distinct from the modern brass instrument with valves called Bombardon. The wooden bombarde is of great antiquity, and is found illustrated almost as early as any of the shalms. In Gower's *Confessio Amantis* (end of the Fourteenth Century, VIII, *l.* 2481, 2) there is a reference to it:

In such acord and such a soun
Of bombard and of clarion,

and in the *Squyr of Lowe Degre* (*l.* 1072) the " Bumbarde " is mentioned. It should be noted that on the Continent the word Bomhart or Pommer was applied to several members of the shalm family, each distinguished by a prefix indicating the pitch; even the shalm was occasionally called the Bombardino (*v. also* SHALM).

BORE: A dance that attained to great popularity in England. There can be no doubt that the statement of Hawkins—" the Bourrée seldom occurs but in compositions of French masters " —has misled a great many readers. The fact is that a large number of Bourrées, or Bores as they were more generally called here, can be cited, composed both before and after the date at which Hawkins wrote. Some of them, it is true, were but reprints of foreign examples, but as soon as the dance became better known the native musicians speedily supplied original music for it. Musically the Bore usually consisted of the common form containing two repeated sections of four or a multiple of four measures each, and marked with a *caesura* every two measures to adapt it to the steps of the dance. Its rhythm was dactylic (an accented crotchet followed by two quavers), and the first and third beats of each measure received marked stress. Altogether the accentuation was rather vehement, assisted as it was by the stamping of saboted feet. According to the almost common rule, the dance was frequently accompanied by voices, and in general it may be said that the form was originally a very gay one, eminently suited to rustic sports. That the Bore ever became a fashionable dance abroad is very doubtful, although later in its history society dancing-masters published chorography for it.

Its popularity in England began at the middle of the Seventeenth Century, and three specimens of it are to be seen in John Playford's *Musick's Delight on the Cithren* (1666), called " Bore," " Boree," and " The Running Boore," the last-named being reprinted in the same publisher's *Musick's Hand-Maide* (1678). By the end of the century a large number of French specimens had been imported, and many of them were included in the " French dances used at Court, and in the Dancing Schools," given by Playford in his *Apollo's Banquet* (1690). It was at about this period that the English composers began to imitate the French productions, and soon a large number were available for use. Typical examples of the form at that period in England are given by Humphrey Salter in his *Genteel Companion for the Recorder* (1683), one called " Mr. Farmer's Borey." A printed book in the British Museum (K. 1, c. 5) contains a " Borry " in manuscript by Henry Purcell. It persisted until the Eighteenth Century, being mentioned by Swift: " From thence came all those monstrous stories that to his lays, wild beasts danc'd borees " (*Ovidiana*). Tomlinson described it in 1726 and gave the steps for it. Even when the dance itself fell out of favour, the *pas de bourrée* remained for use in other dances. Handel often uses the name, and *arie* of his are to be found headed *Tempo de Bourrée.* Its eclipse as a dance did not cause the complete disappearance of the form, for it was still used as an instrumental piece in the Suite, where it occupied the place between the Saraband and Jig usually filled by the guests of the Partita (the *Intermezzi*).

The Bore is generally accepted as a native of the Auvergne, though Taubert, and after him, F. L. Schubert, thought the Spanish province of Biscaya to have been the birthplace of the form. The earliest examples I have been able to trace come from the French province, although the possibility remains, of course, that it was evolved from an earlier Biscayan dance. Both may conceivably have had a common origin in one of the forms of the Branle (*q.v.*), or in one of the local modifications of that dance. In any case, the Bourrée was still being danced in the Auvergne when Rousseau wrote his *Dictionary of Music* in 1764, and De Felice his *Encyclopedia* in 1770. Later writers assert that in Central and South France the form is used at the present day, but how far the old traditions connected with it have been preserved, I cannot determine.

The vigorous character and forceful rhythm of the Bourrée caused it to be used very frequently in the French opera, more as incidental music than specifically for dancing. Lully's ballets and operas contain it very often, and Marais, Destouches, and Rameau all welcomed it in their works.

Taken into the German suite towards the end of the Seventeenth Century, the Bourrée was naturally treated with greater freedom than was the case when it was written for dancing. Some writers, while using the rhythm of the form, entirely forgot its dance-origin. The *Florilegium Primum* (1695) of Georg Muffat contains a Bourrée in each of six suites, all in regular form; while the second series of Suites by the same composer (1698) gives another two, one of them an imitation of a French example. In these works, too, we meet with the phrase *Tempo di Borea*, showing that the dance had been so far accepted as to cause the rhythm and movement to be applied to other pieces. Johann Krieger (1697), Niedt (1706), and Johann Mattheson, followed, and the form became thoroughly naturalised in Germany. Bach's use of it proves how much the form had been developed on the Continent, and some of his examples are typical of the manner in which the great Cantor of Leipzig used the ancient dance-forms. In its final development, as exemplified in Bach's work, the Bourrée consisted of Bourrée I, followed by Bourrée II, and closed with Bourrée I da Capo. The Italians also used the form, though in not nearly so popular a manner as the English did, nor in so dignified a way as the Germans. G. B. Vitali (*Balli in Stile Francese*, 1685) and Corelli (*Opera Quarta*, 1692) may serve as typical writers of the Italian "Borea"—although the former frankly imitated the French style.

BOREA *v.* BORE.

BOREE. *v.* BORE.

BRALL. *v.* BRANLE.

BRANLE: A French dance-form, much in favour during the Sixteenth and Seventeenth Centuries, especially in England, and one of the ancestors of musical form. The name was derived from the French *branler*, to sway, and no doubt the form itself took origin in one of the uses of the Bassedanse, in which the movement of the body may have named the dance. This Bassedanse seems to have been the progenitor of practically all the European dances, and having been evolved so early in the history of music, we cannot be astonished if we find a lack of consistency in its form. Whatever the reason—whether terpsichorean or other—the fact remains that the Bassedanse of the early Sixteenth Century was often to be found written in duple and triple time, the choice being apparently left to the whim of the dancer, who frequently changed from one measure to the other, according to the steps of his dance. This question of the early dances *à double emploi* is a very interesting one. But to return to the Branle. Evolved and developed in France, we find it mentioned there as early as 1529 (Antonius de Arena), and in 1588 Jean Tabourot (Thoinot Arbeau) gave a good deal of information concerning it in his *Orchèsographie.* According to most descriptions it was danced in a circle as a round-dance, and was called by Rousseau, Furetière, and other French lexicographers an air *en Rondeau.* Like most of the ancient dances, the Branle was sung as well as danced, was of gay character, moderate tempo, and, latterly at any rate, of duple measure. Examples in triple time are not unknown; notably Mersenne (*Harmonie Universelle,* 1636) gives specimens in 3/2, but by then the form had been widened into a sort of ballet, and between these triple Branles and the triple form the dance had very early in its history there can be no connection. The reigns of Louis XIII and XIV saw the Branle in universal use. At court the form became a dance of ceremony, and for some time it served to open every ball of importance.

Germany and Italy did not seem much attracted towards the dance, but England received it with open arms. Modified to suit the Elizabethan taste, the Branle, more often called Brawl, attained to such favour as it had perhaps not known even in the country of its origin. Its introduction into England must have taken place before the middle of the Sixteenth Century, for David Lindsay's play *Diligence* (1540) mentions it in the epilogue: "Minstrel, blow up one Brawl of France. Let's see who hobbles best." Thence onwards it grew in popularity, until we find it mentioned in the works of our famous writers in a way which suggests that the word must have become household property. Spenser alludes to the form in the *Faerie Queene*, and Shakespeare (*Love's Labour's Lost*, III, 1) could not overlook so beloved a diversion: "Master, will you win your love with a French Brawl."

The changing of the ruling house did not affect the Branle's popularity. In 1607 Sir John Davies refers to it in his *Orchestra*: "Whereof a thousand brauls he doth compound," and John Day, in *Humour Out of Breath* (1608, II, 2) has: "Love's nothing but . . . a French brawl." It is quite possible that in Stuart times the Branle had grown into a sort of pantomimic diversion, for we find Philip Massinger (1629, *The Picture*, II, 2) saying: "'Tis a French brawl, an apish imitation of what you really perform in battle."

James I and Charles I used the Branle a good deal at the court in Whitehall, and after the Restoration it was revived by Charles II. Samuel Pepys, after gracing Whitehall with his gossiping presence on December 31, 1662, went home and wrote in his *Diary*: "By and by, comes the King and Queen, the Duke and Duchess, and all the great ones: and after seating themselves, the King takes out the Duchess of York; and the Duke, the Duchess of Buckingham; the Duke of Monmouth, my Lady Castlemaine, and so other lords other ladies; and they danced the Brantle." On November 15, 1666, the diarist entered as follows: "I also to the ball. . . . Presently after the King was come in, he took the Queen, and about fourteen more couple there was, and begun the Bransles." It is a peculiar circumstance that the Branle, as a dance, outlived by a good many years, its own offspring.

BRANSLE.
BRAWL. } *v.* BRANLE.

BREAKING THE GROUND: Christopher Simpson, in his *Division-Violist* (1659), speaks of "Breaking the Ground" and defines the phrase as "dividing its notes into more diminutive notes." He also gives, at some length, an account of the differences between Breaking the Ground and Descanting upon a Ground (*v.* Descant). Thomas Campion, in his little treatise on *The Art of Descant, or Composing Musick in Parts* (1674 *ed.*), says: "Moreover, it is to be observed; that in composing of the Bass, you may break it at your pleasure."

BREVE: The name of a note now but very rarely used, and when employed is the longest note of the series, being equal to two semibreves. In ancient (mensurable) music the value of the Breve varied according to the Time of the composition; being equal to two semibreves in "imperfect time" and three in "perfect time." As its name implies, the breve was looked upon as a short note; a legacy of the early days when only two sorts of note were employed—a long and a short. In the era of mensurable music the Breve was the recognised standard of measurement; it was called a *Tempus*, and was considered the shortest time in which the voice could develop a full tone (*minimum tempus in quo potest formari plenitudo vocis*, Marchettus of Padua; and Franco of Cologne says the same in slightly different words).

In transcribing old manuscripts it will be well to remember that the breve written black had a different value from the same note white (*i.e.* written in outline). The difference lay in the circumstance that a change from black to white notes indicated a change of measure from triple to duple, and *vice versa*, the blackening of the breve reducing its value commensurately. This use of the black and white notes dates from the turn of the Fourteenth to the Fifteenth Century; previously the breve were written black only. John Playford (*Introduction to the Skill of Musick*) probably alludes to this when he says that "swifter Triple Time is sometimes prick'd in Black Notes," and although no change of rhythm was understood, the idea of writing a rapid semibreve or minim black, may have been derived from the older custom. The Breve was written as follows:

(*v.* MOOD, TIME, *and* PROPORTION).

BROKEN MUSIC: A term with many uses and meanings. Shakespeare, in *Henry V* (V, 2), says: "Come, your answer in broken music"; and in *Troilus and Cressida* (III, 1): "Fair prince, here is good broken music." In such cases, "broken music" means music in parts. But it can also mean the sounding together of instruments belonging to different families. In the Lord Chamberlain's Record we read of a violinist engaged to perform in the "broken consort" (Vol. 477,

June 16, 1660), and in an entry under date October 16, 1660, we have the phrase again. Here it no doubt meant a consort which included instruments of different categories, such as viols and lutes, strings and wind. Francis, Lord Bacon (*Essay of Masques and Triumphs*), has : "I understand it that the song be . . . accompanied with some broken music," *i.e.* supported by an instrumental accompaniment. The term was also applied to such instruments as harps, guitars, lutes, *etc.*, which could not sustain their notes, and on which the chords had to be "broken."

BUMBARDE. *v.* BOMBARD.

BURDEN : The "burden" of a song was a recurring refrain, sung generally in chorus, at the end of each verse and sometimes at the close of every line. Occasionally the burden was an intelligible motto or phrase, but more often it was composed of nonsense syllables such as "Hey, troly, loly," mentioned in *Piers Plowman.* Coverdale, in his "Address to the Christian Reader," prefaced to his *Goastly Psalms and Spirituall Songes* (1538), says : ". . . they should be better occupied than with 'Hey, nonny, nonny,' 'Hey, trolly, lolly,' and such like fantasies." In Stuart times the burden was reduced to a simple *Fa-la-la* or something like it. Shakespeare, in *Much Ado About Nothing* (III, 4), uses the term : "Clap us into the 'Light o' Love,' that goes without a burden ; do you sing it and I'll dance it."

Etymologically the term has nothing to do with the word meaning anything borne, but is from the French *Bourdon* (Late Latin, *Burdo*, a drone bee), the drone of the bagpipe, or the held bass. A continuous, droning pedal-note, like an undercurrent, was called a *bourdon* (as was one of the organ-stops), and from this the insistent burden of the song was named.

Shakespeare employs the term "Holding" in a similar sense in *Antony and Cleopatra* (II, 7) :

> Make a battery to our ears with the loud music ;
> The while I'll place you ; then the boy shall sing ;
> The Holding every man shall bear as loud
> As his strong sides can volley,

unless he uses the word in place of "Hold" (*q.v.*), and intends that all present shall join in at the close. Ben Jonson's use of the word Burden is characteristic: "I will have a canzonet made, with nothing in it but sirrah; and the burthen shall be, I come" (*Cynthia's Revels*, IV, 1).

BYSSYNGE SONGES: Very early English cradle-songs or lullabies. The name is to be derived from *Bissyn*, to lull children to sleep (Halliwell, Dictionary of Archaic Words, 1847; citing the *Promptorium Parvulorum* with the variants Byszyne and Byssynge).

CADENT: A Seventeenth-century ornament used to bridge the space between two descending notes and leading to a close by anticipating the closing note. Although musically and etymologically allied to "Cadence," the Cadent must not be confounded with the word still in use. Playford gives the sign for, and the manner of performing, the ornament as follows:

The Cadent could also be "Shaked" in the following way:

CANARY: A dance-form in jig-rhythm that became very popular in England and which is frequently mentioned by the writers of the Sixteenth and Seventeenth Centuries in a way that suggests it to have been in common use. After much research in this subject I am inclined to think that musically the Canary was little more than a jig (*q.v.*), and that the reason for the special name lay in some difference in the dance. Shakespeare's ". . . but to jig off a tune at the tongue's end, Canary to it with your feet" (*Love's Labour's Lost*, 1588, III, 1), seems to support this theory. In *All's Well that Ends Well* (II, 1) we have the form mentioned again:

I have seen a med'cine
That's able to breathe life into a stone,
Quicken a rock, and make you dance Canary
With spritely fire and motion . . .

Fletcher's *Bloody Brother* (1639, II, 2) gives the dance with a quaint conceit:

> I'll make you a dish of calves' feet dance the Canaries
> And a Consort of Cramm'd capons fiddle to 'em.

Literary mention of the form, then, is fairly early compared with the dates of the Canary abroad; yet early specimens of the music are very rare. Though examples of the dance are to be found in the Eighteenth Century, there are none in the Fitzwilliam Virginal Book, or in the Virginal Books of Lady Nevell, Will Forster, and Benjamin Cosyn. My conjecture is that the Canary could be danced to any jig-tune, and that, as I have already said, the differences between the two forms were terpsichorean differences only. After the Restoration of Charles II we meet with music labelled "Canaries"; but it was at a period when foreign names for all things in art were fashionable. It is quite possible that under the old *régime* thees Canaries may have passed as jigs. Thus only can I explain the peculiar circumstance that the form in England should be so frequently mentioned in our literature and so seldom contained in our music-books of equal date. Specimens of the Seventeenth-century Canary are in Playford's *Musick's Hand-Maide* (1663) and in the sixth edition of *Apollo's Banquet* (1690). No. 1 of the latter work is called "The New Canaries"; and in *Part* III of the same work is to be seen a short suite consisting of "The Princess-Bore (*q.v.*)—Saraband (*q.v.*)—and Canaries." John Stafford Smith printed in his *Musica Antiqua*, 1812, the Canaries from Tabourot's *Orchèsographie* (1588), and also Purcell's Canary from *Dioclesian* (*c.* 1691). As a dance for the ball-room, with prearranged steps, it is given by Tomlinson in 1735, but such an appearance of the form cannot be looked upon as historical; and the existence of a set dance of this kind need not prove that the Canary lived until then, or even show that it had anything in common with its Sixteenth-century namesake.

The place of origin of the dance is not quite certain, though within narrow geographical limits it can be defined closely enough to serve our purpose. The name is obviously derived from the Canary Isles, and the Spanish influence seems strong upon it. Leo's *Description of Africa* (translated by Pory in 1600) has: "They were and are at this day delighted with a kind of dance which they use also in Spain, and in other places, and because it took origin from there, it is called the Canaries." Pineda's Spanish-English Dictionary of 1740 defines *el canario* as the name of an "old Spanish dance," and Halliwell's statement that the castanets sometimes accompanied it, helps to give colour to the assertion. Moreover, the rhythm of the Seventeenth-century Canary as it appears in a specimen given by F. L. Schubert (*Die Tanzmusik*, 1867), again points to Spain, especially in the last measure of the example:

Halliwell no doubt obtained his information concerning the castanets from Florio's Italian Dictionary of 1598, which gives *Castagnette* as "little shells, such as they use that daunce the Canaries."

On the Continent the form is to be met with very frequently, especially in France; but a detailed account of specimens need not occupy space here, since they differ very little, if at all, in rhythm, measure, or character, from the jig or gigue.

CANTUS: In the older part-writing, the name given to the upper voice, generally that performing the melody. In the two-part harmony of the Twelfth Century this upper part, written above the Tenor (*Cantus firmus*) was known as the *Discantus*. It should, however, be remembered that the English term "treble" should not—in the majority of cases—be applied as a synonym for either Cantus or Discantus, for this voice takes the place of the ancient *Triplum*, which was the third voice above the *Cantus firmus* in medieval three-part compositions.

CANZONET: A little song. A popular form of composition taken from the Italian Canzonetta. The word was frequently used in England, Shakespeare having it in *Love's Labour's Lost*, and Ben Jonson in *Cynthia's Revels* ("I will have a Canzonet made, with nothing in it but sirrah," IV, 1). Towards the end of the Sixteenth Century a large number of books containing Canzonets appeared, but Morley's *First Booke of*

Canzonets to Two Voices (1595) may serve as an example. Half a dozen numbers from this book may now be seen in a modern reprint, a little over-barred perhaps, but otherwise excellent and useful (Curwen, edited by Sydney Grew).

CARMAN'S WHISTLE: A term frequently used in Elizabethan and Stuart music-books, having its origin in the circumstance that the carmen of that period enjoyed a reputation for musicianship and whistled all the tunes they heard. Shakespeare makes Falstaff say of Shallow, ". . . sang the tunes he heard the carmen whistle, and sware they were his fancies (*q.v.*) and his good nights" (II *Henry IV*, 3). Ben Jonson in *Bartholomew Fair* (I, 1) also alludes to it: "I dare not let him walk alone, for fear of learning of vile tunes, which he will sing at supper, and in the sermon-times! If he meet but a carman in the street, and I find him not talk to keep him off on him, he will whistle him and all his tunes over at night in his sleep!" A tune called the "Carman's Whistle," very popular in its day, is given in the Fitzwilliam Virginal Book, and also in *My Lady Nevell's Virginal Book* (1591), both harmonised by William Byrd.

CAROL: A song, the text of which was in some way connected with Christmas or the Nativity; a part of the ancient Miracle-Play; a jovial drinking-song; a dance in the nature of the German *Reigen* or the French *Branle*;—all these things the Carol has been in turn. The name, coming through Old French *Carole*, a dance, and later French *Carolle*, "a sort of dance wherein many danced together" (Cotgrave, French Dictionary, 1660), from the Late Latin *Choraula*, a side-form of *Choraules*, the flute-player who accompanied the chorus-dance—was first undoubtedly applied to a dance of the Rondo type. How old this dance is, it would be almost impossible to guess, for it has been used in the Miracle and Mystery Play for nearly a millennium, and the verb "to carol" by our most ancient writers. The possible derivation of the word from the Breton *koroll* need not influence the other etymology in the slightest, for both can easily be from the same source; at all events, the Breton word, like the one of Romance origin, meant a round-dance. It is quite conceivable that this round-dance (German, *umme-genden Tantz;* Norman *karole*) was the very germ of all artistic dancing, since it was not the spontaneous tumbling of irresponsible savages, but the outcome of a premeditated plan.

Accompanied by voices as well as by instruments—sharing this peculiarity with many of the old dance-forms—the carollers stepped round in a circle, holding hands. This dance naturally soon gave its name to the song which accompanied it, and the word Carol was, in England at any rate, applied indiscriminately to both. In Fourteenth- and early Fifteenth-century England, carolling meant singing as well as dancing,—but a subtle distinction was made between carolling and dancing. France observed a similar distinction between *caroller* and *danser*, as did Germany between *reihen* and *tanzen*—in each case the former being less lively than the latter, and indicating a stepping round rather than leaping. "Faire is carole of Maide gent," we read in *King Alisaunder* (after 1300; Weber's *Metrical Romances*, 1810, *l.* 1845), and also, in the same work: "There was maidenes carolyng."

It was no uncommon thing for dancing to be used in the religious services of ancient times, and the dance was admitted on occasion even into the ceremonial of the Christian Church. This being so, no surprise need be expressed at the finding of the Carol incorporated in the mysteries performed within the walls of the churches themselves. Although there were carols set to words appropriate to most seasons of the year—such as summer carols in Wales and winter carols in England; Easter carols in addition to Christmas carols—the application of the name soon became limited to those songs which made the Nativity their theme. At one time roistering drinking-songs were written to well-known carol tunes, and although later on the form became more reverent, the carol never ceased to be half-secular and essentially the property of the masses. A distinction was ever drawn between the Christmas hymn and the Christmas carol—as if the terpsichorean origin of the latter were just sufficient to deprive it of the highest honours—and while the former was more serious and devotional in the words, and grave and solemn in its music, the latter was always more rhythmical, more joyous, and often quite worldly. It was nothing unusual for the congregation to trip home carolling all the way after having sung the prescribed Christmas hymns within the church. It may therefore not be too much to say that the carol has kept a devotional spirit alive in masses of people who might never have been influenced by the hymn which, although of deeper meaning, was harder to understand and feel.

One of the oldest English carols traceable is preserved in the British Museum and dates from the Thirteenth Century, but earlier uses of the form can be shown, for it was given in the Miracle plays performed at Christmastide during the reign of Henry II (*c.* 1170). This song and dance, performed before the mangers erected in the churches, probably constituted the first step towards limiting the carol to Christmas. Many authorities suggest that the Christmas carol, like the holly and mistletoe, was the survival of some heathen custom; but I think we need go no farther afield than the popular dance for its origin. If ever there was a product of the Middle Ages, it was the carol, song and dance; and very few things, taken by themselves, reflect so thoroughly and so faithfully the medieval spirit.

CATCH : A canon for three or more voices, so constructed that a great deal of skill was necessary for each voice to "catch" up his part at the right point. This was rendered more difficult by the circumstance that the composition was at first written out in a continuous strain, with little indication as to where each part should enter. Later, however, signs were given to assist the singers. A further development lay in writing the text in such a way that the various entries caused very amusing word-combinations, but often of a suggestive and indecent character. Indeed, some of the best specimens of this class of composition have to be banished from the repertoires of respectable catch-singers on account of the questionable words to which they were set. In the Seventeenth Century the Catch was a very popular form of musical entertainment, and later on societies were formed for the performance of these works and others of a kindred nature.

CATLEEN. *v.* CATLING.

CATLING : The highest, or treble, string of the lute; the name being no doubt a diminutive of cat from the supposed origin of the strings. Shakespeare uses the word in *Troilus and Cressida* (III, 3): "What music will be in him when Hector has knocked out his brains, I know not: but I am sure, none; unless the fiddler Apollo get his sinews to make Catlings on."

And, by analogy, "Simon Catling" in *Romeo and Juliet* (IV, 5) would be the name of a luter, and not a fiddler as Nares supposes, since "James Soundpost" would play on the viol. The term is often found spelled Catleen, and an entry in the Lord Chamberlain's Records for October 20, 1688 (*Vol.* 752, *p.* 342), mentions the payment of £1 "for catleens." Mace (1676) speaks of "Venice-Catlins," probably because good ones were imported from Italy.

CEBELL: An old English dance, very like the Gavotte in construction and measure. How the form obtained its name and whence the latter was derived are alike unknown. The Cebell may equally well have been a modification of the French Gavotte, or an independent invention similar by coincidence to the better-known form. On the other hand it may have been considered identical with the Gavotte from the musical point of view, the differences between them having been terpsichorean only. It appears to have been danced slightly quicker than the Gavotte. Examples of the dance may be seen in *Lessons and Aires for the Harpsichord and Spinnett*, by J. Eccles, D. Purcell, and others (headed "Cibell," and commencing at the half-bar, *alla breve*), and, curiously, one by a French composer writing for an English publisher, in *Lessons for the Harpsichord or Spinet*, by Lully, with the same characteristics. In the last-mentioned work both the Gavotte and the Cebell are used.

C-FA-UT. *v.* GAMUT.

CHACCON, CHACONNE: An imported instrumental piece consisting of a number of variations on a ground-bass, a slow and stately movement, and the characteristic rhythm:

Although a few examples of English origin are to be found, the Chaconne did not attain to very great favour in this country.

The source of the Chaconne is not quite clear: it may be descended from an ancient dance-form of Mauro-Spanish origin, travelling to France *via* Italy. On the other hand, it can easily be the product of the Motet of the Twelfth and

Thirteenth Centuries—or, at least, have been influenced by it. It is even possible that both of these two distinct sources supplied factors towards making the form, which eventually met and became merged. The Italians, and still more the Germans, of the Eighteenth Century, made of the Chaconne a test of originality and imagination almost without equal in its musical importance; and why the composers of England made so little use of the form is a mystery. It is possible that they had had a surfeit of "Divisions" and desired a rest from the endless variations.

The few composers who did use the form in England—among them being Purcell and William Richardson (*Lessons for the Harpsichord or Spinet*, 1704)—were no doubt influenced by the craze for imitating foreign fashions. In the Lord Chamberlain's Records for July, 1675, there is an entry referring to a payment "For the fair writing of a Chaccon," probably copying one of the examples set by the French opera.

The Chaconne filled a very important place in the history of musical form, and was to be met with, danced, sung, and played at different periods in its career;—but its English use was too slight to justify more space being devoted to it here.

CHACOON. *v.* CHACCON. CHACONNE.

CHAIR-ORGAN: An old name for the Choir-Organ, some authorities holding the view that the term was a corruption of this. Their argument is based upon the circumstance that in cathedrals the choir-organ frequently formed the back of the organist's seat. But it can quite easily, and more logically, stand for "Cathedral Organ" (though French *chaire*, from the Greek *kathedra*). An interesting entry in the State Papers (Lord Chamberlain's Records) referring to the Chair-Organ is to be found under date February 3, 1636/7 (*Vol.* 739, *p.* 146), where we read that a warrant was issued to the Signet for "a privy seal of £140, to be impressed unto Mr. Edward Norgate, to be employed for the altering and reparation of the organ in the Chappell at Hampton Court and for the making of a new Chayre organ there conformable to those already made in the Chappells at Whitehall and Greenwich."

CHAPEL ROYAL: The clergy and musicians who perform divine service for the sovereigns of England. The earliest information we have of the English Chapel Royal is contained in the *Liber Niger Domus Regis* (British Museum; Harleian MSS. 293 and 642, *temp.* Edward IV), and this valuable source gives much material for a history of the Chapel. From it we learn under what conditions the members lived and what food was allowed them, *etc.* "Chaplenes and Clerkes of the Chapelle" were expected to be "endowed with virtues morolle and specikatyve, as of the musicke, shewinge in descante . . . suffytyente in organes playinge . . ." For all this the wage of seven pence per day was paid, which was very good remuneration when we remember the value of money in the Fifteenth Century and the fact that clothing, board, and lodging were generally provided. The choir of the Chapel Royal is the oldest of which we have any certain information, and it was probably looked upon as the standard by which other choirs were organised.

During the reign of Edward IV, "Children of the Chappell" numbered eight (later increased), and they were under the direction of a "Master of Songe" who was later known as the "Master of the Children." When their voices broke, the Children were sent at the King's charge to Oxford or Cambridge—"yf they will assente," and the Lord Chamberlain's Records give frequent references to clothing given to boys whose "voices had changed" and who, on that account, had left the Chapel. When their voices merited the promotion they were oft advanced to sing with the "Gentlemen of the Chapel." The first recorded Master of the Children was Henry Abingdon, and his salary of forty marks a year was "for fyndyng, instruction, and governaunce of the children of the Chapelle of our Housholde." Subsequent Masters were Gilbert Banister (1482), William Cornish (1493), William Crane (1510), and later musicians whose names may be found in the Lord Chamberlain's Records.

The Chapel Royal was engaged to officiate wherever the King happened to be, and a good deal of travelling was done; the State Papers containing many entries relating to payments for "riding charges." The Chapels Royal of St. James's Palace and Whitehall, in London, and St. George's, Windsor, are the most important, and at the present time the first and last are the only ones in regular use. That of Whitehall is visited only on Maundy Thursday in connection with the bestowal of alms to the poor (*v.* also E. A. Rimbault, *Cheque-Book of the Chapel Royal*, 1872).

CHAYRE-ORGAN. *v.* CHAIR-ORGAN.

CHEST OF VIOLS: The name given to the complete set of viols and the case in which they were kept. Seventeenth-century England used the whole series of viols (*q.v.*) much as the pianoforte is employed to-day. They were the instruments *par excellence* for chamber use, and thus a chest containing them was part of the furniture of almost every Stuart house. Thomas Mace (*Musick's Monument*, 1676) gives a very good account of such a case, and instructs his readers how to prepare one that would keep their instruments in good playing condition: "First, see that it be conveniently large, to contain such a number as you shall design for your use, and to be made very close and warm, lined through with baize . . . by which means your instruments will speak livelily, brisk, and clear. Your best provision (and the most complete) will be a good chest of viols, six in number, *viz.* two basses, two tenors, and two trebles, all truly and proportionably suited . . ." When a complete set of instruments matching in every detail was not obtainable, Mace recommends that the chest be made up of such as can be picked up, but impressing upon his readers the special necessity for matching them as to size.

The combination of instruments as given by Mace, although the most frequent one, was not the only useful set; some chests contained three trebles and one bass instead of two of each. The compass of the tenor viol was very great and it can easily be understood that, if necessary, the first bass-part of a consort could, with very little trouble, be played by the third tenor, with the added advantage of strengthening the exquisite tone of the tenors.

An advertisement in *Tripla Concordia* (1667) announces the sale of two chests of viols in the following words: "There is two chests of viols to be sold, one made by Mr. John Ross, who formerly lived in Bridewell, containing two trebles, three tenors, and one basse. The chest was made in the year 1598, the other being made by Mr. Henry Smith, who formerly lived over against Hatton House, in Holborn, containing two trebles, two tenors, two basses. The chest was made in the year 1633. Both chests are very curious work." The two makers mentioned in this advertisement enjoyed a great reputation for excellent workmanship; and others high in popular favour as *luthiers* were Eldred, Jay, and Bolles.

CHURCH MODES: The series of type-scales upon which all medieval music was based, and taken for ecclesiastical use—whence the name—from the older Greek system. Perhaps "Modes" describes these octaves of notes better than "Scales"; for although each contained the seven notes of the present-day series, they did not follow each other with the same constancy (as far as the intervals between them were concerned) as is the case with the modern scale. Thus the First Mode which we must consider consisted of a succession of intervals like this: Tone, Semitone, Tone, Tone, Tone, Semitone, Tone (from D to D) and was called the Dorian mode. The second, or Phrygian, Mode ranged from E to E (Semitone, Tone, Tone, Tone, Semitone, Tone, Tone). The Third, or Lydian, lay between F and F, with the interval succession Tone, Tone, Tone, Semitone, Tone, Tone, Semitone. The Fourth, or Mixolydian, Mode had the Final (or *finalis*) G, and the sequence Tone, Tone, Semitone, Tone, Tone, Semitone, Tone. For the purposes of the present article these four series will suffice to commence with. They were known as the "Authentic Modes," and were adopted by St. Ambrose (Bishop of Milan) in the Fourth Century, for Church use. Gregory the Great in the Sixth Century added four more Modes to this quartette—the so-called "Plagal Modes." These were allied to the Authentic Modes in so far that each Plagal Mode lay below its corresponding Authentic partner at an interval of a fourth, its name being distinguished by the prefix *Hypo*- Thus the first plagal mode, or Hypo-Dorian, was pitched a fourth below the first authentic, or Dorian, and ranged from A to A. In other words, the fourth degree of the plagal mode was identical with the *finalis* of the authentic. The second plagal mode, or Hypo-Phrygian, was in the same way separated from and allied to the second authentic, and lay between B and its octave. In like manner the Hypo-Lydian and the Hypo-Mixolydian commenced from C and D respectively.

The modes in use, therefore, during the reign of Pope Gregory the Great were as follows :

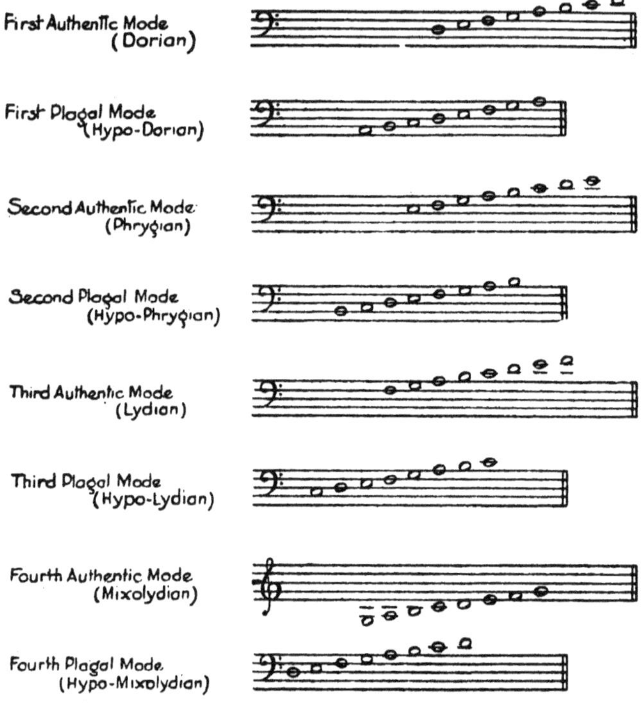

These modes were also frequently numbered consecutively, so that the Dorian was known as the First Mode, the Hypo-Dorian as the Second Mode, the Phrygian as the Third, the Hypo-Phrygian as the Fourth, and so on; besides such appellations as *Authentus Protus*, *Plagius Protus*, *Authentus Deuterus*, *etc.* At some periods a considerable amount of confusion resulted from this varying nomenclature.

Later on more modes were taken from the Greek system and embodied in the set already in use, such as the Ionian, Æolian (with their Plagals) and others. But all were constructed on the same principle, the only difference between them being the varying positions of the diatonic semitones.

CIBELL. *v.* CEBELL.

CINQUE-PACE. *v.* GALLIARD.

CITHAREN, CITHREN. v. CITTERN.

CITOLE : A medieval stringed and plucked instrument, smaller in size than the later lutes, and played with a plectrum as well as with the fingers. The body appears to have been most generally pear-shaped—sometimes oval—and the four strings of wire. The back of the Citole was flat—in this respect differing from the lutes, but similar to the cittern of the Seventeenth Century.

Sculptures, and drawings in medieval manuscripts are the only sources of information we have concerning the instrument. It is mentioned in State use at the beginning of the Fourteenth Century when, in 1306, the future Edward II was knighted. On that occasion a "Citoler" was rewarded for his services with one Mark ; but this was not the earliest known use of the Citole in England. Edward the Third's royal orchestra, such as it was, included a performer on the Citole. The interesting sculptured "Minstrel Gallery" in Exeter Cathedral has a player on the instrument, and Engel, working after a plaster cast of the original, describes the first musician in the series as playing upon the lute or possibly the cittern. But there can be no doubt, I think, that the instrument is a Citole. Several manuscript "Romances" (mostly metrical) of the Fourteenth and Fifteenth Centuries contain references to the instrument, and in one of them the verbal form "Sytolyng" is used. Wiclif erroneously translates the name of one of the Biblical instruments as "Sitol." John Gower mentions the instrument in *Confessio Amantis* (*Lib.* VIII, *ll.* 829, 1487, and 2679). Chaucer has it in the "Knight's Tale" (*l.* 1965) : "A Citole in hir right hand hadde she." Lydgate mentions the Citole similarly in *Reson and Sensuallyte* (*MSS.* Fairfax, 16, Bodleian, Oxford ; and Add. 29729, British Museum) in *l.* 5583. Common variants of the name itself are Cythol, Cytole, Sitole, Sytholle, *etc.*

In mechanical treatment the Citole resembled the lutes, the bar which held the strings being fastened to the belly, and served at the same time the functions of a bridge, keeping the strings at a sufficient height to enable them to vibrate freely. Its origin is not at all certain. It may have been evolved from some form of psaltery by an ingenious musician who conceived the idea of adding a neck and fingerboard. It may quite as easily have been a flat-backed modification of an early lute, possibly of Eastern origin and coming North and West *via* Spain or Provence.

The shape and ornamentation of the Citole varied a good deal, but it does not appear to have enjoyed much development; for with the rise of the Lutes and Gittern it fell into disuse, leaving behind fewer traces of itself than were left by the instruments of Ancient Egypt.

CITTERN: A flat-backed, pear-shaped instrument very popular in England at the end of the Sixteenth Century and during the Seventeenth. Exactly when the Cittern was evolved, and what its source was, would be very difficult to decide. The fact that its back was flat and that the back and table were connected by ribs would rule the lute out at once as a possible source. It is more likely to have been derived from some form of the Citole. Its strings were of wire and strung in unison pairs, most commonly four in number. Playford, in *Musick's Delight on the Cithren* (1666), says: "The Cithren is strung with eight Wyre strings, which are divided into four Course, two in a Course." Mace (1676) also alludes to its "Wyar strings." Metal strings were the characteristic feature of the Cittern and distinguished that instrument from the Gittern, or early Guitar, which were strung with gut. This distinction was noted by Michael Drayton in his *Polyolbion* (1613, *Song* IV): "Some that delight to touch the sterner wire chord, The Cythren . . . strike." As time went on, of course, more strings were employed, and even a "fourteen-course" instrument was known. Thomas Robinson (*New Citharen Lessons*, 1609) speaks of such an one which had seven pairs of strings over a fingerboard, and seven single ones alongside. This, however, cannot be considered as a typical specimen of the instrument, and was no doubt influenced by the theorbo. The ordinary four-stringed Cittern was provided with a fretted fingerboard; and a carved head, often elaborately chiselled, surmounted the peg-box with its eight pegs. A plectrum of quill or whalebone was generally used, but the instrument was also played with the fingers, the resultant tone being softer and less metallic. Its effect must have been quite pleasant, and the quality of tone could be modified and varied according to the distance of the plectrum or plucking

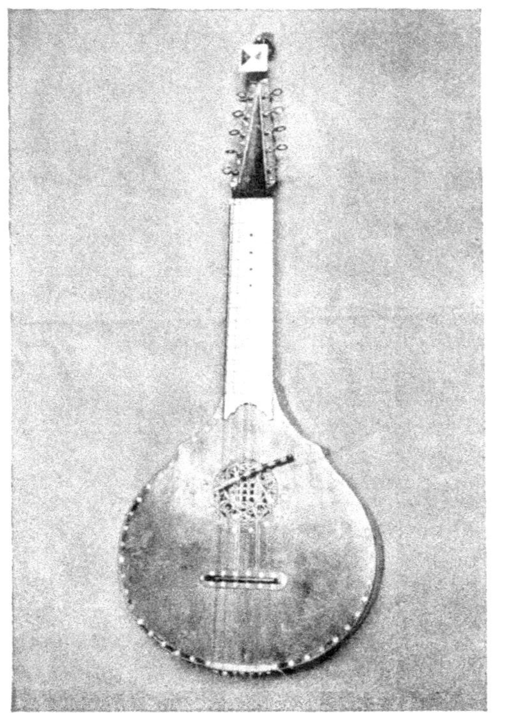

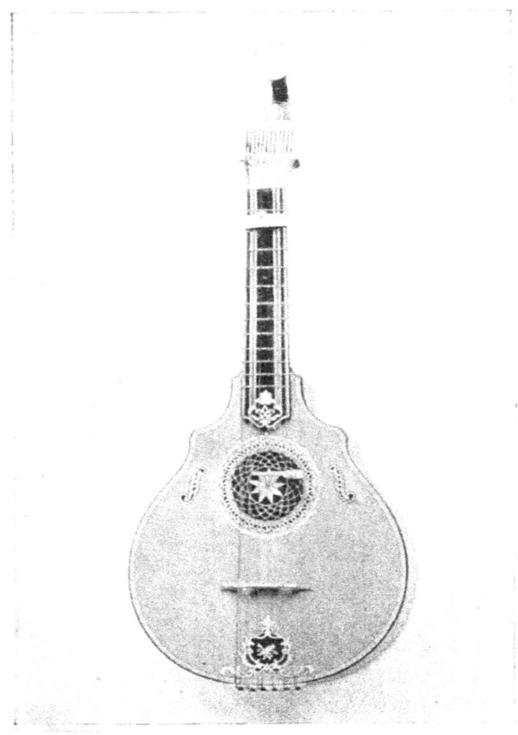

TWO CITTERNS (one with Watch-key tuning head)
(*Victoria and Albert Museum*)

[*face p.* 40

finger from the bridge. The sound-hole was circular and fairly large, often filled with a delicately carved and fretted Rose (or Knot, *q.v.*). The tuning of the Cittern, which varied considerably, was peculiar in that the pitch of the strings did not rise in the order usually followed; the string on the extreme left of the fingerboard being tuned higher than its neighbour. The commonest tuning at the change of the century was:

This arrangement made the performance of certain chords very easy and of original effect. The strings, in the order given here, were named Tenor, Bass, Mean, and Treble, and an illustration of the instrument with these names attached is given on the title-page of Playford's *New Lessons for the Cithern and Gittern* (1652).

The head of the Cittern, already mentioned, was often carved most artistically—sometimes into a head of great beauty, sometimes grotesquely. The popularity of the Cittern was such that its head became proverbial. Thus Fletcher in *Love's Cure* (1622 c., II, 2) says: "You cittern-head! Who have you talked to, ha? You nasty, . . . ill-contenanced cur!" and Shakespeare makes a point of it in *Love's Labour's Lost* (*Act* V):

> *Hol.* I will not be put out of countenance.
> *Bir.* Because thou hast no face.
> *Hol.* What is this?
> *Bir.* A cittern head.

John Ford, in *The Lover's Melancholy* (performed 1628, printed 1629; II, 1), has: ". . . I hope the Chronicles will rear me one day for a headpiece"—". . . Barbers shall wear thee on their citterns." This quotation brings us to a very interesting feature in the social life of the early Seventeenth Century. The barber's shop was not only the "Staple of News," and the exchange of gossip; it was also the place where music of all kinds might be heard, and waiting customers would avail themselves of the instruments kept there for the purpose of passing the time away pleasantly. Before his shop was entered the signs of the barber's music were visible in his windows, for the teeth he extracted were suspended, as an advertisement, at the ends of rejected lute-strings. Of course, the professional musicians were inclined to look with contempt upon the musical pretensions of the barber; and in Morley's *Introduction* we may read: "You sing you know not what; it should seem you came lately from a barber's shop, where you had Gregory Walker, or a Coranto, played in the new proportions by them lately found out." But to the ordinary amateur the barber's cittern gave a good deal of pleasure. At the turn of the century it appears as if no author could write of barbers without mentioning the Cittern. Ben Jonson has:

> . . . He is my barber, Tom.
>
> . . . . .
>
> He got into a masque at Court, by his wit,
> And the good means of his cittern holding up thus
> For one of the music . . . (*Staple of News*, I, 2.)

The circumstance that the cittern in the barber's shop was public property explains one or two otherwise mystifying quotations. In an old play we find a character saying of his wife that she was "a barber's citterne, for every serving man to play upon." In the *Silent Woman* (III, 5) Ben Jonson has: "I have married his cittern that's common to all men." Thus, for a lady to be called a cittern in the Seventeenth Century was no compliment.

The mass of allusions to the cittern can only point to one fact, and that is the immense popularity the instrument enjoyed in this country. And yet Grove's *Dictionary of Music and Musicians* says that "the Gittern and Cithren never appear to have had much popularity in England."

Music for the Cittern was written on a stave of four lines in Tablature (*q.v.*). Such a stave, of course, would only suffice for the four-stringed instrument. There does not appear to have been much music especially written and published for the Cittern; it is quite possible that players helped themselves to any popular tune, or improvised solos and song-accompaniments. The peculiar tuning of the instrument would prevent any other tablature being used than that expressly composed for it; but from ordinary notation the cittern-player could perform anything within the compass of his instrument with comparative ease. What printed music there is for the Cittern is very rare and difficult of access. The Royal College of Music possesses a copy of Anthony Holborne's *Cittharn Schoole* (1597), a work containing thirty-two dances, Ayres, and popular tunes for the Cittern, in addition to twenty-three more pieces with an accompaniment for Treble, Tenor, and Bass Viols. In Morley's *Consort Lessons for the Treble Lute, the Pandora, the Citterne, the Flute, and the Treble-Viol*, 1599, we have the Cittern among its contemporaries. The cittern-part only of this work is in the Bodleian Library. Phillip Rosseter's *Lessons for Consort* (1609) contained music for a similar *ensemble*, the cittern-part of this belonging also to the Royal College of Music. In 1609 also appeared Thomas Robinson's *New Consort Lessons*, containing compositions for two citterns, voice with cittern accompaniment, and others. A few "lessons" are also included for the Cittern with fourteen strings, mentioned earlier. It will thus be seen that although the Cittern was employed in a very frivolous manner in the barber's shop, it was put to more dignified uses by more serious musicians; and Sir William Leighton had a place for it in the accompaniment to his *Teares or Lamentacions of a Sorrowfull Soule.*

Perhaps the most interesting, and certainly the rarest, work on the Cittern is John Playford's *A Booke of New Lessons for the Cithern and Gittern, etc.* (1652). A copy is in the Euing Library (Royal Technical College), Glasgow, and thanks are due to the librarian, Mr. Peter Bennett, for an account of it. The instructions given in the book, according to Mr. Bennett, comprise only the mode of tuning the instrument, the time-signatures, and the value of the notes and rests. *Part* II of the little work contains twenty-four pages of exercises for the Cittern. This book, judging from Playford's preface, appears to have been the second of its kind, the first having probably been a publication of 1650, no copy of which is known to have survived. The Index of the 1652 edition gives the names of fifty-four melodies for the Cittern and nine "Psalms to sing to the Cittern according to the Church Tunes." The secular music consists of the popular airs of the day, melodies that are to be found in many other publications of that period. The rest of the book is devoted to the Gittern.

Playford's venture of 1666 is second in importance only to the foregoing: "Musick's Delight on the Cithren, restored and Refined to a more Easie and Pleasant manner of Playing than formerly; and set forth with *Lessons* Al a Mode, being the choicest of our late new *Ayres*, *Corants*, *Sarabandes*, Tunes, and *Jiggs*. To which is added several New *Songs* and *Ayres*, to sing to the Cithren"; a long-winded title for a small work.

Very early references to the Cittern are rare, and the first I have been able to locate is in a manuscript in the British Museum (Additional 30513). This dates from the reign of Henry VIII, and contains nine pieces for the Cittern in Tablature. An early official allusion to the instrument is made in 1556, when among the New Year's gifts received by Queen Mary was "a faire Cyterne." Kendall's *Flowers of Epigrammes* (section headed *Trifles*, 1577) makes another Tudor reference to it:

> On Saterday I will you send
> some Lessons for your Lute:
> And for your Citterne eke a few
> take leaves till time of fruite.

The Cittern, thus, was in almost every kind of use and in the hands of every class of player. From Henry VIII to Charles II, from Timothy Kendall to Samuel Pepys, the instrument was a source of pleasure; and whether its environment was the royal palace or the barber's shop, it was popular everywhere.

CLARICHORD, CLARICHORDE. *v.* CLAVICHORD.

CLARICON. *v.* CLAVICHORD.

CLAVICHORD: One of the earliest of the keyboard instruments, differing from the others in many particulars. It was contained in a rectangular case and was played by means of brass or copper pins or elongated studs which set the strings in vibration by contact. The shape of these studs, or tangents, as they were termed, was slightly conical, the flattened end being upward. Placed at the end of a balanced key farthest from the player's hand, the tangents fulfilled the functions of the hammers in the modern pianoforte. The most noticeable feature, however, of the method employed in constructing this instrument lay in the circumstance that in very early specimens each string was provided with several tangents which operated on the string at different points. This divided the string into sections of varying length and caused it to produce different notes. Whatever may have been the defects of such a system, it proves that much thought and scientific study must have been devoted to the subject; and, for its period, the idea was highly ingenious. The instrument, then, emerging from scientific hands, was most probably developed from the monochord, or one-stringed instrument used for the determining of pitch for the church singers of the Middle Ages. The process of evolution is clearly defined. Once a number of notes could be produced from a single string, more strings were added to give a greater compass. But it was soon discovered that it was easier to add extra strings than to multiply the tangents. So it came about that the number of the latter was reduced to two, and each string made to play a note with the semitone above it. In this form the Clavichord remained until the Eighteenth Century. The term "fretted" was applied to those instruments with a number of tangents to each string (German, *gebunden*). Later specimens became bichord and even trichord, and the strings, which earlier were of brass, were afterwards more commonly of steel;—sometimes the bass strings were made of brass and the treble of steel. There were even specimens with octave strings added to the lowest bass notes, probably to assist the latter and to fill the bass.

Exactly when the Clavichord was sufficiently developed to merit its name, is not clear; but it must have been a serviceable instrument by the end of the Fourteenth Century. Yet it was not until the commencement of the Eighteenth Century that there was a separate string for each key and note, and the instrument became "unfretted." Its tone was soft and suitable to small apartments, and the instrument survived as long as it did chiefly on that account, and because of the circumstance that it was capable of an interesting effect known in Germany as "Bebung," an effect which might be called *vibrato* to-day. It was produced by repeating the finger-pressure on the key several times after the note had been struck, pressing the tangent on to the string, and thus, incidentally, slightly raising the pitch of the note. This effect, added to its capability to produce fine tone-gradations, made it the favourite it was with the Eighteenth-century composers.

The compass of the Clavichord varied considerably according to the period and the number of tangents and strings used. Generally a note was omitted from the regular sequence at either end of the keyboard, so that the highest and lowest notes that could be played should be notes of frequent occurrence.

Although the Clavichord does not appear to have been as popular in England as were the Virginal and Spinet, there are sufficient historical and literary allusions to it to show that it was used to a considerable extent by artistic musicians. In the Latin form of the name—Clavicordium (*clavis*, a key)—we find it mentioned in English printed books before the end of the Fifteenth Century, though in Germany it appeared in the first years of that century. A Clavichord of this period also is carved in the roof of St. Mary's Church, Shrewsbury. This specimen possesses six strings but shows nine keys; thus arguing that some of the strings were operated upon by more than one tangent. John Skelton, poet laureate and tutor to Henry VIII, was a great lover of this instrument, and wrote a good deal about it; in his "Agaynste a comely coystrowne, *etc.*," we read: "Comely he clappyth a payre of clauycordys" (*l.* 36);—the word "pair" showing that the custom of using a second and smaller instrument, generally tuned an octave higher, simultaneously with the larger one, was very old (*v.* also Virginal). In Stephen Hawes' *Historie of Graunde amoure and la bell Pucel, called the Pastime of Plesure* (1506), and other works, we meet with the spelling Claricorde, but there can be no doubt that the same instrument is meant. The Privy Purse Expenses of Henry VII give some very interesting information: "1502, January 7. To one that sett the Kings Clevecords xiiis. ivd." "1504, March 6. For a paire of Clavycords, xs." A similar account-book dealing with the expenses of Elizabeth of York (*ed.* N. H. Nicolas, Camden Society, 1830) contains the entry: "1502, August 19. To Hugh Denys for money by him delivered to a straungier that gave the Quene a payre of Clavycordes in crownes for his rewarde . . . iiij*li.*"

In 1663 (November 6) John Hingston, as keeper and repairer of the king's instruments, was paid a sum of money which included a reward for "mending a Claricon." This also was doubtlessly a Clavichord. The change in name was only a passing fancy, probably due to the ignorance of a clerk; and using Clarichorde as a connecting link, Claricon is not so far from Clavichord. Moreover, we similarly find Harpsicon for Harpsichord at the same period.

English specimens of the Clavichord are extremely rare, and

the only one I have ever heard of by an English builder was the late Dr. T. L. Southgate's example (1700) by Peter Hicks (*v. also* WREST).

CLAVICYMBAL: An old English form of the Italian Clavicembalo (Harpsichord). This instrument was so named on the Continent long before the harpsichord was developed into the form it acquired in the Eighteenth Century, and appears to have been little more than a Psaltery (*q.v.*) with a keyboard. The name Clavicembalo or Clavicymbal may have been applied to instruments played with metal plectra as distinct from those later forms which used leather or quill for the same purpose. At any rate the name is found in Germany as early as 1404. The English "Cymbal" was doubtlessly suggested by the bell-like tinkling produced by these instruments. Stephen Hawes has "Claricymbals glorious" (with the same variation of spelling as is often to be met with in the case of the Clavichord) in his *Pastime of Plesure* (*chap.* 16, 1506).

CLAVICYTHERIUM: A keyboard instrument of the Spinet (*q.v.*) type, differing from the Spinet, however, in that the body, sounding-board, and strings, were set vertically instead of horizontally, thus foreshadowing the upright pianoforte. In every other respect the Clavicytherium was a Virginal or Spinet, and was played by means of jacks and plectra. The latter, in a specimen of the early Sixteenth Century illustrated in Hipkins and Gibb's *Musical Instruments*, appears to have been of metal.

CLEAVE. v. CLIFF.

CLIFF: The old term for Clef. It was (and is) the sign prefixed to a composition to indicate its pitch; in other words, it gives the position on a stave of music for a certain note from which "all the other notes in your song or lesson are understood" (Playford). Derived from the Latin *Clavis*, a key, the term is used to determine which voice or instrument shall perform the music which follows it. The old English spelling varied considerably; Cotgrave (*A French and English Dictionary*, 1660) defines the French *Clef* as "a cliffe in musick," and Ford, in the *Lover's Melancholy* (1629), has: "Whom art had never taught cliffs, modes, or notes." In John Playford's *Introduction to the Skill of Musick* we meet with another application of the term. He speaks of a *B Cliff*, belonging to all parts of the polyphony, and used as we should employ the words " key-signature " to-day, making the note it refers to " half a tone or sound lower (or higher) than it was before." When this so-called B Cliff was used to sharpen a note it was known as *B mi* or *B sharp*, and when written to flatten, it was called *B fa* or *B flat*. In this usage the term Cliff, by its etymology, forestalls our key-signature.

CLOSE-PLAY : A technical term employed by the lutenist to signify that fingers once down on a string should not be removed, in view of the possibility of their being required again in the same position. In Close-Play a finger would remain where it fell on the string until needed elsewhere. An explanation of it is given in Barley's *Lute-Book* (end of the Sixteenth Century) : " Thou shalt not need but to remove those fingers which thou shalt be forced, which manner of handling we call *close* or *covert*-play." Thomas Mace (*Musick's Monument*, 1676) is more explicit : " Then take up no stopt Finger, till need so require ; for any stopt Finger, remaining still upon its stop, gives you a better advantage, than if it were taken off, as being a sure Guide, to any other stop following. . . ." Be it noted that the violinist of to-day very frequently uses close-play, although the term has fallen completely into desuetude.

CLOSE SHAKE. *v.* SHAKE.

COMPOSURE : A word frequently used in place of the more usual " Composition." An example of such use is to be found in Roger North's *Memoires of Musick* (1728), where, speaking of the music written during the reign of Charles I, he says : ". . . some plain-song consorts I have seen of so late composure."

CONCENT : Used as a noun and verb by the Elizabethans to mean harmony or concord. Spenser speaks of " A lay of love's delight, with sweet concent," and :

> Such musicke is wise words with time concented,
> To moderate stiffe minds disposed to strive.

Milton, in *At a Solemn Music,* writes : " That undisturbed song of pure concent." The word is derived from the Latin *Concentus* (*concinere ; con* and *canere,* to sing together).

CONSORT : 1. The equivalent of the modern word concert.

2. Earlier, it signified the simultaneous playing of different

instruments in parts, such as could "consort" together. A "Consort of Viols" would be a party of instrumentalists playing the various members of the viol family. Often as many as six together—two trebles, two tenors, and two basses, or two trebles, three tenors, and one bass (the usual combination in a "Chest of Viols")—would perform *ensemble*. A composition for one of these combinations of instruments was similarly known as a Consort. In Stuart England there was also a consort of wind instruments, the Lord Chamberlain's Records containing entries relating to the engagement of musicians for the "Consort of wind musick." Seventeenth-century music-books often contained music for a consort of Viols, Lutes, Citterns, and other instruments.

When Spenser (*Faerie Queene*, III, *l*. 40) speaks of the singing of a number of birds together, he says: "That wonder was to heare their trim consort." Fletcher (*Bloody Brother*) alludes to a "consort of cramm'd capons" in a line quoted in full in the article on the Canary.

CONSORT-VIOL: A bass-viol "of the largest size, and the Strings proportionable" (Playford). It was used for playing in Consort, *i.e.* in *ensemble* music. It found its most appropriate place in the four, five, and six-part Fancies (*q.v.*) so popular at the time of the Viol's vogue. The reason for the Consort-Viol being of the largest size will be apparent when it is remembered that it required the greatest possible amount of sonority when playing against two, or perhaps three, tenor viols, each capable of producing a grave tone of very full quality. Playford also uses the name Consort-Viol (the music for which was "play'd from the Rules of the Gam-ut," *i.e.* from ordinary notation) to distinguish the large chamber-music bass from the smaller Lyra-Viol (*q.v.*) which was played "by Letters or Tablature" (*q.v.*), and tuned Harpway (*q.v.*). For the tuning of the Consort-Viol, see VIOLS.

CORANTO: A dance-form supposed by some to have been introduced into France from Italy by Catherine de Medici, and brought to England during the reign of Elizabeth. It became exceedingly popular in Sixteenth-century England, although it was soon divested of most of its original characteristics, and converted into a merry, sprightly measure. Its speed certainly increased, and if not actually as quick as the Galliard and Jig, it was at least as full of vivacity as both of these forms. The Queen herself was celebrated as a Coranto dancer, and her court was not slow in following suite. As the speed changed, the solemn *terre-à-terre* of the French gave place to a "lofty sprightly dance" (Johnson); and, says Walsh, "I would as soon believe a widow in grief for her husband because I saw her dancing a Coranto about his coffin." The popularity enjoyed by the Coranto in Shakespeare's time accounted for and caused the many allusions to it in the literature of the period. The reference to it in *Twelfth Night* may be seen in the article on the Galliard, and Ben Jonson mentions it also.

In Stuart times the favour shown the Coranto seems to have increased; indeed, it appears that it played the part of the late Victorian waltz in Stuart society, and some writers began to show signs of restlessness under the monotony of the ever-lasting Coranto. Pepys, attending a court ball on November 18, 1666, observed so little variety in the dances that "the Corants grew tiresome." The ball in question was given in honour of the Queen's birthday, and there were present the King and Queen, the Duke and Duchess of York, Prince Rupert, and the Duke and Duchess of Monmouth. On this auspicious occasion the King led off the dance with the Queen. Some four years earlier the genial diarist recounted his experiences at another ball, where ". . . the King led a lady in a Single Coranto . . . and very noble it was and a great pleasure to see" (*Diary*, December 31, 1662). Pepys's entries bear out Selden's statement: "At a solemn dancing, first you had the grave measures, then the Corrantoes and the Gaillardes" (*Table Talk*, 1689).

Remembering the popularity of the Coranto in England, it will not be surprising to find a great many examples of the dance in the works of English composers from the time of Elizabeth to the period at which the form ceased to be danced, and remained only in the instrumental suite. Many of these were original compositions, of course; but the greater number were French Corantoes modified to suit English requirements. It is, in some cases, difficult to recognise the nationality of many forms printed in England, especially in the Stuart period. The later specimens occurred at a time when the music of the cultured classes was largely influenced by French fashions, and thus a great many Corantoes with French names may well be purely English ones deliberately misnamed to secure favour for them. The works of Thomas Robinson, Matthew Locke, John Playford, Thomas Morley, Ferrabosco (Stuart members of the family), William Corkine, and a host of others, all contain specimens of the Coranto. Of the two hundred and forty-five dances and airs contained in Playford's *Court Ayres* (1655), no fewer than fifty-five are Corantoes.

The later Suite and Sonata writers used the form in the accepted Continental manner, following the Almain (*Allemande*).

A rapid sketch of the Coranto's foreign history and original form may assist in making the differences clear between the early French form of the dance and its English use. Whether it had its origin in France or Italy, it was in my opinion first suggested by the Galliard. The fact that some authorities describe the original Courante as one of the most serious, solemn, and dignified of dances, need not disprove this theory; every period and country had its own way of treating the dance-form.

The name, derived from the French *courir*, to run (or from its Italian equivalent), describes one species of the Courante; that which consisted of a succession of running notes. There were three forms of the dance bearing the name, each differing from the others in rhythm. The Italian form, called Corrente, had as its distinguishing feature a succession of running quavers, a circumstance which may prove that the original form may have been taken from the Italian version of a Galliard with the dotted rhythm smoothed out. The French shape (Courante) contained the rhythm dotted-crotchet, quaver, crotchet, and thus shows a remarkable likeness to the Galliard and its successor the Jig. A hybrid form containing both rhythms is to be met with, and was occasionally used, chiefly by Handel. Bach, Mattheson, and Couperin, to mention only three composers, used both the Italian and French forms, but kept them apart and adhered to the distinguishing titles (*Corrente* and *Courante*). The time-signature was generally 3/4 or 3/2, a characteristic of the 3/4 measure being that the last measure was written in 6/4, a change that may have been called for by some terpsichorean requirement. Later, when the form ceased to be danced, the 6/4 measure was used for the whole of the composition. Its form was the usual one of two or more sentences of eight or a multiple of eight measures, each repeated, and it usually began on the up-beat. The early German writers insisted upon many academic points, but when the form became more elastic, Courantes were evolved that were as unlike the original dance as they could possibly have been. Taking all these circumstances into consideration, then, and remembering the different rhythms employed in the writing of the dance, we may take it that the Coranto formed the connecting link between the early Galliard and the later Canary and Jig on the one hand, and led to the Menuet, and possibly the Waltz, on the other.

CORNEMUSE. *v.* BAGPIPE.

CORNET: A wood-wind instrument very much used in Tudor and Stuart England (the German *Zinke;* but not to be confounded with the modern brass instrument). It was a horn-like instrument made of wood, generally covered with leather, and often elaborately ornamented with ivory and silver. Finger-holes enabled it to produce the different notes within its range. It was made bent or straight, though the curved specimens seem to have been more common. Its tone, according to most contemporary writers, was bright and pleasing when the instrument was well played. Its place of origin is somewhat uncertain, though the very early appearance of allusions to it in English manuscripts would seem to suggest England as one of the first countries to use it, if it was not actually evolved here (Harleian MS. 603; end of the Tenth Century; British Museum; and a Psalter dating from A.D. 1000 in the Cambridge University Library). Harleian MS. 1419A contains a list of musical instruments belonging to Henry VIII, and among them were: "Twoo gitteron pipes of Ivorie tipped with silver and gilte they are caulled Cornettes . . .," and, "xiiij gitteroune pipes of woodde in a bagge of leather they are caulled Cornettes." An account of the Cornet is afforded by one Randle Holmes in Book III of his *Academy of Armory* (British Museum, Harleian MS. 2034, *c.* 1688): "It is a long and somewhat bending Instrument made of an Horn, and some tyme garnished at the mouth, middle, and end with plates of silver, but generally plaine. It hath six holes above for the fingers, and two under for the thumb. It is a delicate pleasant wind musick if well played and Humored."

Laneham, in a letter of 1575, already speaks admiringly of its tone. It appears that Holmes's Seventeenth-century experiences gave him specimens made of horn, though the leather-covered wooden instruments seem to have been the commonest, at any rate in Tudor times. Stainer and Barrett's *Dictionary of Musical Terms* is not correct when it gives the Cornet as "an obsolete reed instrument not unlike a hautboy . . .", persisting in also calling the *Zinke* " a coarse reed instrument " (article WAITS).

A complete set or consort (*q.v.*) of cornets contained a Treble, a Tenor or Common Cornet, and a Grand Cornet. This set was known as a " nest of cornets." Its compass extended a little over two octaves, the Tenor being pitched a fifth below the Treble, and the Grand Cornet an octave below. The tenor instrument was by a long way the most frequent pitch and it was used in every conceivable form of music all over Europe for at least half a millennium.

Allusions to the instrument become more frequent as we approach the Elizabethan and Stuart writers. " The musicke of Cornettes " is mentioned in the tragedy of *Gorboduc* (1561) and in *Jocasta* (1565). Spenser refers to it in the *Shepherd's Calendar* (1579), and in John Howes' *Familiar and Friendly Discourse* (1587) we read : " I also think it convenient that the children should learne to sing and play uppon all sorts of instruments, as to sound . . . the cornett, *etc.*," which shows the value placed upon the instrument. Ford (*The Sun's Darling*, II, 1) has : " The way is windy and narrow ; for, look you, I do but wind this cornet, and if another answers it, she comes." Dekker's masque *The King's Entertainment* shows by a stage direction : " A noise of Cornets, a Consort, a set of Viols," that the cornet was reckoned among the high-class instruments of the day. In the Seventeenth-century drama it was very frequently utilised for sounding at the beginning of the acts, and Beaumont and Fletcher, Drayton (1607), Nathaniel Field (1612), Shakespeare, and Ben Jonson all speak of it or order its use in the stage directions. Marston in *Sophonisba* (Prologue to *Act* I) says : " Cornets sound a march."

The uses to which the Cornet was put were many and highly important. In the orchestra of wind-instruments it held an indispensable place, from the time at which the combination of instruments had taken some regular form. In the band it can be traced back as far as the Fourteenth Century, and in a work of that century (*Octavian Imperator*, Weber's *Metrical Romances*, 1810, *ll.* 67, 68) it is already mentioned in the lines: "Ther myghth men here menstralcye, Trompys, taborns, and Cornettys crye." The instrument was much used at court, and the King in 1503 sent his cornettist, Bonatus, with his daughter Queen Margaret of Scotland, to play before her royal friends.

In sacred music the Cornet was much used, and when boys' voices were not available it was pressed into service to supply the parts these should have sustained. In the official account of appointments to Canterbury Cathedral (1532) there are mentioned two performers on the instrument. That they improved the tone of the service there can be no reasonable doubt; "an intelligencer from Rome" was "struck with amazement and admiration" upon hearing "the solemn music, with the voices and organs, cornets and sackbuts" (*Life of Archbishop Whitgift; Biogr. Britt., p.* 4255). The *Well-Tuned Organ* of J. Brookband (1660) tells us that the services which Charles I attended at Oxford were much improved by the use of Cornets. The particular functions of the instrument are made clear by Laud after he had held a visitation of Canterbury in 1634; he found "in lieu of a deacon and sub-deacon, whose office it was to read the epistle and gospel . . . are substituted two corniters and two sack-butters, whom we most willingly maintain for the decorum of our quire, though with greater charge than we might have done the other." During the Commonwealth the training of boys' voices for the Church service was neglected, with the result that after the Restoration cornets were employed to fill their places. Matthew Locke's *Present Practice of Music Vindicated* (1673) informs us that "For above a year after the opening of His Majesty's Chappell the orderers of the musick there were necessitated to supply the superior parts of their musick with cornets and men's feigned voices, there being not one lad for all that time capable of singing his part readily." Roger North (*Life of the Lord Keeper*), speaking of the cathedrals of York and Durham, says: "In these churches wind music was used in the choir, which I apprehend might be introduced at first for want of voices if not of organs; but as I hear, they are now disused. To say the truth nothing comes so near, or rather imitates so much, an excellent voice, as a cornet-pipe ; but the labour of the lips is too great, and it is seldom well sounded."

The English players on the cornet enjoyed a high reputation for excellence, and they were engaged to occupy important posts in many a foreign court. The Duke of Lorraine, for example, sent his cornettist Jean Presse to engage players in England (1604) and acquired the services of John Adson and William Burt. Adson remained abroad for almost thirty years, and then returned to the English court as a "musician for the flutes and cornet." The Stuart kings secured themselves against any dearth of good performers by always having two boys in training. Their instructor was Andrew Lanier, and in 1630 he received the sum of £29 16s. 8d. for this service. His two boys, having passed through their apprenticeship, were immediately replaced by two more : ". . . because the two boyes he lately had . . . are, because enabled, preferred to His Majesty's service, these are to certify that in their room I have appointed two others, to be bred by him in musique" (*Lord Chamberlain's Records*, 1639/40). The salaries received by the Stuart cornettists compared very favourably with those enjoyed by the other members of the royal music. John Adson, before mentioned, received £46 per annum (1640), while another method of remuneration is exemplified in the case of Thomas Lanier, who was paid 1s. 8d. a day, in addition to £7 11s. 8d. a year for board-wages and £29 9s. 2d. "for apparrell." This last-mentioned item is unusual, for the common allowance "for livery" was £16 2s. 6d. per annum.

The prices paid for specimens of the instrument at the time of its active use varied according to the amount of work put into them. An example bought for Trinity College (Cambridge) in 1595 cost £1 (a large sum in those days), and the *Household Accounts* of Sir Thomas Kytson, for 1573/4, show that £4 was expended for seven cornets. Andrew Lanier purchased a number of them for use in the royal music, and in 1630 was paid £16 10s. for six specimens—three tenors at sixty shillings and three trebles at fifty shillings. In 1632 as much as £13 was paid for a single cornet, and taking the value of money in those days into consideration, the specimen must have been highly ornamented and loaded with silver.

The rise of the violin and the improvement in the reed-instruments probably caused the eclipse of the Cornet after an uninterrupted artistic use extending over at least three hundred years.

CORTHOL. *v.* CURTAL.

COUNTER: To Counter a song or instrumental composition was, from the beginning of the Sixteenth to the end of the Seventeenth Century, to perform *extempore* divisions (*q.v.*) upon it. John Skelton uses the verb in *The Bowge of Courte* (*c.* 1515), saying of Riot that "Counter he coude O Lux upon a a potte" (the text alluded to being that of the hymn *O Lux beata trinitas*). The term Countering is to be met with very frequently, and was used in the same sense.

COUNTERING. *v.* COUNTER.

COUNTER-TENOR: 1. The highest male (adult) voice; the Alto. The spelling *Contratenor* (suggestive of its Latin origin) is given in the State Papers, examples being contained in the Lord Chamberlain's Records for May, 1633. In the entry for April 14, 1674, these singers are given as "Counter Tenners."

2. The term was also applied to one of the Means (*q.v.*), or inner strings of the viols; the fourth string counting downwards from the treble being so named.

COUNTRY CRIES. *v.* CRIES.

COUNTRY DANCE: A terpsichorean diversion, purely English, that seems to have been distinguished from other dances by its steps and manner of performance. The music written for it cannot be said to have possessed any peculiarities, for it could occur in practically any dance-rhythm. It is a remarkable thing that English writers of the past should have attempted to explain the name by deriving it from the French *Contredanse*, while French authorities said it "paroit venir de l'Anglois, *country danse*, danse de campagne." The fact is that this form is of undoubted native origin, and is mentioned in our literature at a very early date. It was, in its original state, the merry frolic of the countryman and his lass, free in performance, and gay in character. It was not saddled with the traditions of the semi-ceremonial Morris Dance, or the artistic restraint of the ball-room forms.

John Essex, in the Preface to his treatise *For the Further Improvement of Dancing* (1710), says that "Every Country has had some Particular manner of Dancing peculiar to itself since ye beginning of the World, but this which we call Country Dancing is originally the Product of this Nation, and is used in most of the Courts in Europe . . ." ; and John Weaver, following in 1712, added: "Country Dances . . . is a Dancing the peculiar Growth of this Nation." Where and when this "peculiar growth" had its roots would be almost impossible to decide; most probably in some of the varied forms of the Branle, developed or adapted to suit the requirements of the dancers. But whatever may have been the *fons et origo* of the Country Dance, the Seventeenth Century saw it at the height of its glory, with John Playford taking advantage of the opportunities it presented. The *Dancing-Master* (1651 and almost a score of further editions) contained a large number of tunes suitable for this form of dancing, together with directions for performance. Only the melody of each piece is given, and this was in all probability played on a viol, violin, bagpipe—or, more certainly earlier—on the pipe and tabor. These tunes were not new in Playford's day, and many were then already traditional. They included such well-known melodies as "All in a Garden Green," "Adson's Saraband," "Blew Cap," "An Old Man is a Bed Full of Bones," "Bobbing Joe," "Dargason," and a host of others. Many of these and similar airs were used as thematic material by the virginal composers of the late Tudor and early Stuart periods, and "Sellenger's Round," "Trenchmore," "Greensleeves," *etc.*, were treated by the composers represented in the Fitzwilliam Virginal Book. And when it is remembered that the earlier editions of the *Dancing-Master* appeared during the Commonwealth, it will be realised how little the Puritan *régime* interfered with the innocent pastimes of the masses. Playford's instructions show that some of the dances were arranged as "Longways for 6," "Longways for as many as will," "A Square dance for eight," and so on. The last-named was, of course, the Seventeenth-century ancestor of the Quadrille.

The Stuart court, although compelled by some regard for etiquette to open their balls with the recognised forms, such as Pavanes, Galliards, Corantoes, or Branles, according to period, nevertheless brought the evening's proceedings to a conclusion with a bout of jigging and Country Dances. The passing of Merry England and the introduction of foreign forms, though many of the latter were influenced by the Country Dance, caused the decline of "the peculiar growth" of this nation. So complete was the change, and so great the mania for things with a foreign name, that, placing the vehicle before the tractor, the scribblers of this country converted the Country Dance into a descendant of the French *Contredanse*.

COURSE: In the language of the lute-player a Course was a string, and in the old books dealing with the lutes we read of "eleven course" instruments (*i.e.* lutes with eleven strings), and so on. The derivation of the word, used in this sense, is not clear. It is possible that the strings, drawn taut and straight, like a running-track, were named by the latter (Middle English, *Course;* Old French, *Cours;* Latin, *Cursus* from *Currere*, to run). The fact that the strings were used in unison-pairs helps to increase the similarity. There is just a possibility of the term being connected in some way with the German *Chor;* Praetorius (*Theatrum Instrumentorum*, 1620) using the expression "Sechs-Choerichte Cither" for a six-stringed cittern.

COURT MUSIC. *v.* ROYAL MUSIC.

COVERT-PLAY. *v.* CLOSE-PLAY.

CRACKLE: A direction belonging to the lutenist, and referring to one of the methods of striking chords on the instruments of the lute family. It would appear that "to Crackle" a chord was to divide it arpeggio-fashion, although Mace's definition is not as clear as it might be. In *Musick's Monument*, 1676, he says: "To Crackle such to three part stops, is only to divide each stop, with your thumb and two fingers, so as not to lose time, but to give each crotchet its due quantity." If the three-note chords were to be distributed between thumb and two fingers "so as not to lose time," it would seem that a solid chord were intended. But the phrase, "give each crotchet its due quantity," suggests that the three notes were to be played separately, though equally. I favour the arpeggio interpretation, not only on account of the last-quoted sentence, but also because Mace gives two other methods of striking, one of them called "Full-Play" (*q.v.*), and the other "Raking" (*q.v.*), which latter appears to me to have come somewhere between a chord in "full-play" and one "crackled" in effect.

CRIES: The "crying" of their wares by itinerant trades-folk is a very ancient institution, and each article had its own traditional melody, the origin of which is lost in the mists of the past. During the Seventeenth Century in England, a popular species of composition took the form of these Cries threaded together to make a sort of vocal Fancy in four or more parts. The *ensemble* sections were interspersed with soli, and the whole was often accompanied by a consort of viols. Thomas Weelkes, for example, wrote *The Cryes of London*, as also did Orlando Gibbons, both compositions being contained in Additional MS. 29427 (*c.* 1616; British Museum), the same volume including the *Country Cryes* of Richard Deering. The last-named composition is given, with slight differences, in Additional MS. 17792. A full account of the separate cries, with their tunes, is given by Sir Frederick Bridge in *The Old Cryes of London* (Novello, 1921).

CROWD: A stringed instrument of great antiquity, originally plucked with the fingers or plectrum, and later—in some forms of the instrument—also played with the bow. A careless comparison between early references and illustrations has often forced the student to the conclusion that between the Crowd, the Rote (*Rotte* and *Rotta*), the Cruit, and the Crwth, there must have existed a close connection. For one thing, they were all played in practically the same way, although later in the history of the individual forms differences were developed that tended to keep them distinct. But, in spite of the fact that we may at the present time treat all these instruments together, they existed in at least four distinct forms, which it will be well to keep apart. There was, in the first place, a Rote or *Rotte* with parallel sides and a hole cut in the upper part of the body for the plucking hand. Secondly, there was a form of Crowd with slightly indented sides, a hole, of varying shape for the fingers of the left hand to pass through (but not so large as in the first case), and strings passing over a bridge and fastened to a tail-piece. Thirdly, the Irish form called

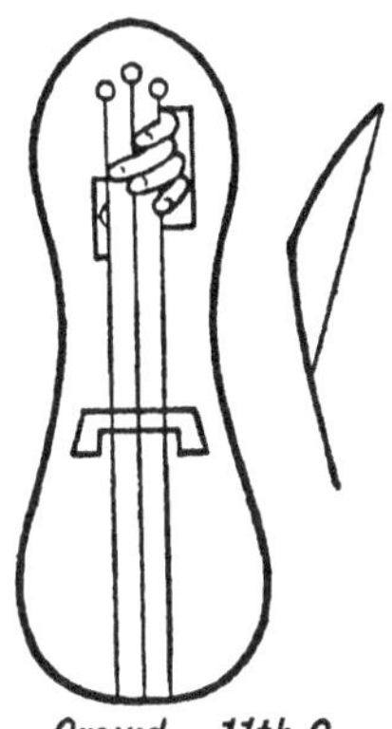
Crowd. 11th C.

Cruit, which appears to be more like the descendant of an early lyre or small harp (the small hand-harp being indeed called "cruit" in Ireland). And fourthly, the Welsh Crwth with bowed strings over a bridge, and plucked strings at the side of the fingerboard. There does not appear to be any close relationship between any of these four forms; and notwithstanding the verdict of many high authorities, I am of opinion that, although the first and second of the forms mentioned may be of common origin, the Welsh and the Irish forms are quite distinct, and may have been evolved in the case of the Crwth from an Eastern lyre, and in that of the Cruit from an early harp. There is nothing extravagant in the latter supposition; commerce between Palestine, Egypt, Greece, Rome, the Levant, and Britannia was very much cultivated even in the remote pre-Christian era. And the parts touched by these travellers were just those which used the instrument in its Welsh or Irish forms.

Every writer on the subject mentions the allusion to the *Chrotta* by Venantius Fortunatus (Bishop of Poitiers, *c.* 609), and it would seem almost heretical to leave it unmentioned here. From the following century an illustration is forthcoming showing the form of the Rote as it was used in England at that time (Cotton Manuscripts, Vesp. A. 1, British Museum). It is a six-stringed instrument, but no bridge or tail-piece can be discerned. The strings simply extend from the bottom of the instrument to the upper end of the hole through which they were plucked. The sides are parallel, and the top and bottom slightly convex. Such an instrument as this could not have been bowed, and similar examples can be seen in other manuscripts. But in another English specimen of *c.* 1400—although in shape it is not at all unlike the one just mentioned—the probability of its having been bowed is not precluded. No bridge is shown, it is true, but the strings (three in number) are affixed by means of a tail-piece. The fingering hand is still inserted through a hole apparently cut right through the thickness of the instrument, but no fingerboard is visible. There can be no possible doubt that there must have been one, for no one in their senses would cut a hole through an instrument unless for the purpose of stopping; because there was a nearer way to the strings from the front, if it was only required to pluck them open. Now, if this Crowd of 1400 was fingered, and had its strings attached to a tail-piece, it was most probably bowed also. It should be noticed that although *Rottes* have been found portrayed with from five to a score of strings, the bowed variety—even in the cases where the bow was certainly used—rarely had more than three. It is important to remember, should there be a danger of confusing these three-stringed, bowed Crowds with the rebecks, that the latter had necks and heads that held the pegs, while the former only had bodies—so to speak—the fingering hand approaching the strings by means of an opening in the instrument.

So far the shape of the Crowd has been oblong, or oblong with slightly curved top and bottom. Another form must now be considered : that of the specimen portrayed in bas-relief in Worcester Cathedral (Choir), and dating from the Thirteenth Century. This variety of the Crowd was oval, about two and a half times as long as it was broad, had a couple of primitive, comma-shaped, sound-holes, a tail-piece, and the hole for the fingering hand was still present. But the chief point of dissimilarity between this Crowd and those already described was the fact that its long sides were decidedly incurved, like those of an elongated guitar ; and I can see no other reason for this incurving, at the place it occurs, than to facilitate bowing. Here, again, no bridge is shown ; this being the only link wanting to make of the instrument one that might be easily bowed. But a French specimen of the Eleventh Century exhibits even this feature ; and in the example in question it is perfectly flat. This would argue that the three strings were bowed simultaneously as chords ; a fact that need not prove the falsity of the bowing theory, for the Welsh Crwth, which was demonstrably bowed, had a bridge of equal flatness.

Now, whether the two forms of the Crowd (or Rote) already treated had a common origin or not, cannot be determined with certainty to-day. They may be related, but so many of the intermediate stages in the evolution appear to be missing, that no advantage can be gained by wasting time on profitless speculation. But one point may be noted ; and that is, at the time of the incurved specimens a distinction seems to have been made between the plucked variety and the bowed. Perhaps the name Rote was applied to the former, and Crowd reserved for the other. Certain it is that, in spite of their similarity, contemporary writers of the Fifteenth Century mention the two forms together, and they would not do this if *Rote* and *Crowd* had been applied to one and the same instrument. My own observation brings me to the conclusion that the Rote was not bowed and that the Crowd, in its later medieval development at any rate, was so played.

Literary mention of both names is not rare in England ; in *Sir Tristrem* (Thirteenth Century) the " Croude " is referred to, and Wiclif has " Crowde " in his Testament. In the *Kyng of Tars* (Ritson's *Metrical Romances, l.* 485) we read :

Nas munstral non with harpe ne crouthe.

In *Octavian Imperator* (Fourteenth Century, *l.* 69) we meet with the form Roowte. *Sir Degrevant* (*l.* 37 ; *Thornton Romances, ed.* J. O. Halliwell, Camden Society, 1844) has the line :

Well to play in a rote,

where the preposition may mean a misprint or slip of the author's pen. *Lybeaus Disconus* (*l.* 138) also uses the term Crouthe. Chaucer frequently made his characters musical and wrote of one who could sing well and " pleyen on a Rote," while John Lydgate (*Reson and Sensuallyte*, MS. Fayrfax 16, Bodl., and British Museum MS. Addit. 29729) has : " Harpys, fythels, and eke rotys " (*l.* 5579). In the *Squyr of Lowe Degre* the same name occurs, as it does also in John Gower's *Confessio Amantis* (*l.* 829). Stephen Hawes refers to " Harpes, Lutes, and Crowdes right delicious " (*Pastime of Pleasure*, 1506, *chap.* xvi.). In Scotland, too, the word used was the English one (Crowd ; mentioned in Gavin Douglas' *Palace of Honour*, 1501, printed 1579). Exactly when the instrument fell into disuse would be difficult to determine. The evidence of poets goes for nothing in such cases, for lutes are mentioned by present-day writers. So that when Spenser writes of the " trembling crowd " in his *Epithalamion* (1594) he may have only used the word with a poet's licence. It must be mentioned in passing, too, that the words Crowd and Crowder may have been applied to the instruments of the Rebeck and Fiddle type and their players, by writers who had no very exact knowledge of earlier distinctions.

In the case of the Irish Cruit we have an instrument that, in its earliest forms at any rate, appears to have been more like a lyre or small harp than were any of the crowds and rotes. A small Cruit, represented on a sculptured cross of the Eighth Century, and a larger one in a similar place dating from the Ninth Century, were both clearly of the harp-type, and could only have been played by plucking. No doubt later developments along certain lines enabled a bow to be used, but under what influences these alterations were made is not clear. It must be noted that authorities on Ancient Irish music look upon the Cruits on the sculptured crosses mentioned above as early harps and nothing more. There is plenty of justification for this ; but it does not prevent the instrument having been developed along two distinct lines—one leading to a bowed Cruit, and the other to the Irish harp.

The Welsh form, although persisting in a highly improved shape until the end of the Eighteenth Century, is not mentioned very early ; indeed, we have allusions to bowed Crowds in England much anterior to bowed Crythau. Whatever may have been the form of the earliest Crwth used in Wales (and it will be seen later that it was most probably the three-stringed Crowd), the last development of it came after considerable outside influence had been exercised. It is mentioned in a poem by " Gruffydd ab Davydd ab Hywell " (*c.* Fifteenth Century), and an extract from it is given by John Jones (Idris Vychan) in *An Essay on Penilion Singing* (1885). From the description of the Crwth given in this extract it is not quite clear that it refers to the instrument as we know it from existing examples ; and the bow that is mentioned may not be a bow for playing so much as some curved part of the instrument. Gruffydd says that it had " a fine wooden chest " and that its value was " one pound " ; further that it had six strings, " one for each finger and two for the thumb." The sentence of which I can make very little is : " Its frontlet (or diadem, chaplet) is round as a wheel and the bow is across its short point."

Hipkins and Gibb in their beautiful work on old instruments illustrate the final form of the Welsh Crwth, and a specimen may be seen in the Victoria and Albert Museum (London). In these the instrument had a hollow body made of a single slab of wood, with the belly glued on to it. Attached to this shallow box was an arch which held at its centre the finger-board and the tuning-pegs. Two circular sound-holes were cut in the belly, and the lower ends of the strings were fastened to a tail-piece. Between the end of the fingerboard and the tail-piece was placed a bridge of peculiar construction. The right foot rested on the table, while the left, much longer, passed through the left sound-hole and rested on the inside of the instrument's back, thus fulfilling the double function of foot and sound-post. This use of the bridge foot is not an isolated one. A third foot in the centre of the bridge rested, like the right foot, on the belly. Over the fingerboard were mounted four strings, and running alongside were another two; this use of additional strings to be plucked by the thumb was again quite common in many instruments (*e.g.* in the Viola di Bardone or Barytone, several varieties of the Lute, *etc.*). The tuning varied, and the commonest appears to have been:

the first two notes being that of the plucked strings. This accordance was still used in the Eighteenth Century (Edward Jones, *Musical and Poetical Relicks of the Welsh Bards*, 1794) An alternative tuning was:

given by William Bingley (1804) who met a Welshman a Carnarvon in 1801 who played on a Crwth thus tuned. Th Hon. Daines Barrington also speaks of a John Morgan wh played at Carnarvon in 1801, probably referring to the sam performer. The flatness of the bridge is a feature reminiscen of the bridges used on the three-stringed Crowds; individua strings could not have been bowed, and chords chiefly mus have been produced. With the peculiar tuning of the instru ment some most effective combinations must have bee possible.

A three-stringed Crwth—*Crwth Trithant*—is frequentl mentioned, which Engel thinks was "a sort of violin, or mo properly a rebeck"; and Hipkins is "disposed to agree" wit him. Why Engel should think thus is not clear when the three-stringed Crowd above-mentioned can much more probably be the instrument alluded to. Moreover, Hipkins says that the tuning of the Crwth Trithant was the tonic, the fifth, and the octave, which was that of the Organistrum or primitive hurdy-gurdy, very popular at the period from which date the references to the three-stringed Crwth.

CRUIT. *v.* CROWD.

CRWTH. *v.* CROWD.

CURTAIN-TUNE. *v.* ACT-TUNE.

CURTAL: An obsolete instrument, playing the part of the modern bassoon. Its chief characteristic was the doubling of the long tube upon itself so that the finger-holes at either end became equally easy of reach, and so that the fingers and thumb of the same hand could work together. This bending of the tube naturally shortened it, and this circumstance gave the instrument its name (French *Courtaut* or *Courtaud*, shortened or squat). A form still shorter than the ordinary Curtal was used, and called the Racket or Sausage-Bassoon. The Double Curtal was pitched an octave lower than the ordinary Curtal.

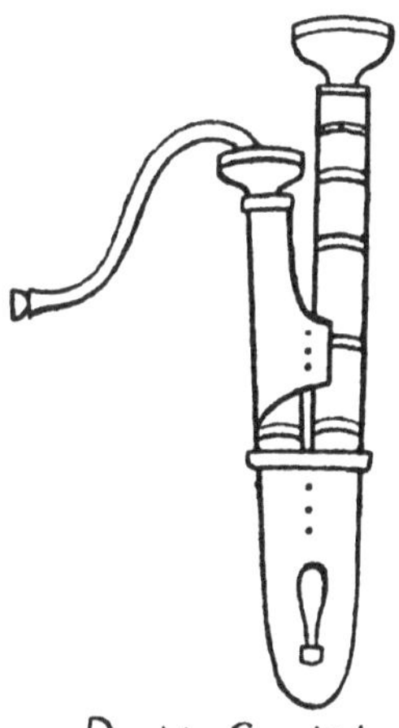

Double Curtal
(Randle Holme. Academy of Armory
British Museum Ms. Harleian 2034.
Bk. III 17th Century)

The only old-English account of the instrument which seems accurate, is that given by Randle Holme in his manuscript *Academy of Armory* (British Museum, *Harl. MS.* 2034, *Bk.* III, *c.* 1688). A sketch of the instrument is also included, and from it we see that the Curtal was composed of a sort of knee-piece into which two tubes were fitted in such a way as to form a continuous air channel, bent like a hair-pin. The two tubes were of unequal length, the shorter being connected with the mouthpiece by means of an S-shaped tube. Holme describes it as follows : " A Double Curtaile this is double ye bigness of the single . . . and its play is eight notes deeper. It is as it were two pipes fixed in on thick bass pipe, one much longer than the other, from the top of the lower comes a crooked pipe of Brass . . . in which is fixt a Reed, through it the wind passeth to make the instrument make a sound. It hath six Holes on the outside and one Brass key called the double *F fa ut* on that side next the man or back part and two Brass keys the highest called double *La sol re* and the other double *B mi*." The curious names for the keys of the instrument were probably those of the notes that these keys produced (*v.* Gamut). Carl Engel mentions a specimen of the Fifteenth-century Curtal in the Conservatoire of Music at Paris, and the existence of this example may account for the full description given in the Encyclopedia of de Felice (1772). Although the instrument was very much used, especially in England, specimens of it are very rare ; and good contemporary accounts are all the more welcome. De Felice says of it : " Courtaut is nothing different than a shortened fagotto or bassoon, which can serve as bass to the *musettes.* It is made out of one piece of cylindrical wood and resembles a thick stick. It has eleven holes, seven on top ; the eighth, ninth, tenth, and eleventh are underneath. The instrument is pierced throughout its length by two holes ; the seventh hole indicating the connecting-point at which these two tubes meet. In order to make of these two tubes one continuous canal, a small box is adjusted, by which means the wind is carried from the reed to the eleventh hole, in such manner that the air descends and remounts. Besides the holes already mentioned, there are six others : three on the right for those who play on this instrument from the right side, and three on the left for the others. Those that are not used are closed with wax. On the others are placed little funnels of wood called " udders " (*tetines*), which penetrate as far as the second canal, into which the holes under the instrument open. Of all these holes, two of the under ones, 9 and 10, give the highest sounds : the six holes, 1 to 6, follow, the sixth hole making the seventh note. The tenth is called the thumb-hole, because it is closed by that member ; it opens into the first canal, just as the six which follow it. The seventh hole gives no sound at all, whether it be open or closed; it merely effects or interrupts the continuity of the tube. The udders form the eighth, ninth, and tenth holes, the eleventh serving for nothing but as an exit for the wind."

The date at which the instrument was first used in England cannot be determined with any degree of certainty. Judging from the circumstance that it was enumerated among the instruments in the possession of Sir Thomas Kytson, of Hengrave Hall (*c.* 1600), the second half of the Sixteenth Century may be a reasonable date to assign to its *debut* in this country. In the *Household Accounts* of the knight just named we read under date December, 1574: "For an instrument called a Curtall, xxxs."; and the way the entry is made seems to suggest that the instrument was not well known, or we might expect to find the item "For a Curtal." References to the instrument are not sufficiently numerous to afford materials for an unbroken history of its use, but enough can be gleaned from what we know to enable us to form a fair idea of its functions. In the Chapel Royal the Curtal was used regularly, and at a festival service of the Knights of the Garter at Windsor the instrument in question took part in the accompaniment.

The Lord Chamberlain's Records give a good deal of information concerning the engagement of performers on the Curtal for the Royal Band. In 1663 (June 20) a warrant "to pay Edward Strong, musician, the sum of £50 for three good Curtalls, by him bought and delivered for his Majesty's service" was issued, and in 1669 (November 30) Robert Strong was to receive £52 for "two double Curtolls . . . given to Segnior Francisco for the service of the Queenes Majesty." An entry dated August 30, 1662 (*Vol.* 741) orders Robert and Edward Strong "to attend with their double Curtolls in his Majesty's Chappell Royall at Whitehall." We can form no opinion as to how many players on the Curtals were employed in the royal orchestra, for the entries in the State Papers are not always clear on the point; several musicians made a habit of playing upon two or more instruments and were often entered simply as "for the wind-music." It is most probable that some of the players on the hautboy performed on the Curtals when the necessity arose. Such a doubling was not unusual, and there is nothing extraordinary in a musician, who understood the treble of an instrument, playing also on the bass of the same species. Only three or four more references to the instrument—that is to say, references able to add to our knowledge of the subject—are known to me. The double Curtal was represented in the Coronation procession of James II, and the municipal books of the Edinburgh Town Council have an entry dating from 1696, giving the information that the Cornets (*q.v.*) of the Town Waits (*q.v.*) were changed for the "French Hautboye and double Curtle, instruments far more proper. . . ." The instrument persisted well into the Eighteenth Century, and in the "grenadier music" of the Honourable Artillery Company it had a place as late as 1731. At a date not much anterior to this Dr. Robert Creyghton wrote the well-known verse in Additional MS. 37074 (British Museum) containing the lines:

> I hear a Thunder rolling here beneath,
> Where Curtals and Bassoons their murmurs breathe.

Another manuscript in the British Museum (Additional 36710; not later than 1732) states that Handel's pastoral *Acis* needed a "double Curtal" for the accompaniment to some of the songs.

There can be no doubt that the Curtal was, for some time, used side by side with the bassoon which was soon to displace it. Grassineau's Musical Dictionary of 1740 still gives: "Curtail, *double*, a musical wind instrument like the Bassoon, which plays the bass to the Hautboy." In this way—as the bass of the hautboy family—the Curtal was used during the whole of its career in England, and although, as we have seen, the instrument was known here in the days of Queen Elizabeth, it did not seem to be very widely used until the middle of the Stuart period.

DESCANT: A term used to signify a disquisition on a theme or ground (*q.v.*). Tyndale (before 1536) has: "Twenty doctours expounde one Text xx wayes as children make descant upon Playne Song." Richard Edwards (*Damon and Pythias*, 1571) uses practically the same simile: ". . . your playne song to sing descant upon." Shakespeare employs the term as a verb in *Richard III* (I, 1): "Unless I spy my shadow in the sun, and descant on my own deformity." In the *Squyr of Lowe Degre* the word is spelled *dyscant*.

At the period from which these quotations have been taken,

the term had a fairly wide application. In the first place it could mean the part or parts added to a plain song or *canto fermo*, in the nature of divisions; and thus Tyndale's use of it was musically quite correct. North (*Memoires of Musick*) says "the early discipline of musick in England was . . . to sing plain-song at sight, and moreover to descant, or sing consort parts at sight . . . and this not only of one part onely, but art was so farr advanced that divers would descant upon plaine-song extempore together. . . ." Christopher Simpson in 1659 speaks of "Descant, or Division."

In the Thirteenth and Fourteenth Centuries the word meant the simultaneous sounding of two or more different themes in harmony, and thus was the forerunner of harmony and counterpoint. In this sense John Playford employs the term until near the end of the Seventeenth Century: "The Art of Descant, or Composing Musick in Parts."

Both senses of the word were used at the same time in the middle of the century. Christopher Simpson (*Division-Violist*, 1659), in speaking of the differences that existed between Descant and Breaking the Ground (*q.v.*), says: "Division, or Descant-Diminution, is that, which maketh another distinct, and concording part unto the Ground. It differs from the former (Breaking the Ground) in these Particulars. That, breaks the notes of the Ground; This Descants upon them. That, takes the liberty to wander sometimes beneath Ground; This (as in its proper sphere) moves still above it. That, meets every succeeding note of the Ground, in the Unison or Octave; This, in any of the Concords."

DIALOGUE: A composition, as its name implies, for two voices, very popular in the Seventeenth Century, not only in England, but all over the Continent of Europe. Its form was rapidly developed and "dialogues" are to be met with in three or more parts. Additional MS. 11608 (British Museum, *c.* 1656) contains a "Dialogue of Juno, Venus, Pallas, and Paris" in two and four parts, by John Hilton; and another by Ramsey called "A Dialogue between Saul, ye Witch of Endor, and Samuell's Ghost." *Ayres and Dialogues* were published in large numbers during the second half of the Seventeenth Century, the texts being chiefly pastoral in character. Of especial interest and importance were the sacred dialogues of the period, which in all probability had their origin in the antiphonal singing of the Middle Ages.

DIAPASON: A Greek term meaning to pass "through all" (the notes) and thus arrive at the octave, whence it came to be the name of the octave itself. Playford explains Diapason as "a perfect Eighth, and contains five whole Tones and two half Tones." It is easy to see how a word applied to a duplication of a note came to mean, in a general sense, concord; and in this way it is employed by many writers. Shakespeare uses the word in *Lucrece* (*l.* 1132) and Milton, in the poem, *At a Solemn Music*, has: ". . . whose love their motion sway'd In perfect diapason." In its stricter meaning, John of Trevisa (translating Ranulf Higden's *Polychronicon*) used it as *dyapason;* and so it is printed in Wynkyn de Worde's edition of 1495. The last-mentioned work also contains the "Duplex Diapason" or double octave, although the example printed with the text contains a note too many.

In England "open" and "stopped" diapason are terms used in connection with the organ.

DIAPHONY: According to accounts given by Hucbald, Guido d'Arezzo, and other writers of works printed by Coussemaker (*Scriptores, etc.*), Diaphony may be said to have been, for all ordinary purposes, the same as Organum (*q.v.*). This early attempt at harmony produced long successions of fourths or fifths, which, to modern ears, sound intolerable; but Guido gives examples in which seconds and thirds are more frequently used, with the result that the music is proportionately more interesting. Diaphony had become fairly free by Guido's time, and the only interval studiously avoided was the tritone (the *diabolus in musica*).

DIMINUTION: 1. In Mensural Music, the halving of the value of the notes, or doubling their speed, by an alteration in the time-signature (*v.* TIME, *Tempus*).

2. In music of a contrapuntal character, Diminution consists of the restatement of a theme in notes of a smaller value—*i.e.* a subject that has been given in minims or crotchets, being repeated in crotchets or quavers, respectively.

DIRECT: A sign placed at the end of each line of music, and later at the foot of every page, to give the performer notice of the next following note, fulfilling the functions of the "catch-word" in early printed books. Playford gives the sign as follows:

and says that it "serves to direct to the place of the first Note on the next line."

DISCANT. *v.* DESCANT.

DIVIDE. *v.* DIVISION.

DIVISION: To "divide" a piece of music meant to write a variation upon it by dividing the long notes into a larger number of short ones, and generally embellishing it in order to exhibit technical dexterity in writer and performer. In *Lingua* (I, 1) we read: "'Tis plain, indeed, for Truth no descant needs, Una's her name, she cannot be divided." Spenser (*Faerie Queene*, III, I, 40) has:

> And all the while sweet Musicke did divide
> Her looser notes with Lydian harmony.

Shakespeare uses the noun in *Romeo and Juliet* (III, 5): "Some say the lark makes sweet division."

The Seventeenth-century instrumental composers in particular were very fond of this form of writing, and the variation-style was exceedingly popular. The majority of the virtuoso show-pieces for the viols consisted of a theme with a number of "divisions," Christopher Simpson having written some interesting specimens. Even the exercises or "lessons" for beginners took the form of some popular tune such as "The Lark," or "John come kiss me now," with simple variations. Thus Playford's *Introduction to the Skill of Musick* (1674 and many other editions) gives "*John come kiss*, with Division to each Strain." The same publisher's *Division-Violin* (1688) prints a number of Grounds suitable for playing division. The division of a ground was often termed "Diminution" (*v.* GROUND *and* DESCANT).

DIVISION-VIOL: A bass-viol of medium size suitable for the performance of ornate divisions (*q.v.*) or variations on a ground-bass. These compositions were often of a very exacting nature, and an instrument that was fairly easy to manage afforded the virtuoso the best chances of success. Both John Playford and Christopher Simpson are unanimous as to the size of instrument best suited to this class of music. The former says: " a Bass Viol for Divisions must be of a less size (than the Consort-Viol, *q.v.*), and the Strings according "; while the latter (*Division-Violist*, 1659) has: " I would have a Division-Viol to be something a shorter size than a Consort-Basse that so the Hand may better command it " (*v.* also VIOLS).

DOMPE. v. DUMP.

DOT: In old English music a term less frequently used than Prick or Point (*q.v*).

DOT-WAY: A species of Tablature (*q.v.*) used in writing music for the Recorder and the Seventeenth-century Flageolet. It consisted of as many lines as the instrument had finger-holes, and each dot placed on a line represented a finger placed on the corresponding hole of the instrument. Humphrey Salter's *Genteel Companion for the Recorder* (1683) and Thomas Greeting's *Pleasant Companion* (for the Flageolet, 1682) both give their lessons and pieces in this tablature. Salter says that some writers used a seven-lined stave and others six; he employs six only, adding a " short line underneath " in the nature of a ledger-line when he requires it; his idea being that " more do but hinder the readiness of sight." The top line of the system referred to the under hole which was stopped with the thumb; the second line belonged to the first hole above the instrument; the third line to the second hole, and so on. These holes were stopped with the fingers of the left hand in regular rotation, and when the digits of that hand were all employed, those of the right followed in the same way. The Pinching-Notes (*q.v.*) were indicated by the dot being crossed with an horizontal line, thus forming a plus-sign. Salter's instructions are rather quaintly worded, as for example, " stopping all the holes is eight dots, up with the little finger of your right hand is seven dots, *etc.*" The last three measures of a short piece given in the *Genteel Companion* are as follows, the

the second stave containing the same three measures in ordinary notation :

DOUBLE : Very similar to a simple division (*q.v.*), consisting of an embellished version of a short instrumental movement. Such simple variations on the stereotyped dance-forms were often called Doubles, and the works of Bach and his contemporaries abound in examples. The term persisted until well into the Eighteenth Century.

DOUBLE BACKFALL. *v.* BACKFALL.

DOUBLE CURTAL. *v.* CURTAL.

DOUBLE FALL. *v.* FALL.

DOUBLE RELISH. *v.* RELISH.

DOUBLE SACKBUT. *v.* SACKBUT.

DOUCET, DOUCETTE. *v.* RECORDER.

DRIVING NOTES : Syncopated notes were named Driving Notes in Seventeenth-century England ; that is to say, they were urged or driven through the ensuing accent. John Playford defines the term with " *Syncopation* is when the beating of Time falls to be in the midst of a *Semibreve* or *Minim, etc.*, or, as we usually term it, Notes driven till the Time falls even again "—" Driven Notes " being a common variant for Driving Notes.

DROMSLADE : A variant spelling of Drumslade (*q.v.*) probably betraying the Dutch origin of the word.

DRUMSLADE : A term derived from the Dutch *Dromstade,* a drummer, and used in England to designate that class of musician, and also, through error, the instrument itself. When the word was first used here is difficult to determine. The State Papers speak of Tabrets until the first half of the

Sixteenth Century, and in an account for expenses connected with the funeral of Henry VIII (Lord Chamberlain's Records, February 21, 1547/8) a " Drume player " is mentioned. In the Privy Purse Expenses of Henry VIII (May 14, 1532) we read : " Item . . . Paied to hans Pyper and Bartholomew his ffellawe Dromslades for their lyverayes xlv.*s*.," while on September 6th of the same year a similar sum was paid to " Christopher Drombeslade and his fellawe for ther lyveray coots." Queen Elizabeth's accounts show the employment of three *Drumsteds* at " fee apeece 18*l*. 5*s*.," the word here exhibiting a spelling very like the Dutch original. Later in the Sixteenth Century the terms Drumplayer, Timpanist, and Drumslade alternate, and are often to be found used in reference to one and the same performer.

D-SOL-RE. *v.* GAMUT.

DUB : An old name for the Tabor (*q.v.*) and used colloquially. Its derivation is doubtful, but may be onomatopoeic ; George Gascoigne in his *Flowers* (Sixteenth Century) having : " The Drummes crie dub a dub, the braying trumpets blow." Beaumont and Fletcher likewise have : " how the drum dubs." Just as the word Drum itself comes to us from the Dutch, so may Dub come from the East Frieslandic *Dubbe*, a blow, and *Dubben*, to strike.

DULCIMER : An ancient stringed instrument almost identical, in its earlier forms, with the Psaltery (*q.v.*), except that it was always played by striking the strings, generally of metal, with small hammers or beaters made of a flexible material to give resiliency, while the other was played with the fingers or a plectrum. The Dulcimer thus became the ancestor of the modern pianoforte with hammers. Sometimes the strikers of the Dulcimer were provided with double heads, one being covered with soft, and the other with hard, material, so that different shades of tone could be obtained. The strings ran over continuous bridges in the earlier forms, and over small, separate, bridges—one for each string—in the later. Being divided by the bridges into parts of unequal length, the strings could be struck on either side of one of the bridges, each part producing a different note. Some of the sections were unfit for use, and a certain amount of skill and practice was necessary to hit off the correct notes at will. The tuning-pins ran along one of the short sides of the instrument, and the sounding-board was not infrequently perforated with one or more fretted circular sound-holes. The tuning varied in different countries ; generally to a diatonic scale in England, and, later, on the Continent, to a chromatic scale. The strings, divided by the bridges, naturally gave different series of notes, those obtained with the commonest tuning being between :

with F natural, in one set ; the same an octave higher in the next set ; and from the D on the fourth line of the treble stave to its octave, with the F sharp, in the rest of the strings used.

The instrument is mentioned as the *Dowcemere* in the *Squyr of Lowe Degre* (*l.* 1075) and as *Doucemer* in Stephen Hawes' *Pastime of Plesure* (*chap.* xvi, 1506). Historical references to it are frequent enough, and as an example it may be mentioned that at the Westminster entertainment of 1502 the " dusymer " was played by female musicians. Pepys (May, 1662) speaks of it as a novelty, the Virginal and the Spinet having probably robbed it of much of its vogue : " Here among the fidles I first saw a dulcimere played on with sticks knocking of the strings, and is very pretty." A month later he heard it again in a tavern.

The name " Dulce Melos " appears as early as the end of the Fourteenth, or the beginning of the Fifteenth Century, and was applied to a keyboard instrument (*v. Vierteljahrschrift fuer Musikwissenschaft*, 1892, *p.* 95). The Psaltery may have been first played with hammers in Germany, since the Italians call the Dulcimer the *Salterio tedesco.* The German name for it, however, is *Hackbrett* (" chopping-board " ; so called from the movements of the beaters). The Dulcimer is still used in Hungary as the *Cimbalom.* In Italy it was known at *Cembalo,* whence " Clavicembalo " for Harpsichord. I have heard it played in so-called Hungarian Bands in England, and one musical mendicant of twenty-five years ago lingers in my memory, for I used to hear him play a rather shabby dulcimer in the suburban trains of the Great Eastern Railway.

DUMP : A form of dance of which very little is known, and its peculiarities as a dance are equally obscure. Shakespeare mentions it twice ; once in *Lucrece* (*ver.* 161) : " Distress likes dumps when time is kept with tears " (which would lead us to the conclusion that the form was a melancholy one), and again in Romeo and Juliet (IV, 5) : " O, play me some merry dump to comfort me," where the " merry " may be a joking play on words. Humphrey Gifford's *Gilloflowers* contains a poem entitled " A Dolefull Dumpe," and two more labelled " A Dumpe " and " A Dumpe by his friend G.C." It is possible that the term was applied in the Sixteenth Century to elegiacs and thence to similar music. At the same time, the rhythm of a Dump called *Lady Carey's Dumpe* (about 1600) cannot be said to be particularly dismal :

DUPLA : In Mensurable Music a doubling of the speed, generally indicated by the figure 2 next to the signature (*cf.* DIMINUTION, 1).

E-LA-MI. *v.* GAMUT.

ELEVATION : An ornament leading up, as its name suggests, from a low note to a higher one :

A variant of this embellishment was the " Shaked Elevation " :

(John Playford, *Introduction to the Skill of Musick*).

Christopher Simpson, in the *Division-Violist* (1659), speaks of a different kind of Elevation applicable to the Viols only :

"Sometimes a note is graced by sliding to it from the Third below, called an Elevation, now something obsolete. This sliding a Third is . . . alwayes done upon one String."

ENTRY: A term used in the Seventeenth and Eighteenth Centuries for what we call a Prelude to-day. It was sometimes applied fairly loosely to the opening movement of a Suite or Set of short pieces, having been doubtlessly suggested by the French *Entrée*. Roger North (*Memoires of Musick*, 1728) writes of pieces beginning "with an entry," and praises "the entrys of Baptist."

FA. *v.* ARETINIAN SYLLABLES and GAMUT.

FABURDEN, FA-BURDON. *v.* FAUX BOURDON.

FADING: Another name for the Burden (*q.v.*) or refrain of a song in Elizabethan England. J. O. Halliwell (*Dictionary of Archaic Words*, 1847) says that the Fading was the name of an Irish dance, "and also the burden of a popular Irish song of a licentious kind." Its use in England as a popular designation for the refrain of a song may have been extended from this sense. See also the quotation from Beaumont and Fletcher's *Knight of the Burning Pestle* in the article JIG.

FA-LA: A vocal (polyphonic) composition of a popular character with these Solmisation syllables as text. In some cases the whole work was sung to these syllables, sometimes only the refrain. It dates from the end of the Sixteenth and the commencement of the Seventeenth Century, *i.e.* during the vogue of the Madrigal, and some of the most celebrated of English musicians wrote in this form. As vocal accompaniments to ancient dances, monodies on such syllables date from the early Middle Ages.

FALL: The Cadence or Close of a musical phrase was, in Shakespeare's day, termed a Fall (*cf.* "That strain again, It had a dying fall," *Twelfth Night*, I, 1). John Playford gives a "Plain Fall" as an ornament connecting a note with another of lower pitch, and a "Double Fall" as one which descended to a note below the next chief note. "A Fall to take breath" is given in the *Introduction to the Skill of Musick* as one in which a short rest is inserted between the high note and the commencement of the ornament.

FANCY : A free form of composition for instruments, which may be looked upon as an English invention of the middle Sixteenth Century. The fact that Fantasies existed on the Continent of Europe does not influence this statement, since the method of handling and the nature and character of the true English Fancy differed so much from the foreign Fantasia, that no doubt can exist as to the native origin of the form. The fashion which sanctioned such writing undoubtedly owed its inception to the popularity of the instrumental In Nomine (*q.v.*), and once the writers of the period had broken away from the older conventions, they began to realise that their powers of invention and imagination were quite equal to the demands placed upon them by the new vogue. The sets of dance-forms were becoming too elementary for the great virtuosi of the time, and something more than mere variations (divisions) on a given theme was necessary to afford adequate expression to the growing technique of our instrumentalists. To meet this demand the Fancy came opportunely, and some of the later (middle of the Seventeenth Century) specimens are fine examples of instrumental writing. Though chiefly used for the stringed and bowed instruments, practically any combination could play the Fancy, and for some time it was the principal form of chamber-music.

How popular the Fancy must have been in Shakespeare's day is shown by the allusion to it in *II Henry IV* (III, 2), a use which proves that the meaning of the term must have been familiar to all: "He came ever in the rearward of the fashion: and sung those tunes to the overscutched hus-wives that he heard the carmen whistle, and sware they were his fancies or his good-nights."

Christopher Simpson gives the recipe for the Fancy as it was written before the middle of the Seventeenth Century: "In this sort of Musick the composer (being not limited to words) doth imploy all his art and invention solely about the bringing in and carrying on these fuges according to the order and method formerly shewed. When he has tried all the several ways which he thinks fit to be used therein, he takes some other point, and does the like with it, or else, for variety, introduces some chromatic notes, with bindings and intermixtures of discords; or falls into some lighter humour like a Madrigal, or what else his own fancy shall lead him to; but still concluding with something which hath art and excellency in it."

Although the Fancy allowed the writer a good deal of freedom as far as its actual form was concerned, the rules that convention imposed upon its writing soon made of it something that was looked upon with a certain amount of awe by the lover of the popular muse. It is peculiar that a form of composition intended to break away from stiff and stereotyped forms should itself become almost as formal. The result was that after having enjoyed great popularity for a couple of generations the Fancy began to decline in favour in the middle of the Seventeenth Century ; so much so that we find Simpson saying, " This style of music was much neglected because of the scarcity of auditors that understand it ; their ears being more delighted with light and airy music " (*Compendium*, 1667). This, no doubt, was the result of Charles the Second's peculiar taste in music, and his encouragement of French fashions to the detriment and neglect of the older English forms. Charles I, on the other hand, was a great admirer of the Fancy, and was probably responsible for the writing of a large number of them by reason of the grace with which he received their composers. John Playford tells us that Charles " could play his part exactly well on the Bass-Viol, especially of those incomparable Phantasies of Mr. Coperario to the Organ." Charles I, whatever he may have been as a king, showed considerable talent and taste as a musician, and his love for the Fancy did English music as great a service as Charles the Second's dislike for it sealed the fate of the form, and commenced an era of foreign influence upon our native art.

Examples of the Fancy are very frequent and no difficulty need be experienced in locating them. Lady Nevell's Virginal Book (before the end of the Sixteenth Century) affords two examples by William Byrd. Orlando Gibbons' manner of writing in this form may be seen in the two specimens contained in Benjamin Cosyn's Virginal Book. Richard Deering's work is exhibited in the British Museum manuscript Additional, 17786/91, and Additional 29366/8. In printed form there are seven specimens in John Dowland's *Varietie of Lute Lessons* (1610). In manuscripts dating from the middle of the Seventeenth Century the Fancy becomes so frequent that it is scarcely possible to refer to one without finding examples by such men as Ferabosco, Gibbons, Jenkins, East, Lawes, Cooper, *etc.* Even Purcell still used it ; but by then it was the property of the academician, and it had ceased to make any popular appeal.

Before leaving the Fancy it is necessary to note a great difference of style and character between the examples we find at the end of the Sixteenth and the beginning of the Seventeenth Century, and those present in such huge quantities about fifty years later. The difference is sufficiently great to cause us to be suspicious that the two species may possibly come from different sources. There is always the likelihood that the earlier, Elizabethan Fancies, may be the English development of the Italian Fantasia ; but even if this be so, the English claim to the form as exemplified in the Stuart examples cannot be gainsaid ; and these were the brilliant children of the semi-virtuose, semi-ecclesiastical In Nomine.

FANTASIE. *v.* FANCY.

FAUX BOURDON : A form of discanting on a Plain-Song, consisting in the Treble and the Alto singing at intervals of a sixth and a third above the Tenor. Each phrase, however, opened and closed with the octave and fifth above the *cantus firmus.* The plain-song was not sung, and served only for the other parts to read from, their music being improvised from it. Chilston says of Faburden (or Faux Bourdon) that it " hath but two sights (*i.e.* positions), a third above the plain-song in sight, the which is a sixth from the treble in voice ; and an even with the plain-song in sight, the which is an eighth from the treble in voice. These two accords the faburdener must rule by the mean (*Altus*), *etc.*" Gulielmus Monachus (Coussemaker, *Scriptores,* III, 273 *et seq.*) indicates that Faux Bourdon was very popular in England and gives an example. In this he uses two staves ; the lower gives the unsung plain-song, and the upper the three-part harmony. The tenor part he writes in open notes, with the altus above and the treble below (sung, naturally, an octave higher) in black notes. Faux Bourdon was used in England certainly at the very beginning of the Thirteenth Century, and was most probably of still higher antiquity. Later meanings applied to the term do not concern us here.

F-FA-UT. *v.* GAMUT.

IDDLE: This term, although used to-day as a colloquialism for "violin," was once employed to designate an instrument very different. The name as well as the instrument itself can be traced back to Saxon times (*Fithele;* and *Fithelere,* a fiddler), and illustrations of it, as given in early manuscripts, show it to have been rather broader and shorter than the Rebeck, and strung with four strings. A closer description would involve too much imagination being employed, since the Fithele borders closely on other, kindred, instruments. It is quite likely that in the Saxon period, as to-day, the word was used to mean any bowed stringed instrument. A drawing in Cotton Manucript (British Museum, *Tiber. C. VI*) shows a pear-shaped body, two small sound-holes, a tail-piece, a square head with four pins for tuning, and an arched bow. Whether the back of the instrument was flat or vaulted cannot be determined from the illustration, and we are thus robbed of one of the most important pieces of information. The frequent references to it that are to be found in the literature of the period between the Thirteenth Century and the rise of the true Viols, prove how common it must have been. But whether the word Fiddle or Fithele (or variation) so used, was meant to apply to a flat-backed instrument or to a vaulted one; to a four-stringed fiddle or to a three-stringed rebeck; to a primitive viol or any of the instruments in Virdung's collections of Geigen; is not always clear. The word *Fydelys* is used in the Fourteenth-century metrical romance *Octavian Imperator* (*l.* 70), and the Anglo-Saxon form *Fithele* employed by Chaucer in the Prologue to the *Canterbury Tales.*

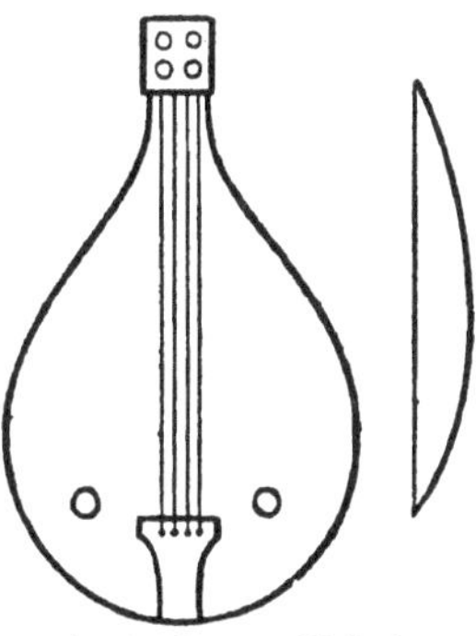
Anglo-Saxon Fithele

'INAL: 1. The note in the Church Modes which occupies the position of the present-day tonic.

2. The last note (*finalis*) of a ligature (*q.v.*).

'IPPLE-FLUTE. *v.* RECORDER.

'ITHELE. *v.* FIDDLE.

'LAGEOLET: A small, high-pitched member of the fipple-

flute family, and the last survivor of the instruments of th Recorder (*q.v.*) class. Its head was of the whistle type an the body bored with six holes, four stopped with the fingers i front, and two at the back for the thumbs. The fingering which was peculiar, is given in Thomas Greeting's *Pleasan Companion for the Flageolet* (1682). The instrument wa played from a Tablature (*v.* DOT-WAY), and could produc notes outside of its natural series by a certain manner o blowing (*v.* PINCHING NOTES). The Flageolet was exceedingl popular in the Seventeenth Century, and Pepys refers to it n fewer than thirty-one times, had his wife taught, and playe alone and in duets with her whenever he had the opportunity In the ale-house he would produce his instrument from hi pocket and kill time with it; on moonlight nights he woul play it in his garden. On January 20, 1667/8 the diarist wrote "... did stop at Drumbleby's, the pipe-maker, there to advis about the making of a flageolet to go low and soft; and he d shew me a way which do do, and also a fashion of having tw pipes of the same note fastened together, so as I can play o one, and then echo it upon the other, which is mighty pretty.' Since the uses to which Pepys put the instrument are typical there will be no need for multiplying quotations. The Double Flageolet mentioned was probably different from the instru ment made by Bainbridge at the beginning of the Nineteent Century. The innovation, which did not live long, consiste of two flageolets, differently holed, set into an adapter whic united them to a single mouth-piece. The ordinary Flageole —of the true fipple-pipe type—is not yet extinct.

FLAT: The state in which a note is too low in pitch. As noun the term is the name of a sign used to lower the pitch of note by a semitone. As in the case of the expression "Sharp (*q.v.*), Flat replaces Playford's "B fa cliff." It was used i the Seventeenth Century to indicate a minor interval, chord tuning, or key, just as Sharp meant the same in the majo Thus a "Flat Third" was a minor third, and the tuning of viol "Harpway Flat" one to a minor chord (*v.* HARPWAY.)

FLOURISH: A military trumpet-call, for signalling purpose The term is of far too frequent occurrence to necessitate description of its uses. "A Flourish of Trumpets" is a ver common stage direction in Elizabethan literature. Shakespeare in *Antony and Cleopatra* (II, 7), follows the observation, ". . . sound and be hang'd, sound out," with the direction, " Sound a Flourish with drums." Later on, the word came to mean any ornamental scale-passage of a showy type. Playford uses it as synonymous with " Graces."

That the Flourish, in its first-mentioned sense, was distinct from the Sennet (*q.v.*), is clearly shown in Thomas Dekker's *Satiro-mastix* (1602) : " Trumpets sound a florish, and then a Sennate."

LUTE DOUCE. *v.* RECORDER.

ORLANE : A dance-form descended from the Galliard, and partaking of the characteristics of the latter. Written in 6/4 or 6/8, the dance varied a good deal in rhythm with the changing eras, but the unaltering feature was the jig-rhythm of dotted-quaver, semiquaver, quaver. The form was a localised one in the province of Friuli (Northern Italy) and was only used occasionally in other countries. Whether we meet it in France, Germany, or England, it is always as a novelty and a curiosity. Tomlinson gives it in his " New Dance 'Shepherdess' " (1716) to French music, the whole thing probably being a simple imitation of the Venetian gondolier's dance. John Stafford Smith's *Musica Antiqua* (1812) affords another example which, says the editor, " was printed in England in 1711, and called 'The Furlong,' used probably by the Waits of London and Southwark."

RETS : A method of mechanically dividing the fingerboards of stringed instruments into semitone intervals. This was effected by a variety of means—either by inlaying thin strips of metal, ebony, or ivory, across the fingerboard, or by tying lengths of catgut round the neck of the instrument so that they crossed the fingerboard under the strings. Mace (*Musick's Monument*, 1676) gives a complete and lucid account of the method employed in fretting the lutes, and explains how the distances between the frets should be gauged.

When a finger depressed a string on to a fret (either by falling directly over the fret, or just behind it), it stopped the string in such manner as to produce a note the pitch of which depended upon the position of the fret. Such a system of note-finding was mechanical at best, and was a legacy of the lutes, which, owing to the number of strings used, and the various tunings employed, had some excuse for them. Playford says that playing the viols by frets was well enough for a beginner, but advised their removal as soon as the student had gained proficiency enough to find the correct positions for the several notes by ear alone. The fret, although the term has fallen out of common parlance, is still used on the mandoline, guitar, and kindred instruments.

The derivation of the word is doubtful. Three possible sources for it are the Old French *Frete*, a ferrule; the Spanish *Frete*, a narrow band (used in heraldry), and *Freter*, to cross (J. B. B. Roquefort, *Glossaire de la Langue Romane*, 1808). A meaning suggested by one of these may have been "to encircle with narrow bands," a sense in which we find the verb employed in *Piers Plowman* (*Vision of Lady Meed*): "Fairly her fingers were fretted with rings." The catgut frets of the viols "fretted" the neck of the instrument in this way, and a specimen of the Tenor Viol (1652) in my possession clearly shows the marks left by these frets.

The word was used so frequently in old English literature that we are forced to the conclusion (if further proof were needed) that music must have been so universally cultivated that the technical term was used in everyday speech. Shakespeare (*Taming of the Shrew*, II, 1) has: "I did but tell her she mistook her frets. . . . Frets, call you these? said she I'll fume with them"; and in *Hamlet* (III, 2) we read "Though you can fret me, you cannot play upon me." These two examples are typical of an enormous number of quotations that could be instanced.

The use of Frets made a system of notation, other than the one in general use, possible (*v.* TABLATURE).

FULL-PLAY: In lute playing the performance of full chords struck right across the strings, and used to differentiate chords from single-stop playing.

FURLONG. *v.* FORLANE.

GALLIARD: A dance of Italian origin that came to England by way of France and enjoyed an immense vogue here. A great number of examples are extant, and may be seen in practically any of the Elizabethan music-books—some of England's most celebrated composers writing in the form. In the Arundel Collection of Manuscripts there is a Galliard called, with the

Saraband which it follows, " The King's Masque " ; and this specimen undoubtedly dates from the reign of Henry VIII, a very early date at which to find these two forms together. *Parthenia* contains ten Galliards by William Byrd, Dr. Bull, and Orlando Gibbons. It is naturally represented in the Fitzwilliam Virginal Book, and one example by Peter Phillips (1592) is noteworthy as containing ten sections, each of eight measures ; the penultimate part being labelled *Saltarello*, a name which is in this case, I suppose, to be taken in its etymological sense only and may have been suggested by the prevalence of the Volte (*q.v.*). Robert Dowland, in his *Varietie of Lute Lessons* (1610), gives seven most interesting specimens of the Galliard ; six of them by his father, John Dowland, and the seventh—unsigned—is, like the seventh Pavane, by Robert himself. All the examples quoted are in Tablature.

How popular the Galliard was in England may be more readily gauged from the fact that its name was used by most of the contemporary writers without any further explanation, proving that its meaning must have been familiar to all. Thus Shakespeare, in *Twelfth Night* (I, 3), intersperses Sir Toby's utterances with many illuminating passages referring to the dance : " What is thy excellence in a Galliard, Knight ? "—and, later—" Why dost thou not go to church in a Galliard, and come home in a Coranto ? " ; and yet again—" I did think by the excellent constitution of thy leg, it was formed under the star of a Galliard." An interesting allusion to a variant name for the form is given in *Much Ado about Nothing* (II, 1) : " Wooing, wedding, and repenting, is as a Scotch Jig, a measure, and a cinque-pace. The first is hot and hasty, like a Scotch Jig, and full as fantastical ; the wedding mannerly modest, as a measure, full of state and antientry ; and then comes repentance ; and with his bad legs falls into a cinque-pace, faster and faster, till he sinks into his grave." The *Cinque-pace* was the Galliard, so called because of the five steps (*cinque pas*) of which the dance was composed. Another form of the same variant was " Sink-a-pace." Finally, in *Henry V* (I, 2), we have :

And bids you be advised there's nought in France
That can be with a nimble galliard won.

Shakespeare's frequent use of the word compels us to the

conclusion that in the poet's day it had already become the property of the merry reveller of the middle classes. Yet, at a not much earlier period it was used as a court-dance in England, as it was in France during the reign of Henri III (1574/89), where it was hampered by all the restrictions of the true court measure.

In conformity with the first law of artistic endeavour—the demand for variety—the Galliard was always used to follow the stately and dignified Pavane (*q.v.*), and in this order we generally find them written as well as danced. The lives of the two forms practically synchronised, for when the one vanished, at about 1650, the other fell out of favour also. Their places were taken by the Saraband and Jig. Occasionally a Galliard is to be found following a Saraband during the period of transition, and to prove that the former gave place to the Jig it will only be necessary to mention that we find Galliards and Jigs wedded to Pavanes and Sarabands indiscriminately—the two names being applied to what was in effect one and the same form.

The popularity of the Galliard on the Continent was, if possible, even greater than in England. Its name was derived from the French *Gaillard, Gaillarde,* "merry," "joyous," "gay," and the original dance was usually written in 3/2 time. Later we find it in almost any triple measure. Arbeau (or Tabourot, to give him his correct name) gives a good deal of information concerning the manner of the Galliard's performance in his *Orchèsographie* (1588). It should be noticed, in passing, that another name frequently applied to the form was *Romanesca*, or *Romanesque*, a term used to show that the place of the Galliard's birth was Rome.

The form was fairly popular in Germany also, but the majority seem to have been the work of foreigners to that country. As was also the experience of the Galliard's daughter —the Volte (*q.v.*)—the mother-dance was the subject of much criticism. Praetorius, sombre monk, condemned it as "an invention of the devil, and full of shameful and obscene gestures and immodest movements." Even the genial Tabourot mentions a Galliard that he witnessed, which was "so abandoned, and the extravagance of its steps such, that the bare knees of the dancer would have been visible at each leap, had she not with her hands held down her dress." Which goes to prove that the beautiful dances of the olden times suffered equally with the less beautiful ones of to-day at the hands and feet of dancers like the one alluded to by the Abbé Tabourot.

GAMUT, GAM-UT: In ancient music the Gamut was the range or compass of the sounds in common use. It referred more particularly to the twenty notes from the G on the first line of the bass stave to the E in the top space of the treble, together with the various hexachords which covered these notes. The whole system, which was to our forefathers what the scales and keys are to us, was presented to the student in some such form as the following, which is taken in part from Morley's *Plaine and Easie Introduction* (1597):

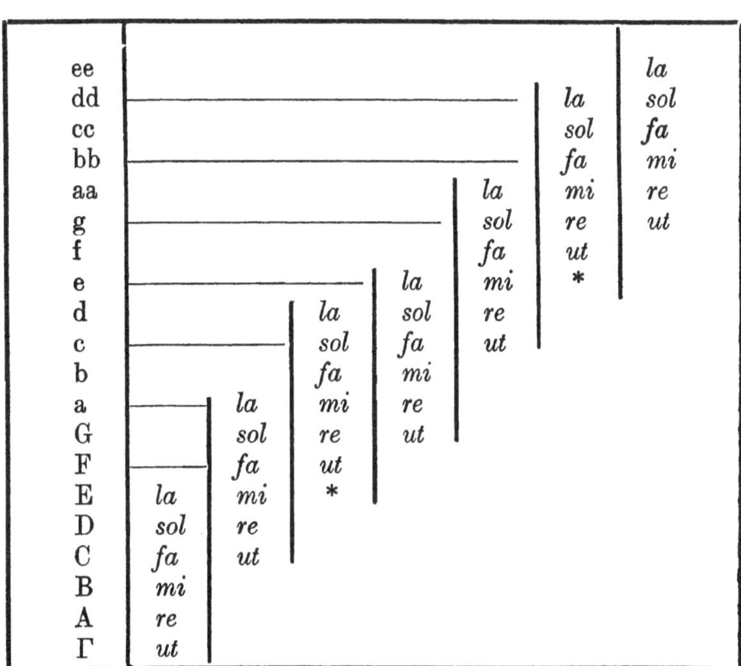

ee							*la*
dd						*la*	*sol*
cc						*sol*	*fa*
bb						*fa*	*mi*
aa					*la*	*mi*	*re*
g					*sol*	*re*	*ut*
f					*fa*	*ut*	
e				*la*	*mi*	*	
d			*la*	*sol*	*re*		
c			*sol*	*fa*	*ut*		
b			*fa*	*mi*			
a		*la*	*mi*	*re*			
G		*sol*	*re*	*ut*			
F		*fa*	*ut*				
E	*la*	*mi*	*				
D	*sol*	*re*					
C	*fa*	*ut*					
B	*mi*						
A	*re*						
Γ	*ut*						

In the hexachords marked with an asterisk, the B is flattened for reasons given in the article HEXACHORD SYSTEM (*q.v.*).

The lowest note of this series was called *Gamma* (the Greek Γ) and this, in conjunction with the Ut to which the note was sung (*v.* SOLMISATION), gave the system its name. *A-Re* was the note above it, *B-Mi* the next above, followed by *C-Fa-Ut*, and so on. These designations thus not only named the notes, but also gave their absolute pitch. With the above chart in view such titles as "Suite in *D-Sol-Re*" or "*a-la-mi-re*" (or *a-lamire*), *etc.*, are easy to understand.

"Gamut I am, the ground of all accord," says Hortensio in *Taming of the Shrew* (III, 1), and a study of what has been said on the subject will explain the many musical allusions made in this play. Skelton already speaks of "alamyre" in *Colin Clout* (*l.* 107).

GAMUT-STRING. *v.* TENOR STRING.

GAMUT-WAY: A term used in the Seventeenth Century to distinguish music set in ordinary notation from that written in one or other of the Tablatures (*q.v.*).

GAVOT: A dance of French origin which became very popular in England. Appearing in this country soon after it had been taken up in the French opera, we find a specimen by John Banister in Matthew Locke's *Melothesia* (1673), consisting of four sections of four and eight measures alternately. The *Tempest* music of Locke (1675) also included a Gavot of sixteen measures repeated. The form does not seem to have been very well known as yet, for Humphrey Salter, having probably received faulty information, wrote a "Gavot" in 6/4 (*Genteel Companion for the Recorder*, 1683). Further early examples of the form are contained in Playford's *Musick's Hand-Maide* (*Part* II, 1689), and in *Apollo's Banquet* (*Part* II, *Ed.* 6, 1690). In the last-named work the Gavot is included in a composite set called "Branle" (*cf.* the set of Branles in Arbeau's *Orchèsographie*). Since the French forms were so fashionable in England at the end of the Seventeenth Century and the beginning of the Eighteenth, the Gavot was industriously danced in English society; but that it rivalled the Menuet in popularity I should not be as ready to assert. All things considered, I am of opinion that the Gavot in England was more often used as an instrumental piece than as a dance.

Deriving its name from the natives (*Gavots*) of the Pays de Gap (Dauphiné), the Gavot is much more ancient than most works of reference would have us believe. Arbeau's set of Branles, to which "they gave this name of Gavotte," dates from 1588, and taking into consideration some of the customs that Arbeau connects with the performance of the dance, there can be very little reason for doubting that the Gavot, which became so popular in the Eighteenth Century, had its origin in the older duple Branles. In Besarde's *Thesaurus Harmonicus* (Cologne, 1603) the Gavottes are all given as parts of the Branles, and Praetorius is one of the first to use the form independently (*Terpsichore*, 1612). A Gavotte by Henry le Jeune (before 1600), and transcribed by Mersenne (*Harmonie Universelle*, 1636), completes the list of very early specimens.

It was not until the last quarter of the Seventeenth Century that the Gavot received its regular form. It consisted, as did nearly all the other old dances, of two sections of four and eight measures, each repeated, in 2/4 time. One of the accepted rules of the dance was that it should commence at the half-bar, and its character was generally gay. Historically the Gavot followed the path of the Menuet, but stopped when it had reached the dignity of use in the Suite ; its dance origin was then lost sight of, and pieces bearing the indication *Tempo di Gavotta* followed, to remind musicians that a popular dance of that name once existed.

In the country of its birth the Gavot was changed from a joyful country measure into a true Court-dance. Originally employed at fancy-dress balls to create the correct atmosphere for the revellers appearing as *Gavots*, it became so much liked that soon every Menuet was followed by a Gavot. In this use it maintained the artistic aims of a century earlier by wedding contrasting forms for the sake of variety. And if a dance did not possess the contrasting spirit by nature it was modified to do so ; a circumstance that accounts for the same dance having differing characteristics in different countries and at different periods. So it came about that the stately, shuffled, and triple Menuet was rounded off by the performance of a duple dance which, though also a *danse grave*, allowed of the feet leaving the ground. It is possible that when the Gavot was used alone as a show-dance it was invested in more dignity, and even touches of deeper expression and tenderness entered into its composition. As time went on the Gavot became more stately, and eventually it differed but little from the Menuet, except in measure. In all its forms the Gavot was very popular, and not less so because it brought into high society all the customs attending a kissing-dance. Although the bestowal of bouquets or chaplets sometimes took the place of the kiss, there were many who thought the exchange an unfair one, and adhered to the older custom.

Coming into vogue during the reign of Louis XIV, we find the Gavotte represented in many of the works of Lully. They are generally in regular form, and in these cases we can be tolerably certain that they were actually danced. In other places we meet with specimens containing, for example, nine measures, which were less suitable for terpsichorean purposes. The example in Lully's *Roland* is followed by another marked *Lentement.* Under the fifteenth Louis the Gavotte was produced in greater numbers, and in some cases the form was already much widened. By the time Gluck wrote *Paride* we find a Chaconne which had an interpolated Gavotte to relieve the monotony of the ever-recurring varied theme. This example consists of six sections of eight measures each, after which the Chaconne is resumed. *Iphigénie en Aulide* (1774) contains a Passecaille treated in a similar manner, and probably for the same reason. Here the Gavotte in the major is followed by one in the minor in true Trio form, the major section being then repeated. The Gavotte in *Alceste* (1776) is also in its most complete form, and is made up of a major and a minor section, followed by the first *da Capo.*

The dance that under Louis XV had been rigorously kept on the stage of the Opera, was brought into the salon by Marie Antoinette, and the introduction of the Gavotte into the State balls ensured for it the homage of society. The national upheaval that succeeded, swept all things artistic into an abyss of wantonness and vandalism. The Reign of Terror seized upon it, and in grim irony it was employed to dance to the death-song of the thousands who fell under the triangular knife. During the Directoire an attempt was made to revive the forms that were fashionable before the national suicide; but the response was feeble, and the Gavotte, though in use for some time, gradually died out.

Germany was the first of the neighbours of France to receive the Gavotte. Dancing-masters travelling from France to Germany soon after the form's inception, brought it with them to be taken over by the German musicians. In such a way Praetorius learned that another of the age-old dances had been given fixed shape. The result in his case took the form of six Gavottes which he included in one of his Branles (1612). The year 1668 still found the Gavotte used in the Branle (Becker's *Musicalische Frühlings-Früchte*) ; but in 1695 it is seen in the instrumental Suite. Moffat's *Florilegia* may consist of very loosely and irregularly constructed sets ; but they are suites nevertheless, and the Gavotte is used alone as a purely instrumental form. Here the shape is generally the strict one of four repeated measures in the first section, and eight in the second, though there are some exceptions where the number of measures is a multiple of four. Mattheson increased the tempo considerably, and generally wished to have them very quick (some even *Prestissimo*). Later specimens will be familiar enough. Every player of the Bach suites, for whatever instrument, will know them. A second Gavotte was frequently added to the first, and this, in some of Bach's Partitas, was written *à la Musette* (*i.e.* with a persistent drone-bass).

Handel often used the Gavot as he did the Menuet—to close the Overture (*e.g.* in *Semele*). In this, as in many other examples by both Bach and Handel, the form was very unlike the original dance in its treatment, and very often a large and irregular number of measures was written ; and to show how utterly these composers severed the form's connection with the dance, it will only be neccssary to cite the Gavotte in *Joshua*, where it serves as an *Aria*.

A curious rule applied to the form early in the Eighteenth Century is quoted by Walther in 1732. He says that "the first section should not end on the key-note of the Gavotte, but on the Third or Fifth ; if it end on the key-note it is as if a Rondeau were being made." A glance at a few of the examples will show how often this rule was observed.

The Gavot, although it enjoyed so long a life, cannot be said to have influenced music very much ;—it added a new form to the Suite (where it was placed between the Saraband and Jig, side by side with, and often in place of, the Menuet) it is true ; but its influence stopped there.

GHITTERN. *v*. GITTERN.

GIGGE, *GIGUE*, *GYGGE*. *v*. JIG.

GIMEL : An early form of harmony (descant), in which two voices moved in similar motion, at varying intervals according to the period, as an accompaniment to a *cantus firmus*. When these parts were anything but a Third apart, the Gimel was known as "ad modum Faux Bourdon" (*v.* FAUX BOURDON). According to Monachus (Fifteenth Century) the Gimel was a purely English manner of writing. Gawine Dowglas (Gavin Douglas) mentions "Gemmell" as late as 1579 (*The Palice of Honour*).

GITTAR. v. GITTERN.

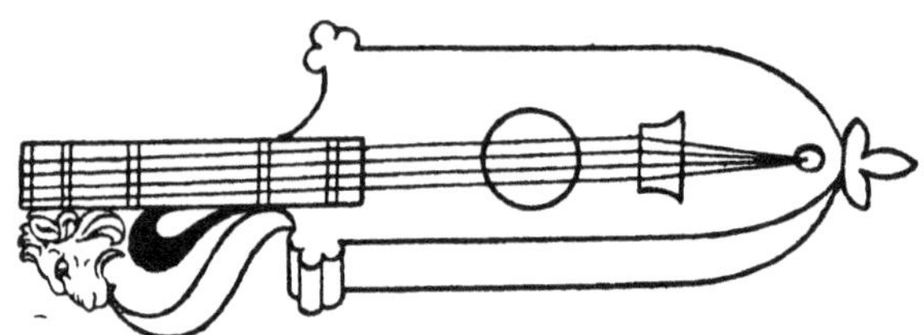

Gittern *Medieval Form*
(British Museum Ms Arundel 83 fol. 134b)

GITTERN: Instruments bearing this name have been found mentioned in manuscripts and printed books from the beginning of the Fourteenth Century until well into the Eighteenth; descriptions and illustrations differ to such an extent, however, that a great deal of care is necessary to prevent confusion. The advent of the Guitar added to the muddle in which the history of the Gittern found itself, and the similarity of the two names caused many instruments to be misnamed. Placing all the evidence at our disposal side by side with whatever pictures, sculptures, and descriptions are left us, we must come to the conclusion that the history of the Gittern (using this name for convenience as most historians have used it—to designate the forerunners of the modern guitar), falls into at least three distinct and clearly-defined periods: In the Middle Ages an ornamental instrument of quaint design and curious handling; in late Tudor and Stuart times one closely akin to the Cittern (*q.v.*); and, thirdly, the form with indented sides. It must be clearly understood that the salient feature of a Guitar is the incurvation of its sides—the rounded "waist," or hour-glass shape. The Gittern of the Middle Ages and the Gittern of John Playford's day did not exhibit this feature. The first was a rather elongated instrument, unlike either of the others; the second was pear-shaped like the Cittern. If, then, these three forms are treated together, at this place, it is not done in order to evade the task of distinguishing between them; but, rather, to collect the material into one spot and thus be better able to see what connection the one may have had with the other. It should not be supposed that I am accepting the three forms of the Gittern as chronologically successive, or that any one of them can be said to be descended or derived from another. It is my opinion that all three forms had distinct and different origins, and that it was only the practice of the masses to call any plucked instrument a Gittern or a Guitar, as soon as they were sure that it was not a lute, that caused the confusion that exists.

The Medieval Gittern is an instrument concerning which not much doubt can exist. It probably came to England during the Thirteenth Century in the hands of wandering minstrels, for in the so-called Ormesby Psalter (Bodleian Library, Oxford) there is an illustration of it. From a number of early drawings we can tell that the Gittern of this period was strung with four strings, most probably always of gut, passing over a bridge and terminating at a tail-piece which was fixed over an end-button that was often highly ornamented with carving. In this feature the Gittern of the Middle Ages differed largely from the lutes (where the strings were fixed to a bar on the table), from the Cittern (where each string had its own button or stud on the bottom rib of the instrument), and from the modern Guitar (where we once more have the strings fastened to a bar fixed to the belly—a survival of the method used in the lutes). As far as can be seen from the drawings, the strings were vibrated by means of a plectrum. Most peculiar was the manner in which the neck, head, and body of these Medieval Gitterns were connected. The neck appears to have had an enormous depth so that it reached to the plane of the flat back of the instrument, which was continued to form one unbroken line with the back of the neck. An oval hole in this deep neck permitted the hand of the player to encircle the fingerboard. Arundel Manuscript 83 (British Museum, early Fourteenth Century) illustrates the feature I have been attempting, inadequately, to describe in words. There is still preserved an actual example of the Fourteenth-century Gittern. It is at Warwick Castle, and a facsimile (from which Carl Engel knew the instrument) is in the Victoria and Albert Museum (London). The date 1578 in the Warwick Castle specimen was added at one of the periods of restoration through which the instrument had to pass. This Gittern is elaborately ornamented with carving, and the music it produced during its prime must have been quite good for its era. Such was the instrument of which Langland wrote (*Piers Plowman*), and to which Chaucer alluded several times: "And as wel coude he playe on his giterne" (*Miller's Tale, l.* 3333), and again: "And Absolon his giterne hath y-take" (*Id., l.* 3353). It is also mentioned in *The Cokes Tale* (*l.* 4396), and the plural form *G释ernes* is to be found in *The Pardoner's Tale* (*l.* 466). Chaucer employs the verbal form of the name in the *Miller's Tale* (*l.* 3363): "Ful wel acordaunt to his giterninge." In the *Squyr of Lowe Degre* we meet with the form *Getron* (*l.* 1070), and in *Octavian Imperator* (*l.* 69; Fourteenth Century) the spelling *Gyterne.*

The late Tudor and the Stuart form of the Gittern was pear-shaped, and it was treated at that period much as the Cittern, with the important difference, however, that the strings were of gut instead of wire. Henry the Eighth's list of instruments contained "four gitterons, which are called Spanish Vialls." It is quite possible that these Gitterns had nothing to do with Spain, and that since they were—in a different form—as popular in Spain as the Viols were in England, they were named Spanish Viols. However this may be, the fact remains that John Playford's *A Booke of New Lessons for the Cithern and Gittern* (1652) treats the two instruments as kin. Laneham says: ". . . sometimes I foot it with dancing, now with my Gittern, and else with my Cittern," and this, together with Playford's title-page, should suffice to point out the error to those who state that the Gittern and the Cittern were one and the same instrument. The shape of this Gittern was certainly very like that of the Cittern, but other differences must have existed beyond that of the strings. Very late specimens of the work of Preston were still called Gitterns, and sometimes Guitars, although to all appearances they were Citterns. Such a pear-shaped Gittern had keyboard mechanism applied to it early in the Nineteenth Century, but the innovation did not prosper. Variant spellings of the name in Tudor times were Gitterne, Ghittern, and Gythorne. It should be observed that in every one of these references, and in every one of these quotations, whatever form of the word has been used the final *n* has been present. I merely wish to draw attention to the fact, because when the instrument with the incurved sides arrived in England, it was called a Gittar in a host of variant spellings ;—but in all of them the *n* is absent. Is it not possible for the Guitar with indented sides to have been derived from an entirely different source and to have obtained its name similarly?

We now arrive at the true Guitar. How early it came to England is not quite clear ; but it is highly probable that it was introduced early in the Sixteenth Century. Returning to the four Gitterons or "Spanish Vialls" of Henry VIII, it is quite likely that these were Spanish Guitars ; the *Vihuela*, which probably suggested the "Vialls," having been the name of a particular kind of Guitar (with six strings instead of four). Just as the Stuart Gitterns and Citterns were strung with unison pairs of strings, so were the Seventeenth-century Guitars ; thus combining two features—the unison pairs of strings of the older instrument and the incurved sides of the newer ;—differing from the other in shape of body, but being similar in stringing. Of course, the fact that these strings were gut and not wire, made the playing of them with the finger more pleasant, and it is possible that the softer tone of the finger-plucked gut strings was so superior to that of the plectrum-twanged wire that the instruments of the Cittern family owe their demise to this circumstance. But though the Guitar still adhered to the unison pairs of strings common to the Gittern, the most frequent number was now five instead of four. It was not until the last quarter of the Eighteenth Century that the five unison course gave way to the single strings, and their number raised to six. A few comparatively early references to the Guitar (*i.e.* the newer instrument with the incurved sides) are to be found in the State Papers, and I think we shall be fairly safe in accepting all references that contain the name spelled without the final *n* as relating to the modern, or Spanish, Guitar. In the list of "musicians in the Mask, 1674," were the names of four players on the "Gittars" ; in the list of materials supplied for their costumes they are spelled "Gytarrhs" ; and in the bill for making the same they are referred to as "Kittars." Now, I submit that at this date the instrument mentioned could easily have been the Gittern ; but that the spelling of the word indicates that the more recently imported Guitar is meant. In the Lord Chamberlain's Records for 1686 there is an "Order that the sum of £10 be paid to John Abell, musician in ordinary to his Majesty, for a guytar by him bought for his Majesty's service in his bed-chamber." Here we have the name in what is practically its present-day form; and yet, at that time, Gitterns were still being used, as well as Citterns.

The improved tone produced by the Spanish Guitar when used for accompaniment probably caused the older instrument to be displaced, but there can be no case in favour of the Guitar having had its origin in the Gittern. The Gittern was the predecessor of the Guitar, just as the viol was the forerunner of the violin; but in neither case was the one the ancestor of the other, for this honour is shared by many forms.

GITTERON PIPES. *v.* CORNET.

GLEE: A form of vocal composition, peculiarly English, in three or more parts, most commonly for male voices. The characterising feature of the Glee was that each of the parts was a solo part, and was not to be doubled. Despite the suggestion of its name, the nature of the composition could be grave or gay, for the word was derived from the Anglo-Saxon *Gle*, which simply meant "music." There is no especial reason for supposing, as some authorities do, that the Glee was originated in some way to fill the place of the Madrigal, or that it was a development out of that form. It is far too recent for that, and the interval which elapsed between the Madrigal's popularity and the rise of the Glee was too great for any direct connection to be established. Moreover, the two differed enormously in form, contents, and construction. The continuous contrapuntal treatment of the Madrigal, and the "fuges," as the Elizabethan writer terms them, are alike absent from the Glee, which harmonised more frequently vertically, and loved to hasten to a multitude of cadences. This latter characteristic was caused by the circumstance that the Glee contained a large number of subjects, with hardly any development worth mentioning. The true Glee, as illustrated by its best examples, needed no instrumental accompaniment, although many compositions appeared bearing the name and provided with an accompaniment. These should not be termed Glees at all. The word is used as early as John Playford's time, and many collections of part-songs were published containing what are labelled "Glees," but which bear little resemblance to the Glee of a century later. The composition, true to name, belongs properly to the Eighteenth and beginning of the Nineteenth Centuries, and the most popular writers in this form (alphabetically arranged) were: Attwood, Battishill, Bishop, Callcott, Cooke, Danby, Horsley, John Stafford Smith, Spofforth, Stevens, and Webbe.

LEEMEN: The musicians of Anglo-Saxon England, who derived their name from the Anglo-Saxon *Gle*, music. The word is not to be traced to the Anglo-Saxon *Gligg*, meaning "merry," when used in the musical sense. The term "glee" (=music; and not to be confounded with the more modern Glee treated above), is to be found as *Glew* at the middle of the Thirteenth Century, and as *Glu* (=*armonia*, minstrelsy) in the *Promptorium Parvulorum* (1440). In *Kyng Alisaunder* we have "Orgles, tymbres, al maner gleo"; and in *Havelock the Dane* there is the form *Gleumen*.

The Gleemen in Anglo-Saxon England were the forerunners of the later minstrels, and it was due to their customs and traditions that some very ancient forms were retained and preserved. Their music, added to that which was brought in by the Normans, formed the basis for a national English school of music.

OOD-NIGHT: The name of a form of composition in Sixteenth- and Seventeenth-century England. It was distinguished by no particular characteristics, and was most probably used as the concluding item of an entertainment. In Mason and Earsden's "Ayres that were Sung and Played at Brougham Castle . . . in the King's Entertainment" (1618) there is a piece entitled "The King's Good-night" in lute-tablature. Shakespeare uses the word in *II Henry IV* (III, 2) in the quotation already given (*s.v.* FANCY).

RACES: The older term for Ornaments, still used in the present-day expression "Grace-notes." The English music of the Sixteenth, and particularly the Seventeenth, Century, was embellished with many now obsolete Graces. Chief among these were the Beat, the Cadent, the Fall, the Elevation, the Springer, the Relish, and the Backfall, together with many variants such as certain of the foregoing "shaked,"—*i.e.*

incorporating a trill. An account, and an example, of graces will be found under their respective headings.

GRADUAL: In the Roman Catholic service the *resp graduale* was a psalm sung after the Epistle and ans the choir. It received its name from having been *gradibus ambonis* (on the steps of the *ambo*). This " re style was not always persisted in, and the compos the English musicians of the Sixteenth Century to a different direction.

Another meaning applied to the word was that o containing service-music belonging to a certain (*v.* Antiphonal). In Middle English the form *Grail* was used for this book, and in the Sixteenth Century a common designation.

GRAIL, GRALL, GRAYL. *v.* GRADUAL.

GREGORIAN CHANT: A name applied rather loose music of the Roman Catholic ritual, not because Pope the Great (Sixth Century) composed the chants be name, but rather because during his occupation of t chair the form of the musical service became fixed. M he used was in existence before his time, and a good added later (*v.* Gevaert, *Les Origines du Chant litu l'eglise latine*, 1890). At the same time Gregory was su responsible for the form of this music to justify us in p his memory in the term. There can be no doubt rescued Church Music from the decadent state into v Ambrosian music had fallen. Much of the then obsolete procedure was abandoned, and the musi Church service gained comparative freedom. The newly founded by this Pope was adhered to mor strictly in different countries. In England, whi Roman singers came in the year 604, the clergy was e faithful to Gregory's system—Benedict, Bishop inviting more singers from Rome in 678. It was not Sixteenth Century that serious liberties were taken wi thence onward there was an ever-increasing dange service-music of the Sixth to the Eighth Centuries b in a muddle of slipshod rendering and so-called " ments." In the Nineteenth Century, however, th Benedictines commenced an organised restoration o traditions, and in 1881 appeared the first edition of *Les Mélodies grégoriennes d'apres la tradition*, which has served as the chief source of the Plain-song in Roman Catholic use. Another edition, claiming equally to be after the true tradition of the period immediately following the death of Gregory, is known as the "Ratisbon Edition." A later edition (Twentieth Century) by the authorities of Solesmes, is now the officially accepted one.

GROUND: Originally meaning the basis upon which all things stood, the term later came to be applied to the groundwork upon which the musicians of the Sixteenth and Seventeenth Centuries based their compositions. This foundation, afterwards known as the Ground-Bass, consisted of a short passage of four or eight measures, repeated as often as the ingenuity of the writer could invent fresh divisions (*q.v.*) or descant (*q.v.*) upon it. The melodies were varied and the harmony altered at each re-appearance of the Ground, and the writing of Divisions on a Ground was a favourite occupation of the old English musicians.

GUIDONIAN SYLLABLES. v. ARETINIAN SYLLABLES.

GUITAR. v. GITTERN.

GYTERNE, GYTHORNE. v. GITTERN.

HARP: A plucked stringed instrument of great antiquity and doubtful origin. So many nations of the remotest past used the Harp in some form or other that it is quite possible for the various types to have been developed from separate sources, though coincidentally similar. Very strong claims to the early development of the Harp can be made by Egypt, the ancient Teutonic peoples, and the Keltic nations, and which of these really first used the instrument may be impossible to decide to-day. One thing, however, must be borne in mind, and that is the circumstance that the Harp of Ancient Egypt possessed no front pillar, while the instrument of Western development had this support. Whether this fact points to separate sources for the two types must again be left an open question. As far as the British Isles are concerned, even, it is not at all easy to fix upon the identity of original types. The very names given to the various forms help to complicate the issue and strengthen the supposition that the different species of the Harp were developed very long ago, uninfluenced by one another. Th name Harp is of Teutonic origin (the Anglo-Saxon *Hearpe* Middle English, *Harpe ;* German, *Harfe ;* Old High German *Harpha ;* from the Teutonic type *Harpon :* Anglo-Saxon verb, *Hearpian*, and the performer, *Hearpere*), and would seem to argue that the instrument, like the name, came to Englan with some of those hardy Norsemen who descended upon ou shores very early in our known history. It is also possible and in my opinion highly probable, that even the Romanc countries (Italian, *Arpa ;* French, *Harpe ;* Portuguese, *Harpa*

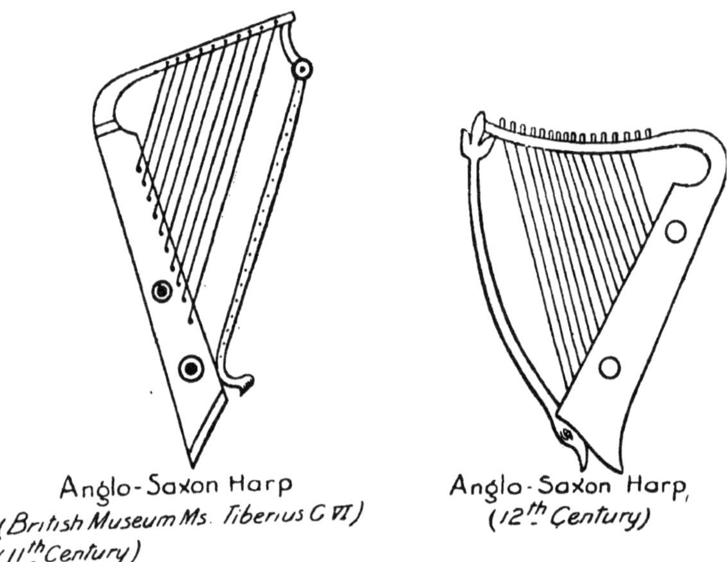

Anglo-Saxon Harp (British Museum Ms. Tiberius C VI) (11th Century)

Anglo-Saxon Harp, (12th Century)

had the name and the instrument from a Northern source, *vi* the Norse settlers in the North of France. In the case of th Keltic peoples, the same similarity of name occurs : Brittany *Telen ;* Wales, *Telyn ;* and Cornwall, *Telein.* The Gaeli sub-division used the distinct name *Clairsech* (Ireland), o variant. Although many eminent authorities on the Har and on Irish music say that the Cruit or Crot, mentioned i the article on the Crowd, was an ancestor of the Western Harp I do not think it had much to do with it. There can be n doubt that the early Crots, figured on the Eighth and Ninth century sculptured crosses, suggest primitive hand-harps but it is my opinion that it developed along different lines from those followed by the instrument that produced the true harps. The Irish Cruit must on no account be confused with the Welsh Crwth or the English Crowd; but at the same time, I think it was developed into a kindred form.

So many pieces of evidence could be produced to prove that the Harp came to England from one of the Norse countries or from Ireland, that it would be very difficult to decide with absolute certainty whence the Anglo-Saxon Harp really came. Personally, judging by the evidence of its form and name, I think it was brought hither from the North-West of the European Continent. There is strong proof of undoubted Irish influence in the early religious settlements in various parts of England; and it is not impossible for the Harp to have been introduced with one of these. Both sources may even have supplied the modified instrument common in the England of the Saxons.

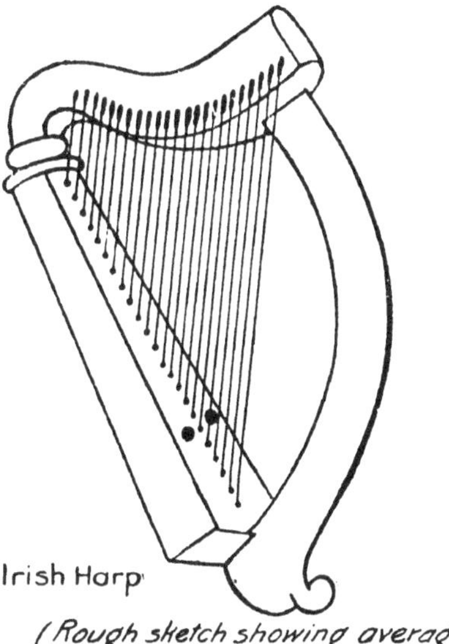

Irish Harp

(Rough sketch showing average 11th Century Irish harp)

Used here at that period, the Harp was a triangular instrument held by one hand and played with the other, generally used by the Gleemen (*q.v.*) to accompany their own or others' singing. In common with the practice prevalent among their kinsfolk on the Continent, the early Saxons in England used the Harp for all festive occasions, the instrument passing round the banqueting hall as one guest after the other accompanied himself in song. So common an instrument was the Harp in England from the Fifth Century to the Eleventh, that the story of King Alfred's minstrelsy in the Danish camp can quite easily be true. The stringing of the ancient Harps varied, of course, very considerably, and the tuning, like that of the organs of the same period, was probably modal, or to a chord;—certainly not chromatic. It is quite likely that the addition of strings to the Harp followed the addition of pipes to the organs, and that as the harmonic system changed, the stringing and tuning of all the instruments in use became altered to suit. With the modern Harp and its transposing mechanism, we can have nothing to do in this work.

HARP-GUITAR: An invention of the late Eighteenth Century, thought out by Edward Light, a London maker who evolved quite a number of such modifications of existing instruments. The Harp-Guitar was tuned and manipulated like the ordinary Guitar, but had a couple of new strings added to the bass side. The shape of the body was altered to approach nearer to that of the harp. The instrument did not enjoy long or great popularity. The music written for it was a sixth above the sounds produced.

HARP-LUTE: A kind of hybrid instrument, between a harp and a lute, strung with gut and covered strings, and treated musically as a Guitar. It was the invention of Edward Light (London, *c.* 1798), and was the subject of subsequent improvements. One of the latter took the form of "ditals" or, as Light himself describes them, "thumb-keys," which were "certain pieces of mechanism, each of which, when pressed upon, will produce the depression of a stop-ring, or eye, which draws the string of the Harp-Lute down upon a fret. . . . This mechanism has the property of holding the string fast in such position as long as may be after the pressure of the finger or thumb is removed." When every string was provided with such keys, the instrument was called the Dital Harp.

HARPSICALL. *v.* HARPSICHORD.

HARPSICHORD: A keyboard instrument of wing-shape (something like a Grand Pianoforte on a small scale) and played by means of plectra made of leather or quill affixed to Jacks (*q.v.*) as in the Virginal and Spinet. For convenience of reference be it noted that the Harpsichord was known as the Clavecin in France and as the Clavicembalo in Italy. The evolution of the Harpsichord is easy to follow. The addition of an auxiliary instrument with strings an octave higher was made in comparatively early times (*v.* virginal *and* spinet). These octave strings were later added to those on the existing sound-board. A stop was then added that could bring these strings into

HANDEL'S HARPSICHORD
By Andreas Ruckers, Antwerp, 1651
(*Victoria and Albert Museum*)

HARPSICHORD
By Thomas Hitchcock, London
Second half of the 17th Century
(*Victoria and Albert Museum*)

[*face p.* 102

action or not, as desired. From such a beginning the rest was simple. By introducing stops that could bring one or all the strings in a bichord or trichord action into operation, some gradations of tone were achieved. Tschudi, by inventing the "Venetian Swell" (1769), added another device which, by opening and closing like a shutter, allowed as much of the tone to emerge as was desired. Another stop would cause a row of Jacks to act on the strings nearer the bridge, and thus produce a peculiar tonal effect. All these stops had names, such as Cymbal, Lute, Buff (a damper-stop), Unison, *etc.* So it came about that by the Eighteenth Century the Harpsichord, with its two keyboards and half-dozen stops (and pedals to put all the stops out of action without removing the hands from the keys), was an instrument capable of a certain amount of variety in effect.

The instrument known as the *Clavicembalo* appeared on the Continent of Europe as early as the beginning of the Fifteenth Century; but exactly when the Harpsichord arrived in England is not quite clear. When it was introduced, it was most probably from the Netherlands. Whether the instruments "with stops" mentioned in the Privy Purse Expenses of Henry VIII were Harpsichords, as we understand the term, is not certain; there is plenty of evidence, though, to make it appear that instruments by the elder Ruckers were brought from Antwerp pretty early (Seventeenth Century). By that century, indeed, the Harpsichord had become fairly popular in England, for we find it mentioned in the State Papers in a way that does not make them look like novelties. It must, however, be remembered that the early specimens were placed upon a table for performance, and were devoid of pedals such as were afterwards added. On November 6, 1663, John Hingston (Organist and Keeper of the King's instruments) was paid for "mending the organs and harpsicords . . . also for mending her Majesty's harpsicord that stands in her own chamber. . . ." And if the word "harpsichord" was used at a period when "virginal" was still being loosely applied to all the keyboard instruments, it must prove that the instruments referred to must have been, in fact, something different. The Lord Chamberlain's Records for August 20, 1663, already mention the Harpsichord. On November 3, 1664, "pedalls" are mentioned in the same records; and since they are not spoken of earlier, we may assume that they were applied at about this time. In the list of musicians for the Mask of 1674, the instrument appears as "Harpsicalls," a not unusual spelling. "Harpsycon" and "Harpsicon" were two more variations of the name, appearing in publications of Playford and his contemporaries. The account for 1675 includes the sum of ten shillings "for strings for the harpsicords and pedalls for half a year," and £2 "to Mr. Haward, the virginall maker, for mending the harpsicords." The same account gives the item: "For a greate harpsichord with three ranks of strings for his Majesty's musick in the hall and in the privy lodgings, £30," probably referring to a trichord instrument. Payments for accessories for, and repairs to, the Harpsichords are entered under date August 19, 1678. In 1685 (August 31) Henry Purcell was sworn in as a musician-in-ordinary for the "Harpsicalls."

John Evelyn mentions the instrument in his *Diary* under date November 20, 1679, when he heard an Italian play. The Harpsichord seems to have been kept more particularly in the hands of musicians and serious students, its cost probably preventing it from becoming as popular with the masses as, say, the Spinet. The higher classes of society, of course, had the instrument in their music-rooms, and rather troublesome they must have found them. The tuning of the strings and the adjustment of the Jacks with the complicated mechanism of the stops and pedals, not to speak of the difficulties provided by the octave-string and its tuning, certainly made the Harpsichord an expensive instrument to maintain in good playing order. Its most important function was to accompany the voice in the opera, and a Harpsichord was always near the conductor's hand at rehearsal and performance.

One or two special specimens of the instrument should be mentioned. The one belonging to Handel, and made by Andreas Ruckers (Antwerp) in 1651, is rather plain in appearance, but must have been excellent in tone when at its prime. It is now in the Victoria and Albert Museum (London). Kirkman also, at the end of the Eighteenth Century, made some excellent specimens of the Harpsichord, and examples of his workmanship are, to my own knowledge, still in daily use. A particularly sumptuous instrument was made by Tschudi and Broadwood for the Empress Maria Theresa in

1733—a specimen representing the highest point in the development of an instrument that had been in use in various forms for three centuries, and which was destined, very shortly afterwards, to be dethroned by the Grand Pianoforte with hammers. A picture of this (the "Empress Harpsichord") is given in *Musical Instruments, etc.*, by Hipkins and Gibb (1888).

HARPSICON. *v.* HARPSICHORD.

HARP-THEORBO: An instrument with a fretted fingerboard and plucked strings invented round about 1800. As its name suggests, it was a compromise between the harp and the lute, leaning more towards the lute. It was one of a number of similar inventions of that period, and probably intended to supply a want felt after the complete eclipse of the last of the lute-family. Like the other instruments of this nature, the Harp-Theorbo did not live long. A specimen may be seen in the Victoria and Albert Museum (London), made by Harley (*c.* 1800).

HARP-VENTURA: A handsome instrument of artistic appearance, named after its inventor, Angelo Benedetto Ventura, Guitarist and teacher of music to Princess Charlotte of Wales. In form it was a peculiar mixture of instruments; the front pillar of a harp, the tuning-pegs of the same; a series of fretted fingerboards; all added to a resonance-chamber that was highly ornamented with painting and gilding. There were no bridges, and the strings were fastened at their lower ends in a manner reminiscent of the lutes. The lower strings, not passing over fingerboards, were only struck open as accompanying chords; while the treble series of strings, running over the fretted fingerboards, supplied the melody. A specimen (dating from the early Nineteenth Century) is preserved in the Victoria and Albert Museum (London).

HARPWAY: A tuning of the bass-viol, differing from the usual one of fourths with an intermediate third. The Harpway tuning was applied chiefly to the Lyra-viol or bass-viol played Lyraway, and consisted of accordance to a regular chord, either major or minor. The phrases "Harpway Sharp" and "Harpway Flat," so frequently seen at the head of Seventeenth-century pieces, mean that the instrument was to be

Harpway Flat

Specimen of tuning given for playing the Viol 'Harpway'.

tuned to the given chord. Indeed, music written in Tablature (*q.v.*) could not be performed at all if the instrument were not tuned as prescribed; for it must be remembered that the signs (letters or other characters) used in the Tablatures do not represent visually the actual notes heard, but indicate only on which frets and on which strings the fingers of the player are to descend. The pitch of the sounds produced are, of course, dependent entirely upon the tuning of the instrument. For the force of the words "Sharp" and "Flat" when used in conjunction with the term Harpway, see the articles SHARP *and* FLAT.

HAUTBOY: A wood-wind instrument with a double reed. The pipe known as the Hautboy in England must not be looked upon as distinct from every other, but rather as one stage in the development of the instrument which commenced its career as a Shalm (*q.v.*) and ended it as an Oboe. During this process of evolution, two features remained constant; the double reed (although in finish and effect it became much improved), and the conical bore of the tube. The plain finger-holes of the early Shalms gave place to a modern system of keys. The name, then, designated the improved Shalms of the Sixteenth Century, and the Oboe of the Eighteenth and early Nineteenth Centuries. It is to be derived from the French *Haut bois*, "high wood," which describes the material of which the instrument was made, and gives its pitch, for, though tenor and other Hautboys were known, the treble was by far the commonest. When the word Shalm was dropped and the other applied cannot be fixed with certainty. It appeared, however, in *Gorboduc*, by Norton and Sackville (first acted in 1560/1), where it was named in "the order and signification of the dumb show before the fourth act." After this date its use became more and more common.

From the first quarter of the Seventeenth Century onwards, the words Hoboy, Hoaboye, Hooboy, or some such variation, are of very frequent occurrence in the State Papers. The instrument occupied an important position in the military music of early times, and under date July 10, 1678, we read: "Account for liveries for two hautboys for the troop of Grenadeers under his Grace the Duke of Monmouth for the war against the French king" (*Lord Chamberlain's Records*).

A more peaceful entry is that of September 29, 1686, where liveries are ordered " for twelve hautboyes . . . for the first, second, and third Troops of Guards, to be made ready against his Majesty's birthday " (*Id.*).

The mere mention of the word Hautboy presumably meant the treble instrument, though occasionally we find the pitch given, as on November 2, 1664, when the " treble hoboy " is referred to (*Id.*). The " Tenner hoboy " is mentioned in 1665 and again in 1684/5 (*Id.*). As soon as the Hautboy became an Oboe it ceased to come within the plan of this book.

HAY: A Sixteenth-century country-dance of the " round " type. Dr. Johnson supposes that it obtained its name from the sense of " to dance in a ring: probably from dancing round a hay-cock." This is not a very convincing derivation, but no better can be advanced. The dance is mentioned in *Martin's Month's Minde* (1589): " Hayes, jigges, and roundelays "; and in Michael Drayton's *Nymphidia:* "There dancing hays by two and three, Just as their fancy casts them." Shakespeare, in *Love's Labour's Lost* (V, 1), has: " . . . or I will play On the Tabor to the Worthies, and let them dance the hay." Sir John Davies also mentions it in his *Orchestra* (1594). James Howell, in the Seventeenth Century, gives the dance in its appropriate atmosphere.

> Shall we go daunce the hay ?
> Never pipe could ever play
> Better shepheard's rondelay.

Survivals may exist locally, and at least one modern composer has revived the name.

HEXACHORD SYSTEM: Although not coming specifically under the heading of " Old English Music "—for the system of Hexachords was in universal use—some knowledge of it is absolutely necessary if many of the matters connected with Medieval music are to be understood. The Hexachord, in the simplest language, was a scale-like succession of six notes, modified, where necessary, always to produce a semitone between the third and fourth degrees. This improvement on the older tetrachord system was introduced in the Eleventh Century and used for the then instituted Solmisation (*q.v.*). The common error of supposing that Hexachords could be based upon any note must be avoided; for, although they were repeated in the octave, there were only three different species. These commenced from three notes in the series treated in the article GAMUT (*q.v.*). It is obvious that a set of six diatonic notes commencing, say, from F, could not contain a semitone between the third and fourth degrees unless the B were modified in some way (for the tritone, F-B, was *diabolus in musica*, and carefully to be avoided). Therefore, the B in this Hexachord was flattened by a semitone and called *B-rotundum* (or, as we should say, B-flat); the B-natural was termed *B-quadratum*. The Hexachord starting from G was known as *Hexachordum durum*, or "hard" Hexachord, that beginning on C the Natural Hexachord, and the one commencing on F, the "soft" Hexachord (*H. Molle*).

Using the series of twenty notes adopted as the complete range in the Eleventh Century, the Hexachords, commencing as they did from the G, C, and F of each octave, would number seven, arranged as follows:

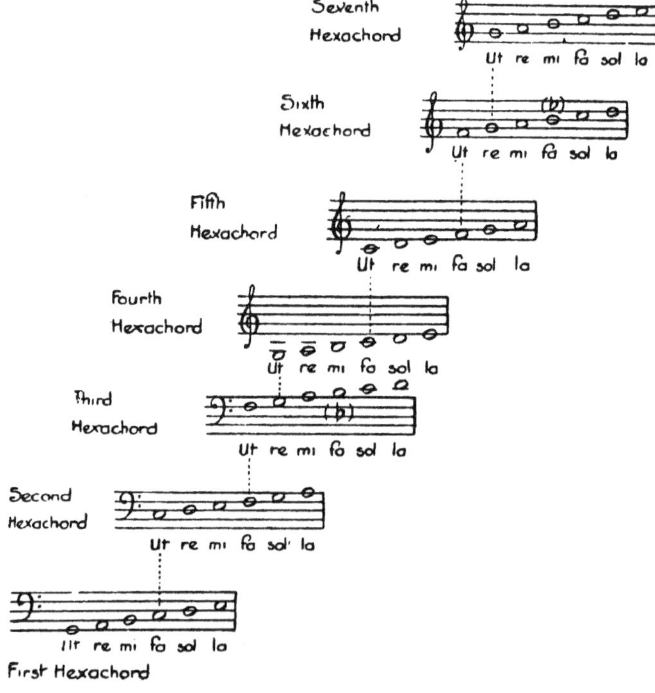

These notes from the bottom G to the top E received at the same time the alphabetic names by which we still know them, and this innovation, like nearly all the musical inventions of the Eleventh Century, was attributed to Guido d'Arezzo. The notes of each Hexachord were sung to the Aretinian Syllables (*q.v.*).

This system of vocalisation answered very well so long as the music remained within the limits of a single Hexachord; when, however, the melody extended beyond those limits, it was found necessary to institute some method of changing the nomenclature of the notes in each Hexachord. The plan evolved was that known as Mutation, and it consisted of naming the first note of each Hexachord *Ut*, and following with the other syllables in their usual order. It will be seen at once that the *Ut* of the first Hexachord (which was G), becomes a C in the second, and an F in the third, and so on—the semitone always falling between *mi* and *fa*. When a vocalist was required to sing a passage which took him from one Hexachord to another, he simply used the syllables proper to the Hexachord from which he started, and changed (*i.e.* resorted to Mutation) when he found the compass too great. A glance at the table given in the article on Gamut will make clear how such passages were sung. In general practice the change between the first and second Hexachords (and their octave duplications) was effected by singing *re* in place of *sol*, and then continuing with the names of the new Hexachord. This when the passage ascended. When it descended, the *mi* of the second Hexachord was replaced by the *la* of the first. Mutation between the first and third Hexachords could not take place in one step, since the B-flat in the third Hexachord would cause endless trouble. Mention of the *B-rotundum* reminds us that another of the reasons for Mutation was to find a name for this flattened B, when it occurred after the notes of a "hard" or "natural" Hexachord. In order to find a syllable that would express the B-flat, Mutation to the "soft" Hexachord was necessary. It is, perhaps, remarkable that once the notes were named from G to E, a seventh syllable was not added to cover the series from one note to its octave, and thus avoid the necessity for Mutation. But this would have anticipated the scale-system which uses a leading-note; and until the modern idea of keys with their attendant signatures was evolved, such a step was impossible. In the changing of *B-quadratum* to *B-rotundum*, however, we see already the germ of this idea. The question of Mutation was probably the weakest spot in the whole Hexachord system, but no other method was possible so long as the scale consisted of six notes. The whole cumbersome series with its Mutations and its *B fa* (B-flat) and *B mi* (B-natural) persisted as long as Solmisation was practised—*i.e.* for over six hundred years (*see also* GAMUT *and* SOLMISATION).

HOBOY. *v.* HAUTBOY.

HOCKET: Sometimes called Hoket or Ochetus. This was a form of composition interrupted by a number of rests, so that the passages were abruptly truncated. The word is in all probability a corruption of *Hocquet,* a hiccup, and in its musical application was used by writers as early as Robert de Handlo (1326; reproduced by Coussemaker in *Scriptores,* I) to refer to music thus haltingly constructed of notes and pauses. An alternative term, much used in the Medieval Latin treatises on music, was *Truncatio* (*Truncatio idem est quod hoket*).

HOKET. *v.* HOCKET.

HOLD: The Seventeenth-century term for a Pause. The sign used for it differed somewhat from the present-day indication, and was made thus: 𝄐. Its function coincided exactly with that of the modern Pause in that it was most commonly set over the concluding chord of a composition. John Playford and Christopher Simpson (1665) both allude to its employment over certain notes in the body of a work which it was desired to lengthen or insist upon for the sake of expression. Variant terms for the Hold were Arch and Stay.

HOLDING. *v.* BURDEN.

HORNPIPE: 1. A wind-instrument of British origin, localised chiefly in Cornwall and Wales. As *Corn-bib,* or *Pib-corn* we find the pipe in Wales; and in Ireland, Cornwall, and Brittany as *Pib-corn* or *Piob-corn.* These three countries using a similar name may point to a Keltic origin for the instrument. The antiquity of the Hornpipe as an instrument can scarcely be determined. A pipe or horn would have been used by pastoral peoples from the remotest periods. A manuscript

Vocabulary dating from the Fifteenth Century (Trinity College Library, Cambridge) translates the Latin *Cornubium* with "Hornpipe," while another such primitive dictionary by a "brother Galfridus" (*c.* 1440) also includes the word.

The Hornpipe was a wooden pipe furnished with finger-holes and a bell of horn. It was played with a reed of the single beating type, which also was covered with horn. This accounts for the early descriptions of the instrument stating that it was a pipe with "a horn at each end." Robert Greene (died 1592) mentions the Hornpipe as an instrument: "and so desiring them to play on a horn pipe, layde on the Pavement lustily with his leaden heeles" (*Greene's Groatsworth of Witte*). Ben Jonson in the *Sad Shepherd* (I, 2) speaks of awakening "the nimble hornpipe and the timburine." In Dryden's day the word was still applied to the instrument, for in his translation of the *Æneid* he has: "The shrill hornpipe sounds to bacchanals." The *Tatler* (No. 157) even has: "Trumpet and Welsh harp; hunting-horn and hornpipe."

2. As a dance the Hornpipe was named by the instrument which accompanied it originally, and for which the earliest examples were doubtlessly written. This being the case, the nature of the dance must have been pastoral. This may come as a surprise to those who only associate Hornpipes with sailors. But during its long career the dance had many forms, and both duple and triple measure. As may be expected, we meet with early mention of the Hornpipe as a dance in those parts of the country that used the instrument—Chaucer already alluding to the "Horne-pypes of Cornewayle." In a Mystery-play of 1485 there is the stage-direction: "Here mynstrellys, an hornpipe." As a written composition, the Hornpipe appears among the works of Hugh Aston, an organist in the reign of Henry VIII, and one of the celebrated men in the history of Tudor music. John Stafford Smith, in his *Musica Antiqua* (1812), gives the example in modern notation. Spenser alludes to the way in which the instrument named the dance in the *Shepherd's Calendar* (1579):

> . . . a lusty tabrere
> That to the many a hornpipe played,
> Wherto they dauncen each one with his maid.

In the days of Queen Elizabeth the Hornpipe was fairly popular, and by that time it had reached a point in its history at which it was an accepted form ; and in a list of fashionable dances, Barnaby Rich (1581) included it. Morley (1597) likewise says there were " many other kindes of Daunces as horne-pypes, *etc.*" Later on the dance became localised; different varieties probably being peculiar to certain districts. Ben Jonson says :

> . . . fetch the fiddlers out of France
> To wonder at the Hornpipes here,
> Of Nottingham and Derbyshire.

The last-mentioned county was noted for its Hornpipes as late as 1709, when the *Tatler* (No. 106) has : " Florinda . . . having danced the Derbyshire Hornpipe in the presence of several friends." In Lancashire, too, the form was very popular. Near the end of the Eighteenth Century it was much used on the Stage as *entr'acte* music, in duple measure. It was mentioned so frequently in Nineteenth-century literature that we may take it to have been exceedingly popular then. H. Martineau, in *The Manchester Strike*, says : " It appeared from the heavy tread and shuffling of feet that some were dancing hornpipes." Lytton as late as 1849 has : " My father . . . could conjure wonderfully, make a bunch of keys dance a hornpipe " (*The Caxtons*). Even Tennyson in *Amphion* wrote :

> The gouty oaks began to move
> And flounder into hornpipes.

Exactly when, and by which means, the Hornpipe became popular with sailors, cannot be fixed with certainty. In the older references it was generally the shepherd or rustic swain who danced the Hornpipe. There is the possibility that the sailors' Hornpipe had nothing to do with the pastoral form at all, and that it was related to the Dutch *Matelotte.*

The earliest specimens of the Hornpipe were practically all written in a triple measure, and examples may be seen in Matthew Locke's *Melothesia* (1673), in Humphrey Salter's *Genteel Companion* (1683), and in Playford's *Apollo's Banquet* (1690). Henry Purcell, in the appendix to *Bonduca* (1695), of which I happen to have a copy of the reprint, gives two triple Hornpipes; one beginning:

and the other commencing:

In *King Arthur*, Purcell wrote two more Hornpipes, this time in 6/4; one with the rhythm:

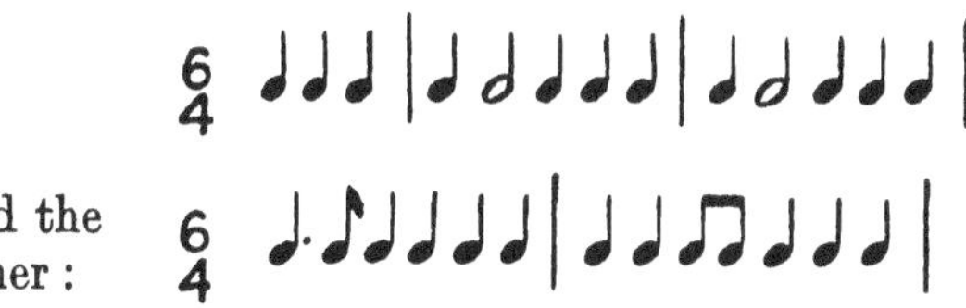

and the other:

Exceptionally, as in Playford's *Musick's Delight on the Cithren* (1666), we meet with a duple Hornpipe, but this was very unusual so early. It is possible that some Seventeenth-century composers were guided more by the spirit of the pieces than by their form, when they chose names for them.

The regular form for the Hornpipe was the usual one of two repeated sections each of four or eight measures. The change of time came about at the middle of the Eighteenth Century, the duple time-signature becoming more frequent until it entirely displaced the older triple form. As a duple dance the Hornpipe was used on the Stage until the middle of the Nineteenth Century.

URDY-GURDY: The idiomatic name for the Organistrum, an ancient stringed instrument with many mechanical contrivances. Essentially it consisted of an oval body with indented sides, and fitted with a wheel turned by a handle—which wheel vibrated the strings much as a violin-bow operates. In its earliest days the number of strings was three, tuned to a key-note with its fifth and octave. The strings could only be vibrated simultaneously, but the continuous repetition of fourths and fifths was not considered unmusical when the Organistrum was popular. Later, a larger numbe of strings appeared, with a couple of Bourdons, or open string playing a persistent drone bass (a fifth). The stopped string were operated upon from a keyboard or similar contrivance and it seems highly probable that this instrument was favourite one for vocal accompaniment from the Tenth Centur to the Twelfth. Variant names, used in different countries were, *Vielle, Bauernleier, Drehleier, Lira Tedesca, etc.*, an the instrument, provided with a chromatic series of notes, an improved action, is still to be seen occasionally in the hand of perambulating beggars. In France some exceedingl elaborate and expensively ornamented specimens were mad during the Eighteenth Century.

IMPERFECT OF THE LESS. v. MOOD.

IMPERFECT OF THE MORE. v. MOOD.

INITIAL: In Mensurable Music the name of the first note in Ligature (*q.v.*).

IN NOMINE: A term applied in the late Sixteenth and earl Seventeenth Centuries to a form of instrumental compositior It was always polyphonic, and its distinguishing feature wa the use of a few notes of an ancient Church chant named after the first words of the text, "In Nomine Domine." Thi ecclesiastical motive was given to one of the inner parts o the consort—generally the tenor—and was carried righ through the piece in long sustained notes as it was in it original (vocal) form. While the instrument performing thi part was thus occupied, the others of the *ensemble* descante freely above and below it; and with the standard of technica workmanship in this class of writing as high as it was at th time, many very interesting compositions bearing the nam were evolved. The practice which the English musicians of th Seventeenth Century had in all kinds of "division," stoo them in good stead here, and there can be little doubt that th In Nomine was the germ from which the English form of th Fantasia (or Fancy, *q.v.*) grew. Many beautiful art-forms wer developed from very simple origins, and the In Nomine consisting as it did of "only descanting upon the eight note with which the syllables (*In Nomine Domine*) agreed" (North *Memoires of Musick*), was the ancestor of perhaps the mos essentially English form of instrumental composition. The name, before this use of the motive became popular, was, of course, applied to many vocal devotional works in the Catholic liturgy.

Specimens of the instrumental In Nomine may be seen in many manuscripts preserved in different libraries; the British Museum including some by Thomas Tomkins, Simon Ives, and John Jenkins, generally in five parts (Add. 17792; first quarter of the Seventeenth Century; and Add. 29290, *c.* 1650). Huge quantities of In Nomines were written, and the greatest difficulty is that of selecting characteristic examples.

NTERLUDE: A term used in many senses at different periods. Employed in the Fifteenth and Sixteenth Centuries to designate a kind of allegorical play, masque, or mystery, it sometimes contained music (as, for example, Rastell's *Interlude* of The Four Elements). In this use it approached the Italian *Intermezzi*, which later were developed to such important proportions (*v.* my paper read before the *Musical Association:* "The Intermezzi of the Opera," printed in the *Proceedings of the Mus. Assoc., Session* 43; 1916/17). In its broadest sense the word meant any piece of music played between two sections of another work.

Organists at one time applied the term Interlude to short pieces sandwiched between the verses of a hymn, a procedure that was followed on the Continent to an even greater extent than in England.

NTONATION: Originally the short phrase that led to the Reciting Note of a chant, and later the opening of precented portions of the divine service. The Intoning of the first notes secured the pitch of the whole, and once the Precentor had done this, the fate of the ensuing chant was not so much left to chance.

NTONING: In Church music the singing of the opening of chanted portions in the service by the celebrant, his deputy, or a very small number of choristers who could be trusted to set the chant in its correct pitch. Although the Intoning of the liturgy was generally of a monotone nature, versions that were harmonised wholly or in part are not unknown.

VTROIT: A text from the Scriptures, set antiphonally, and

sung before and after a psalm, the whole forming the opening section of the Mass. The music of the Introit was modal and chanted (Gregorian).

INWARD PARTS: The inner parts or voices of polyphonic music, between the treble and the bass. Playford uses the term in this sense in the phrase, "be it Bass, Treble, or any Inward Part," and again when he describes the Tenor-Viol as "an excellent Inward Part."

JACK: The upright slip of wood that carried the quill, piece of leather, or metal, used as a plectrum in the instruments of the Virginal, Spinet, and Harpsichord class. The quill was fastened on to a movable tongue at the upper end of the Jack, and after having twanged the string on rising, was taken back by the hinge on the movable part so that it should not repeat the note in descending. When the Jack had returned to its original position—*i.e.* when the other end of the key had risen—a slight spring returned the quill-carrier to its place for the next note. Over the head of the Jack was a slip of cloth which damped the string when the Jack descended (*v.* VIRGINAL).

The word Jack is common in Old English to mean any implement fulfilling the functions of a servant—as, for example, a boot-jack. Shakespeare alludes to the Virginal Jack in Sonnet 128:

> Do I envy those jacks that nimble leap
> To kiss the tender inward of thy hand,

though how the Jack could come anywhere near the "inward" of the player's hand is a mystery; unless the poet is wrong for once in a musical allusion, and speaks of the keys as Jacks. Chapman, in *Monsieur d'Olive* (1606), also refers to it in the lines: "The weaver, Sir, much like a Virginal iack, Start nimbly up. . . ."

JIG: A dance-form of undoubtedly British, and most probably English, origin. In triple time its rhythm was the same as that of the Galliard, whose place it took. There can be very little doubt that such a dance with the rhythm—dotted-crotchet, quaver, crotchet—must have existed very early in the history of civilisation. It was a tripping measure that probably came spontaneously to the first dancer who felt genuinely happy

This dotted rhythm was a characteristic feature of the true British Jig, and it must be borne in mind when a modified form is met with that was developed when the Jig was taken to the Romance countries. A considerable amount of disagreement exists among authorities as to the original nationality of the form. German and French writers of the Eighteenth Century call it "the English Jig," while Grove contents himself by saying that it was "an old Italian dance."

The word is found in a great many forms—Gigue, Gique, Gigua, Giga, Chique, Gig, Gigg, Gigge, Jig, Jigg, Jigge, Jeg, *etc.*—and the general practice is to derive it from *Gigue*, a fiddle, thus forming what was considered a parallel to the Musette, Loure, Tambourin, Hornpipe, *etc.*, by naming the dance after the instrument that was supposed to accompany it. But very little etymological research will be necessary to prove that the one had very little to do with the other; that where the noun *Gigue* or *Giga* was used to mean the instrument, the dance-sense was not applied; while those dialects that used the verb *Giguer*, meaning "to dance," did not have the noun at all.

The earliest references to the word Jig or Gigue deal with the instrument and not the dance. In this sense it is to be found in a German poem of the middle of the Twelfth Century, in Wolfram von Eschenbach's *Parsifal* (*c.* 1220), and in a vocabulary of John de Garlandia (*c.* 1225), in the last-named of which we find the following entries: "Giga est instrumentum musicum de quo dicitur Organicos imitata modos, *etc.*," and later on: ". . . et dicitur Gallice *Gigue*," and yet again, "cum sistro, cum giga, cum psalterio"; statements that leave no room for doubt that the word, at that period, was applied solely to a musical instrument. Not much later Dante (1265/1321) uses the word, in his *Divina Comedia*, in the same sense:

> Et come giga et arpa intempra tesa,
> Dimolte corde fa dolce tintinno.
>
> (*Paradiso*, XIV, 118/119.)

Here, again, no doubt can be entertained that anything but an instrument is meant. A *Nominale* of the Fifteenth Century (British Museum) gives the word *Giga*—still meaning an instrument only—and also *Gigator*, the player. In Middle High German we know the term *Giga* and also its verb *Gîgen* to have been used in connection with the instrument—a word from which the Modern German *Geige*, violin, was derived. Under certain circumstances the word *Gîgen* could mean "to dance after" (*nachtanzen*), and thus a possible connection is found between the two meanings. But what holds good in Middle High German need not necessarily apply in any other country. The Middle Low German language had the diminutive *Gigel* meaning the instrument also, as is proved by the following erroneously translated passage: "De hilligen evangelien noemen se gygelen unde lyren," and also "der Gigelen Klang." We thus see that hitherto the word was used exclusively in Italy, Germany, and England to mean a certain stringed and bowed instrument of music.

In France we meet with both meanings, each in different parts of the country. Godefroi (*Dictionnaire de l'Ancienne Langue Française*) tells us that the *Gigue* was a stringed instrument, usually with three strings, and played with the bow, but that the verb *Giguer* meant "to romp" or "to leap." What connection the noun had with the verb it is impossible to decide to-day; but it is interesting to note that the same occurred in the Middle High German. We cannot agree with the authorities who derive the name of the dance from that of the fiddle on the strength of this evidence alone. There is, on the other hand, the strongest reason for supposing that the noun and verb came from entirely different sources, especially so since some French dialects used the verb and not the noun, and *vice versa*. We find the term (always meaning the same instrument) in the Provençal patois as *Gigua* or *Guiga*. The Norman dialect did not contain the noun *Gigue* at all, but had only the verb *Giguer*, which meant "to leap" or "to dance." Henri Moisy compares it with the English "to Jig." It will be interesting to note how, from now onwards, those dialects derived from, or influenced by, the Romance languages have the noun *Gigue* meaning the instrument, and those having a Northern origin possess the verb *Giguer*, signifying "to caper." Menage (*Dictionaire Etymologique*, 1694) says the *Gigue* was "a piece of music of a merry nature," and adds that in Scotland the word was used to mean a very merry dance-air. This, of course, proves nothing in favour of France having been early to use the word in its dance-sense. The lateness of the dictionary's date would place it out of the question at once.

for we had the Jig in England as a dance more than a century earlier. The fact that the Scotch meaning was known in France is not surprising; the intimate relations that existed between the two kingdoms would account for that. We shall see that neither Italy, Germany, nor France used the name to signify a dance until comparatively late.

Turning our attention to England, we find the word used successively in all its meanings, the last being its dance signification; and since this last stage was arrived at before the close of the Sixteenth Century, we may, with perfect assurance, assert that the dance called *Gigue* or Jig was first used as such, and was first so named in this country, and that it wandered to the various countries of Europe. The first references to the word here as elsewhere dealt with the instrument. But about the middle of the Sixteenth Century a new meaning came to be applied to it. We find it used to mean a kind of ballad. It was a ridiculous metrical composition, sometimes rhymed, sung by the clown, who followed it with a dance—which dance was always performed to music supplied by Tabor and Pipe. Be it noted that the fiddle was not used thus early for the purpose. Here the connection between the ballad and the dance performed to the tune is pretty obvious. Beaumont, at the turn of the century, says: "A Jig shall be clapped at, and every rhyme praised and applauded." Ford uses the word in the same sense: "Petrarch was a dunce, Dante a Jig-maker." So also did Joshua Sylvester, in his translation of "G. de Saluste du Bartas, his devine weeks and workes" (1605):

> If neere unto some Eleusinian Spring,
> Som sportfull Jig som wanton shepherd sing,
> The ravisht Fountaine falls to daunce and bound.

So we see that the rhythm of the sung Jig, or ballad, was one very well adapted to a merry dance. John Florio, an Italian, writing his Italian-English Dictionary in England (1611), although influenced by the English meanings applied to the word, nevertheless gives *Giga* as a fiddle; and this would seem to prove conclusively that in Italy the word came to mean a dance very much later than in England. Christopher Marlowe, in *Tambourlaine* (1587), announces his intention of freeing the Drama "from jigging veins of rhyming mother-wits, And such

Conceits as Clownage keeps in pay." Shakespeare's *Love's Labour's Lost* was an early play, and being that, we find the word still used in its ballad meaning: " but to jig off a tune at the tongue's end, Canary (*q.v.*) to it with your feet . . ."; while in " He's for a Jigg or a tale of bawdry " (*Hamlet*, II, 2) it may have been used in the same sense. Later on in *Hamlet* we find exactly the same use as with Ford: " O God! your only jig-maker "—in a scene where only a merry quip or jingling rhyme can be meant. And Ben Jonson, dedicating his Catilene to the Earl of Pembroke, says: " . . . in these jig-given times, to countenance a legitimate poem." Nash, in 1596, speaks of a " Jigge in English Hexameters " (*Have with you to Saffron Walden*).

Now, these doggerel ballads of the clown were danced;—could not the song used by the mountebank have named the dance? Does not the *Spectator* have it very much later, " a certain jiggish noise to which I dance "? This is at least as logical as to connect the dance with *Giga* the instrument. Even the German, Riemann, says that the name is of English origin and has nothing to do with the instrument.

The fact that the Norman dialect had the verb meaning " to jig " would cause our eyes to turn Northwards for the source of the dance-name. In Scandinavia is to be found the original form of our word Jig. There is the Icelandic *Geiga*, which passing through Middle English (*Gigge*) became the modern Jig, meaning anything round or revolving. Examples of such use are frequent. We have " Whirligig," and " Jig-machine," and the wheels of the light carriage known as a Gig; also a spinning-top, according to Shakespeare's " Go, whip thy gig " (*Love's Labour's Lost, Act* IV). This doublet of Jig was used to mean " to spin " until comparatively late. The writers of the Seventeenth Century still used that word in the last-mentioned sense: " No wonder they'll confesse no losse of men; for Rupert knock's 'em till they gig agen."

What is more natural than to suppose that a word meaning " to revolve " should have been taken to designate the verses with a constantly recurring refrain, and that such a set of verses, being sung by the clown, should have given its name to the dance which was performed to the same tune. A curious inversion of meaning meets us in Scotland. There, " to jig " meant to play the fiddle, a meaning that the language most probably owed to France for the reason already given.

In England we have the last link of the chain—the Jig as a dance. Lady Nevell's Virginal Book (1591) was probably the first work to contain the word as the name of a piece of dance-music (*Galliard Gygge*), and Thomas Robinson (1603) followed closely after. Not much later the writers of the period employed the term in the dance-sense. Thus Fenton: "Those elegant delights of Jig and vaulting," and Beaumont and Fletcher (*Knight of the Burning Pestle*, IV, 1) make the citizen's wife say: "George, I will have him dance fading; fading is a fine Jig, I'll assure you."

Summing up all this etymological evidence, then, we may take it that the word Jig meaning a dance is to be traced to a Northern source *via* the ballad meaning of the late Sixteenth Century; and that it had nothing to do with the *Giga*, or fiddle. The connection that appears to have existed between the two in one or two isolated cases was probably accidental.

The Jig as a dance succeeded the older Galliard in the musical scheme; and having practically the same spirit and rhythm, changed places with the older form almost imperceptibly. It was written in almost any triple measure—3/8, 3/4, 6/8, 12/8, or 6/4—had the light rhythm of dotted-crotchet, quaver, crotchet (or these values halved or doubled according to period), and, before the form was extended by later composers, consisted of two repeated sections of four or eight measures each. The Old English writers usually gave the time-signature as "3 in 1," but the indication "2" or "4" was often used. It must not be supposed from the latter circumstance that the Jig was ever a duple form; the "4," for example, merely meant four beats to the measure, which would reduce a 12/8 bar to four measures of 3/8 each. It is, of course, impossible to say when the first piece of music was written in the English Jig form and rhythm. In all probability such music was sung and danced to long before the name was applied to it. In the reference of Barnaby Rich (1581), "the dances in vogue were measures, galliards, jigs, *etc.*," we see that the Jig and the Galliard were used side by side; and they were doubtlessly used together until their similarity caused the latter to be dropped, and the former developed. The *Galliard Gygge*, already alluded to, was composed by William Byrd, and is the only piece thus named among several other Galliards. In this specimen we probably see one of the fruits of the period of transition, in which the native and alien forms became merged. Benjamin Cosyn's Virginal Book (*c.* 1600) contains several Galliards but no Jigs so-named. Thomas Robinson's *Schoole of Musicke* (1603), on the other hand, contains five Jigs. Robinson's use of the French form of the name—*Gigue*—was most likely caused by the desire to make the work appear more artistic and fashionable; in the Introduction, however, he spells it Iigge. In 1607 Thomas Ford published his *Musicke of Sundrie Kindes*, and includes Galliards and Jigs side by side. If will thus be seen that the Jig had not yet reached the popularity with musicians that it attained to shortly afterwards, and that it had not yet succeeded in ousting the Galliard. Although Ford uses the name *Jigge* on the title-page, only one of the " Lessons " is so named—No. XV, " Whipit and Tripit, M. Southcotes Jig." The other four examples are No. IX, " The Wild Goose Chase " ; No. XI, " And if you do touch Ile crie " ; No. XIII, " Why not here " ; and No. XVII, " A Snatch and away." All of them exhibit the dotted rhythm mentioned above as being typical of the true English Jig. The names bestowed on these specimens suggest that words were added to the tune, and that the Jig, like most of the other old dances, was also sung. The form seems to have been a " popular " one, and the composers of " choice " music were rather chary of using it. Thus, Robinson's *New Citharen Lessons* (1609) only adds one more example to the list; *Parthenia* (1611) contains only Galliards; and the same occurs in Robert Dowland's *Varietie of Lute Lessons* (1610), in Morley's *First Booke of Consort Lessons* (1611), and in William Forster's Virginal Book of 1624. By way of contrast, the Fitzwilliam Virginal Book, although parts of it are earlier, gives us some very interesting examples of the Jig;—specimens that are worthy of notice not only because they were written by some of England's best musicians, but also because they show some deviation from the accepted form. " Nobodyes Gigge " (No. CXLIX) by Richard Farnaby, and Giles Farnaby's " Gigge " (No. CCLXVII) are both in Common time. To find pieces labelled " Jig " in common time is by no means as unusual as might be expected, especially at this period;—in most cases the spirit of the piece would have dictated the title rather than the measure. Such Jigs were intended only as instrumental pieces, and not for dancing. In the same way can the Sixteenth and Seventeenth-century "Marches" in 3/4 be explained. This naming of a piece by its character is also most probably responsible for such movements as the "Gigue-Almaines" which we often see in the late Sixteenth and early Seventeenth Century; they were for the most part duple as the true Almain, but were to be performed in the light, tripping manner peculiar to the Jig. Further examples in the Fitzwilliam Virginal Book are the "Gigge—Dr. Bull's Myselfe," in good form; a "Gigge" in 6/4 also by John Bull, having the typical rhythm, but containing two measures in common time; and a "Jigg" by William Byrd, in 6/4, which is a true English Jig in rhythm and spirit.

It was during the reigns of the first two Stuarts that the Jig seems to have enjoyed its greatest popularity. Although most probably not used as a true Court-dance, there can be little doubt that it was danced occasionally at the royal merry-makings, especially under the Merry Monarch. At the middle of the century the form underwent a change, and it came to be looked upon more generally as a purely instrumental piece, just as were the Jigs in *Parthenia.* Of course, it was still danced on the village-green and at popular gatherings—the different editions of Playford's *Dancing-Master* prove that. The edition of 1652 contains several examples of the form, used as Country-Dances, such as "Kemp's Jegg," "Lord of Carnarvon's Jegg," "Millison's Jegg," "Solomon's Jigge," and others not called Jigs, but which, from their rhythm, may be taken as such. Playford's *Court Ayres* (1655) contains several examples by such writers as William Lawes, Benjamin Rogers, Richard Cobb, George Hudson, *etc.*, while the same publisher's *Musick's Hand-maide* (1663) gives a further selection. Each successive publication now seems to afford more and more specimens, and the name was often not attached. The form had been accepted, and was used, as an instrumental piece pure and simple. Even then the Jig was still used as a dance in ordinary circles, and several extracts from contemporary books prove it. Pepys writes in his *Diary* (October 11, 1665): "My wife and Mercer, and Mrs. Barbara danced, and mighty merry we were, but especially at

Mercer's dancing a jigg, which she does the best I ever did see, having the most natural way of it and keeps time the most perfectly I ever did see." Nearly a year later Mercer once more amused the diarist (August 14, 1666) by dancing a Jig. John Playford suggests that in 1652 "the Gentlemen of the Inns of Court, whose sweet and ayry Activity has crowned their grand solemnities with admiration to all Spectators," also saw in the Jig's sprightly measure a relaxation from their sedentary occupation. This fact may account for the titles, "Inner Temple Jig," "Middle Temple Jig," "Lincoln's Inn Jig," and "Gray's Inn Jig," which we find in Playford's *Apollo's Banquet* (1690) among several other examples of the form. The Jig, therefore, was developed along two distinct lines; one as an instrumental piece, free in form, and the other as a dance. Before the Stuart régime ended the Jig was so popular as a dance that no entertainment or other occasion when many assembled, closed without a Jig.

The passing of the crown to the House of Hanover marked the decline of the popularity of the Jig; and with Handel and his contemporaries the form was considered more the movement that closed the formal Suite and less as a dance. It must not be supposed that Handel influenced the form of the Jig. His early examples are rather in the form that the Jig acquired when it was borrowed by Italy. In that country the dotted rhythm was smoothed out, and returned to England as the Italian *Gigue*, a form of running triplets. In some of Handel's examples the two rhythms are used together, just as this composer employed the rhythms of the *Courante* and the *Corrente* merged into one hybrid form.

The question as to whether Scotland or Ireland was the first to have the Jig from England is easily answered. Dated references give Scotland the earlier possession of the form. Thomas Morley, already in 1597 (*Plaine and Easie Introduction*) says: "And I boldly affirme, that look which he bee who thinketh himselfe the best descanter of all his neighbours, enioyne him to make but a Scottish Iygge, he will grossly erre in the true nature and qualitie of it." This gives us Scotch Jigs very early; and it also shows that these dances certainly possessed a special "nature and quality" of their own, in spite of the authorities who say that the British Jigs did not appear to have had any peculiar characteristics. Shakespeare mentions the Scotch Jig in 1599 (*Much Ado About Nothing*). The form does not seem to have become popular in Ireland until the second half of the Seventeenth Century, no examples bearing that name and possessing the requisite rhythmical character having been found before that time. To attempt to find the original source of so natural a rhythm is an almost hopeless task. If, as Boehme (*Geschichte des Tanzes, etc.*) says, the Jig was a Keltic form, why should not the Galliard, Canary, Siciliano, *etc.*, also be Keltic? for all possessed the same rhythmic figures. The most we can do in regard to the Jig is to discover where the dance with this well-known rhythm was first called "Jig," and where it was first danced. And the answer to these questions, as the above evidence shows, is in both cases, England.

But if Ireland was the last to make it welcome, that island was also the last to retain it in favour. To-day the term Jig is immediately associated with the green isle, and an "Irish Jig" is held to be synonymous with anything light-hearted and gay. Perhaps the best account of an Irish Jig as it was actually danced by the country-folk a century ago is to be obtained from Lady Morgan's *Patriotic Sketches of Ireland* (1807): "In the centre of the field . . . a distaff is fixed in the earth, on which is placed a large flat cake; this cake is the signal of pleasure and becomes the reward of talent. . . . At a little distance from this standard of revelry is placed its chief agent, the piper, who is always seated on the ground, with a hole dug near him, into which the contributions of the assembly are dropt. . . . At the end of each Jig the piper is paid by the young man who dances it, and who endeavours to enhance the value of the gift by first bestowing it on his fair partner; and although a penny a Jig is esteemed very good pay, yet the gallantry or ostentation of the contributor . . . sometimes trebles the sum which the piper usually receives." Such was the natural environment of the Jig—one most suitable to its merry and often riotous movement. It should be noted that it is still a piper who accompanies the dance, and not a fiddler. It would, of course, be very hazardous to say that Jigs were never fiddled; but in the case of nearly every older piece of evidence it is the tabor and pipe or the popular bagpipe that is mentioned.

In France the *Gigue* appears with Lully's early operas and

is mentioned by La Bruyère (*Les Caractères, etc.*, 1688). Sebastian de Brossard, too, speaks of the form and says, "Gigue is an air for instruments, rich in dotted notes and syncopation, which render the melody gay, and, so to say, tripping"; a description that makes it sound very like the true English Jig. The misplaced accent, also, is by no means rare in old English examples of the dance. Lully used the form only in the operas composed between 1682 and 1685, a fact that makes it all the more apparent that it was only an importation into France. Charles II sent many of his private musicians to France to acquire the French style which he admired so much—John Banister and Pelham Humphrey, to mention only two—and these English musicians may quite conceivably have taught the French composers one or two English forms. The dates of these visits and those at which Lully's operas containing *Gigues* appeared, fit so nicely that the probability is very great that they were suggested by the Englishmen. Colasse and Destouches used the form later, but one used some of his master's material, and the other imitated him very closely. Between 1700 and 1710 Feuillet attempted to revive the *Gigue* as a dance, and wrote Chorography for it, employing the Lully music; but these dances had little or nothing in common with the jolly British Jig, being really elaborate ballets for use on the stage by professional dancers.

In Italy there was an even greater scarcity of Gigues as dances, and as a movement in the early Suite it was by no means as common as were many of the other forms. The Italians generally removed the rhythmic characteristics of many of the dance-forms, and nowhere is this more plainly discernable than in the Jig. Just as they omitted the dots from the French Courante and made of it a Corrente, so did they transform the English Jig into a succession of running triplets, a figure of which the Italians were ever fond.

Germany likewise had the Jig from England, but used it almost exclusively as a suite-movement. From Frohberger (1649), Rieckh (1658), and Becker (1668), to Bach, the Gigue was used as an instrumental movement only, and examples of it in this environment need not be quoted.

There can be no doubt that the Jig played an important part in the history of certain musical forms; and from a gay dance-tune of eight measures, it became gradually extended, until it was employed in an important position in the Suite, and suggested the characteristic rhythm of the closing sections in many examples of the Sonata and Concerto.

KIT : A small stringed instrument much used by the dancing-masters of the Eighteenth Century. In this use it had four strings and was shaped like a miniature violin, its pitch varying according to different writers, from a unison with the violin to a fourth, fifth, or even an octave above. Praetorius says that it sometimes had brass or steel strings. Earlier examples were shaped like a baton (without corners or bouts), and during one period of its career it had only three strings. A good deal of confusion and doubt exists in the nomenclature, and we cannot be at all sure when *Poche*, *Pochette*, *Quart-geige*, and Kit were synonymous terms, and when not. The Kit in very early references may have been a pocket-rebeck. The word is mentioned in Rastel's *Interlude of the four Elements* (early in the Sixteenth Century), but we cannot be sure as to which form of the instrument it refers :

Kit (Mersenne: *Harmonie Universelle*, 1636)

> This daunce would do miche better yet,
> If we had a Kit or Taberet.

KNOT : Sometimes called the Rose. The fretted and often elaborately carved circular sound-hole cut in the tables of lutes and similar instruments. A large amount of highly artistic work was often put into this feature, and the *luthier* not infrequently strove here to exhibit his skill in the handling of his tools. Some specimens are exceedingly delicately cut, and beautifully designed.

LA. *v.* ARETINIAN SYLLABLES *and* GAMUT.

LARGE: (*Duplex Longa* or *Maxima*). In Mensurable Music, a note equal in value to two Longs (*q.v.*) and sometimes to three Longs. In form the note was as follows:

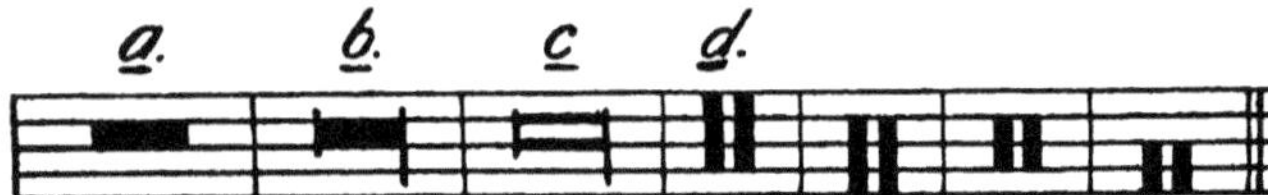

In the earliest manuscripts the Large was written as at *a.* and *b.* (as black notes); about the middle of the Fifteenth Century it appeared as at *c.* (open; white; in outline), and the black note returned for reduced note-values. The corresponding rests were written as at *d.*; covering three spaces when Perfect, and two when Imperfect. The Large or *Duplex Longa* was not evolved until the time of Franco of Cologne, when it was written, as its Latin name implies, as a double Long (*v. also* MENSURABLE MUSIC *and* MOOD).

LAVOLTA, LAVOLTE. *v.* VOLTE.

LESSON: A short composition of no especial characteristics, but which had to be suitable for the purpose of study. In the Sixteenth and Seventeenth Centuries, and even persisting well into the Eighteenth, the Lesson took the place of what we should to-day call an exercise or étude. "Lessons for the Recorder," or "Short Lessons for the Bass-Viol" were common titles at the head of Elizabethan and Stuart pieces. The word was in everyday use in Shakespeare's time and Hortensio, in the *Taming of the Shrew*, disposes of Lucentio with the snubbing remark: "You may go walk, and give me leave a while; My Lessons make no musick in three parts"; meaning to imply that he and the lady could make all the harmony required without the aid of a third part. Only Shakespeare could turn a phrase with such rich and subtle meaning, and it is to him and his literary contemporaries that we owe so much for having kept all account of many old terms from becoming lost.

LETTERS, or BY LETTERS. *v.* TABLATURE.

LIGATURES : In Mensurable Music the Ligature was a species of notational contraction for the music sung to one syllable of the text. This applies to the semibreve and notes of greater value. The Ligature was written in several forms, such as that of the *Ligatura recta*, where the square notes were placed closely together, the *Ligatura obliqua*, in which the first vertical stroke of the first note was connected with the second vertical stroke of the second note by a pair of parallel lines, and a mixed form in which both of the foregoing were used :

Certain clearly defined rules fixed the values of the notes in Ligature, values which varied according to the position of the notes in relation to their neighbours, and according to the presence or absence of tails to the notes. Any number of notes could be tied together (*ligatus*) in *Ligatura recta*, but the *Ligatura obliqua* could contain only two notes, the pitch of which was determined by the position of the vertical strokes that commenced and ended the parallelogram.

When the first note of a Ligature was a Breve it was said to be *cum proprietate* (*i.e.* normal), and when the first note was a Long it was *sine proprietate.* What is *cum proprietate* in an ascending Ligature is *sine proprietate* in a descending one, and *vice versa.* When the structure of a Ligature causes the first note (and consequently the second also) to be read as a semibreve, that Ligature was said to be *cum opposita proprietate.* Franchinus Gaforius (1496) says : " Every ascending Ligature of which the first note has no tail is *cum proprietate ;* similarly every descending Ligature of which the first note has a tail descending on the left side is *cum proprietate.* The first note of every Ligature *cum proprietate* is a Breve. They are therefore in error who read the first note of an ascending oblique Ligature as a Long." A tail ascending makes the Ligature *cum opposita proprietate* and converts the first two notes (and both if there are only two in the Ligature) into semibreves—both because one semibreve by itself could not exist in the days when the semibreve had no fixed value and was *ultra mensuram.* It will be seen from what has been said of the Ligature *cum opposita proprietate* that if the first note (Initial) has a ta ascending on the left side, both that note and the succeedin one are semibreves. All notes in Ligature which have a ta descending on the right side are longs. This rule, howeve does not apply to the last note (Final) of a Ligature. Provide that nothing which has already been said alters their valu all the intermediate notes of a Ligature (*Notae Mediae*) ar breves. If the first note has a tail descending on the left sid it is a breve. When the Initial has no tail it is a long if th second note descends, and a breve if the second note ascend All notes in a Ligature that have a tail descending on the righ side are longs. Every *Finalis* (last note) of an oblique Ligatur is a breve, the same applying to the final of a *Ligatura recta* i the note preceding it is a lower note. If the preceding not however, is higher, then the final becomes a long. The thre conditions just mentioned are upset if in a Ligature of tw notes the first has an ascending tail on the left, in which cas they are, of course, both semibreves. A final that has a ta on the right side is a breve if the tail ascends, and a long i the tail descends. Furthermore, the point of perfectio could be added to any note in Ligature, whether *recta* o *obliqua*.

It will be seen that there are sufficient rules and regulation relating to the correct interpretation of these products of th Middle Ages to cause every intending translator of ancien manuscripts to pause and consider before making the attemp The study of this subject, of which the foregoing is but th barest possible outline, will amply repay the student b opening for him a field of research in which all too few are a present occupied (*v. also* MENSURABLE MUSIC).

LITANY: A prayer of a supplicatory nature, of very gre antiquity. The origin of its later form was most likely in th monotone singing of the *Kyrie* (not as part of the Mass), form that was later developed in bulk and rendered still mo impressive by the addition of rich harmonies. It is interestin to note that the Litany was the first of the prayers to b translated into English. The early English examples of th Litany—*e.g.* that contained in Day's *Certaine Notes, etc.* (156 —and the later specimens by Tallis, followed the tradition the time by keeping the Plain-song in the Tenor part, th preserving the original character of the prayer, while it was beautified by the surrounding harmony.

LONDON CRIES. *v.* CRIES.

LONG: In Mensurable Music a note equal in value to two or three breves (*tempora*), according to Mood (*q.v.*). Like the Large, it was first written as a black note, and later as an open one with a tail on the right side. It may be described as a breve with a tail:

The rest of the same value was written as at *c.* when Perfect (*Pausa Modi*), and as at *d.* when Imperfect (*Pausa Longa*).

The tail of the Long could be placed on either side of the black note; but in the case of the open note it was of the utmost importance that it should be on the right side, and descend. The reason for this will be seen when Ligatures (*q.v.*) are studied.

LUTE: The name of a large and highly important family of plucked stringed instruments. In the Sixteenth Century and the first half of the Seventeenth, the Lutes occupied the position, as accompanying instruments, of the pianoforte of to-day, and were even more ubiquitous. In the physical aspect they were composed of a flat table or belly, and a vaulted, pear-shaped back made up of a number of narrow ribs glued together—the latter being often fluted, ribbed, or inlaid. The fingerboard was fretted, most commonly by having lengths of catgut tied round the neck and passing over the fingerboard under the strings at chromatic intervals. The strings were of catgut and arranged in pairs tuned in unison (*v.* COURSE *and* RANKS); they ran from the pegs to a bar affixed to the lower part of the belly. Each string had its own name, as in the case of the Viols; the highest string on the Lute being called the Catling. No bridge was used on the Lutes, and the strings were kept at the requisite distance from the fingerboard and belly by the transverse bar to which they were fixed. The heads of the Lutes were generally bent back at an angle with the neck, thus offering more resistance to the pull of the strings. The number of the latter varied with the period, but six was the most usual for the stopped strings (*i.e.* those running over the fingerboard); additional strings were added later at the side of the fingerboard, and tuned from a separate peg-box situated at the side of the other, or arranged as an extension from it. But the addition of these bass-strings changed the character of the ordinary Lute and made of it a Theorbo or an Arch-Lute (see these). Mace's *Musick's Monument* (1676) is perhaps the most valuable work for the study of the Lute in its English use, and most of the information we have on this branch of the subject is from its pages. Thomas Mace explains how the instrument is to be handled, treated, and strung; how tuned, and how the frets were to be "laid." The method of tuning varied considerably, and no useful object can be served by occupying space with such a fluctuating quantity. Naturally, as with all fretted instruments, the tuning and the Tablature (*q.v.*) from which the music was read had to go hand in hand.

A history of the Lute, to be complete, would occupy a volume at least as large as the present one, and consequently only the barest indication of its sources can be given. Of Oriental origin (Arabic, *Al'ud;* Spanish, *Laud;* Portuguese, *Alaude* Provençal, *Laut;* Old French, *Leut;* Middle English, *Lute* and introduced into Western Europe at the time of the Crusaders, the form of instrument used in this country would date from the Middle Ages and the Renaissance. By the time the later Tudor craftsmen worked the artistic appearance o the Lute was much improved and some exceedingly beautifu work is to be found. The sound-holes, for instance, varying in number from one to three, were often most elaborat examples of the *luthier's* art, being delicately fretted and carved. Famous makers existed in all the countries of Europe but England was not in the rearward, for Vinzenzo Galile already remarked that the Lutes of English manufacture wer the best (*Dial. della Mus.*).

References to the use of the instrument in England occu very early. Already at the beginning of the Fourteent Century we are told that a luter received forty shillings for h performance at Westminster. Another very early allusion in the Hosteller's account for Durham Priory (1361/2): "I uno viro ludenti in uno loyt . . .," and it is to be hoped th the lutenist's playing was better than the scribe's Latin. Langland in *Piers Plowman* says that Truth "thanne lutede in a loud note," while Chaucer, who mentions practically all the contemporary instruments, has in *The Pardoner's Tale :*

> Wheras with harpes, lutes, and guiternes,
> They dance and plaie at dis bothe day and night.

Gower also alludes to the Lute in *Confessio Amantis* (1390; *l.* 2679).

The "Household Account-Books" of many noblemen under Tudor rule afford a good deal of information on the subject, especially as far as it concerns the instruments in private use. Thus in 1495, "To Hugh Denes for a lewte xiii*s*. iiii*d*.," and in 1501, "For a lewte for my Lady Margaret, xiii*s*. iiii*d*." A Lute which the king gave as a present to his daughter, Princess Mary, cost the same sum (Nicolas, *Privy Purse Expenses of Henry VII*). Elizabeth of York also kept accounts of expenditure, and in the entry for July 5, 1502, we read: "To Giles lewter for stringes for the Quene of Scottes lewte, x*s*."

Henry VIII was a thorough musician, and employed a large number of musicians. In July, 1509, the Master Giles already mentioned is entered in the State Papers as a luter with the salary of 22*s*. 2*d*. per month. The instruments belonging to the king were in the charge of Philip van Wilder and a list of them is preserved in the British Museum (*Harl. MS.*, 1419). On *folio* 202*b* there is entered: "A Lute being in a case cheste fasshion of Timbre covered wt. leather," a further "xxiij Lutes wt. xxiij cases to them," and (*f.* 205*b*): "a litle Venise Lute wt. a case to the same." Henry, as is well known, treated any musician who could show talent out of the ordinary very generously; and the Venetian ambassador, writing home, described a concert at which he met "a Brescian whom the King paid 300 Ducats a year for his Lute-playing." On the same authority we have it that Henry himself played the Lute very well. Society followed the King's example, and the account-books of many of the nobility contain entries referring to payments for instruments and performances. And contemporary literature is just as full of allusions to the instrument as the records are. All of the children of Henry VIII played the Lute, and in saying this it might be remarked that everyone learned the instrument, for no education was considered complete without that accomplishment. If the references to the Lute be any indication, the very air of England must have trembled with the music of that instrument. It was heard everywhere, and it was frequently placed in the hands of the heroine and played on the stage, just as was the viol a century later. Such uses are to be found in Heywood's *Woman Killed with Kindness* and Shakespeare's *Taming of the Shrew*, in the latter a very humorous scene being given in which the Lute and its frets are used very punningly. It is mentioned in *Much Ado about Nothing* (II, 1): "God defend the lute should be like the case." Stage directions often ask for the instrument, as in Marston's *Sophonisba* (*Act* V): "A base Lute and a Treble Violl play for the act," and in Ben Jonson's *Masque of Hymen:* "full music of twelve lutes." So ubiquitous did the Lute become in Elizabethan England that a box of strings for that instrument was a common gift, and it was one that even the Queen deigned to accept from her Court-musicians at New Year. The instruction-books of this period were, *The Science of Luting* (1565) and an edition of Adrien le Roy's *Brief and Easy instruction to learne the tableture, to conduct and dispose the hand unto the Lute* (1588), translated into English by J. Alford. As in the case of the viols, the lutenist had often to content himself with vocal music arranged to suit his instrument, and a typical example of this is seen in Thomas Morley's *Canzonets or litle short Aers to five or sixe voices* (1597), in the dedication to which the editor says: ". . . I have also set them Tablature wise to the Lute in the Cantus Booke for one to sing and plaie alone when your Lordship would retire yourself and bee more priuate. . . ."

The passing of the Crown to the House of Stuart only increased, if possible, the popularity of the Lute. Allusions to it are more frequent in the works of contemporary writers, one of the most interesting containing a scene that is in reality a burlesque on a Lute-lesson. This is Cyril Tourneur's *Atheist's Tragedie* (1611; *Act* IV): "Well said: A lesson o' th' Lute to entertaine the time with till she comes"—"Sol, fa, mi, la,—Mi, mi, mi,—Precious! Dost not see *mi* betweene the two Crotchets? Strike mee full there—So—forward. This is a sweet straine, and thou finger'st it beastly. *Mi* is a laerg there, and the prick that stands before *mi* a long; alwaies halfe your note.—Now Runne your division pleasingly with these quavers. Observe all your graces i' the touch,—Heere's a sweet cloze—strike it full, it sets off your musicke delicately."

The official lists of musicians active at Court give all the information we require respecting appointments to positions in the royal music and the salaries paid. In 1604 Philip Rosseter was engaged as a lutenist with the salary of £20 per annum in addition to £16 2*s.* 6*d.* for livery. Six years later the wage of the lutenists was raised to £40 and then to £50, quite large sums in those days. The celebrated Robert Johnson was appointed in 1604 and received 20*d.* per day and the usual livery money. This musician's father, John Johnson, was one of the most celebrated of the Elizabethan lutenists. Another celebrated player was Thomas Cutting, who succeeded John Dowland in the service of the Danish king. The chief works of the period were three books of *Songs or Ayres of Four Parts* with an accompaniment for the Lutes by John Dowland, the *Schoole of Musicke*, dealing with the Lute and several of its relatives, by Thomas Robinson (1603), and the *Varietie of Lute Lessons* by Robert Dowland (1610). The last-named work is very valuable, since it contains, besides several pieces for performance, an English version of Besarde's classic instructions (from his *Thesaurus Harmonicus*, Cologne, 1603), " a short Treatise thereunto appertayning by John Dowland," and several practical hints. Further representative works giving music for the Lutes were Robert Dowland's *Musical Banquet* (1610) and William Corkine's *Ayres to singe and play to the Lute* (1610).

In the reign of Charles I the instrument still showed no signs of declining from favour. Roger North (*Memoires of Musick*) says: " The Lute was a monopolist of the ayery kind, and master, gentlemen, and ladyes, for the most part used it." The viols were beginning to be serious rivals, but it was some time before the Lutes fell from favour. It will not be necessary to quote largely from the Lord Chamberlain's Records, for these are sufficiently easy of access now, and have been quite well catalogued; but one manuscript (British Museum, Add. 5750) is worth quoting as being typical: " Charles R. . . . Whereas wee have appointed Robert Dowland to be one of our Musicians in ordinary for the consort in the place of his father Doctor Dowland deceased, and are pleased to allow him for his wages twenty pence by the day, and for his livery sixteen pounds two shillings and sixpence by the year; We doe hereby will and command you out of our treasure from time to time remayning in your custody to pay or cause to be paid to the said Robert Dowland or his assigns the said wages . . . from the day of the death of his said father for and during his naturall life, at the four usual termes or feasts. . . . Given under our Signett at the palace of Westminster the six and twentieth day of Aprill in the second yere of our Raigne. . . ." Subsequent names of lutenists include Robert Johnson, Nicholas Lanier, Henry Lawes (1630), Lewis Evans (1633), William Lawes (1635), George Hudson (1641), John Mercure (1641), and many others. The official "stringer" of the Lutes was William Allaby (1641); and in view of the contemporary jest that three-quarters of a lutenist's life was spent in stringing and tuning, the appointment of a stringer must have saved a considerable amount of time. Five pounds a year was the usual sum allowed to the lutenists for their strings. The prices paid for Lutes in the Stuart period varied from £10 upwards according to the amount of ornamentation and the materials of which they were made. A fellow commoner of Trinity College, Cambridge, paid 3*s.* for borrowing a lute for one month, 3*s.* for "two dozen small strings" (Catlings), and 5*s.* for "learning one month on lute."

The publications of the second half of the Seventeenth Century included John Playford's *Select Musicall Ayres and Dialogues* with Lute and Theorbo accompaniment (1652), a similar work in 1653, and another in 1659.

After the Restoration the Lutes began to decline seriously from their popularity, and the great vogue of the Viol family and the growing fashion of the newer Violins soon caused them to be neglected. So much so, that by the time Mace wrote in 1676, he had to bewail the fact that "the world is grown so slight; full of new Fangles, and takes their chief delight in Jingle-Jangle. With Fiddle-Noises; Pipes of Bartholomew. . . ." John Rogers, though already advanced in years, was at that time the Lute's best friend, and with men like John Jenkins still writing, and social butterflies like Samuel Pepys still playing, the Lute could not yet be said to have become obsolete. References to the instrument are contained in the State Papers until the very end of the Seventeenth Century;

and in 1715 a post of lutenist was created at the Chapel Royal, musicians being appointed to fill it until as late as 1752 (John Immyns). During the lifetime of this player the post became a sinecure. Thence onwards it remained only as a means of increasing the salary of the Master of the Children of the Chapel until the death of the last holder of that position—William Hawes—in 1846, when it was suspended (*v. also* ARCH-LUTE, THEORBO, PANDORA, ORPHERION, *and* MANDORA).

LYONS: A name often used in the Seventeenth Century for the bass-strings of the Lutes, probably because the best quality were imported from Lyon (France).

LYRA-VIOL: A Bass-Viol of the smallest size used for solo-performance in showy and technically difficult works. Its small size rendered it easy of manipulation, and its light strings " proportionable " (as John Playford has it) to its size, made it of ready and facile speech. The term was also employed to designate a viol tuned to a chord, and used with music written in Tablature (*v.* HARPWAY, TABLATURE, *and* VIOLS). A work containing such music was Playford's *Musick's Recreation on the Lyra-Viol* (1652), and many books of a similar nature were published at about the same period. John Jenkins was a very celebrated performer on the viol treated in this manner, and Roger North (*Memoires of Musick*) says : " His talents lay in the use of the Lute and Base or rather Lyra-Viol." He was once " brought to play upon the Lyra-Violl afore K. Charles the First, as one that performed somewhat extraordinary. And after he had done, the King sayd he did wonders upon an inconsiderable instrument."

The instrument just mentioned, which was only an ordinary bass-viol tuned in a particular manner, must not be confounded with the Lyra, which had any number of strings, from seven to twenty-four, in addition to *Bourdons* or bass-strings, which in some forms of the instrument ran through the back of the neck and were plucked with the thumb, while the strings passing over the bridge were bowed (*v. also* BARYTONE).

LYRAWAY: Tuning the Bass-Viol to a chord, and playing it from a letter-tablature. This system was possible only so long as instruments were fretted, and it was undoubtedly an idea borrowed from the lutenist. For an unmusical ear this method of performance had certain advantages, for all that was necessary was to drop the finger best able to stop a given fret (indicated by a letter) on the right string (shown by the line of the stave on which the letter stood). But the system had its disadvantages, the chief of which were that tempered intonation was next to impossible, and that in the case of a string being out of tune, no amount of finger-manipulation could compensate for it. John Playford (*Musick's Recreation on the Viol, Lyra-way*, 1669) was of opinion that this manner of using the Bass-Viol was of comparatively late evolution. He says: "The first Authors of Inventing and Setting Lessons this way to the *Viol* was Mr. *Daniel Farunt*, Mr. *Alphonso Ferabosco*, and Mr. *John Coperario*, alias *Cooper*, who Composed Lessons, not only to play alone, but for two or three *Lyra-Viols* in Consort." This latter circumstance shows a big development of the idea, and with the physical characteristics of the Lyra-Viol (*q.v.*) what they were, a consort of these instruments must have been of very fine effect. Examples of Lyraway tunings can be seen in Tobias Hume's *Ayres* of 1605, Ferabosco's *Lessons* of 1609, and Playford's *Musick's Recreation, etc.* (1652 and 1669), mentioned above.

Roger North (*Memoires of Musick*) speaks of Thomas Baltzar, the famous Swedish violinist of the Seventeenth Century who became very popular in England, having used a "lyra-tuning and conformable lessons," for the violin. This would doubtlessly have been a case of the mistuning, or *Scordatura* as it was called on the Continent of Europe, and was probably not used with a tablature, and, in the case of Baltzar, certainly not with frets.

MADRIGAL: A form of vocal composition that became very popular in England, and attained to such a high plane of artistic excellence that it is deserving of the closest study. Some of the English examples of the late Sixteenth Century are as beautiful as they are interesting, and fully worthy of being considered typical specimens of native musicianship at a period when this country stood second to none in the art.

Although various forms were used in different countries and periods, the English Madrigal was treated as a part-song unaccompanied by instruments. It reflected the spirit of the time exactly, and written by such men as Byrd, Morley, Wilbye, Dowland, Gibbons, *etc.*, to the texts that only the Elizabethan era could supply, it was a form of musical art, the passing of which can only be deeply deplored. Contrapuntal writing was a salient feature of the Madrigal—or, as Christopher Simpson (*Compendium of Practicall Musick*, 1667) quaintly puts it: "Of vocal Musick made for the solace and civil delight of man there are many different kinds; as namely, Madrigals, in which fugues and all other flowers of figurate musick are most frequent. . . ."

The Madrigal came to England *via* the Low Countries in the last quarter of the Sixteenth Century, and so great a favourite did it become, and so well suited was it to the taste and talent of the English composers, that it became here a form that could scarcely be improved upon. The music was written in any number of parts, from two to six, or even eight, but there was nothing to prevent these parts being doubled, and the works of this class sung by a small or medium-sized body of vocalists. In this particular (as also in style of writing) the Madrigal differed from the Glee, in which each part was a solo-part. The period of the Madrigal's pre-eminence in England was comparatively short, for by the end of the first third of the Seventeenth Century it was no longer the popular favourite it had been when the House of Tudor made way for that of Stuart. Perhaps the lighter tastes of the latter sovereigns had something to do with the change of style; but a more powerful factor to bring about the decline of the Madrigal was no doubt the changing direction of the national talent, which tended more and more to the dramatic style. At any rate, it was not only in England that the Madrigal fell from favour at this period, for it vanished as rapidly on the Continent of Europe also.

The derivation of the name has occasioned a good deal of speculation, but the etymology that appeals most strongly to me is the one which traces the word from the Greek and Latin *Mandra*, a stable, whence Italian *Mandra*, a sheepfold, herd, or drove. From this source came the Italian *Mandrigale*, a shepherd's song (*cf. Mandriale, Mandriano*, "a herdsman, a grasier, a drover," Florio, *Dictionary*, 1598). This lexicographer already defines Madrigal as "a kind of short songs or ditties in Italie," also mentioning the form *Madrigale* (the suffix being the Latin—*calis*). Assuming this derivation to be the correct one, the pastoral character of the early Madrigals is explained.

Various museums and private libraries possess specimens of English music-books containing examples of the form, but they are not always easily accessible to the ordinary musician. It is therefore an especially fortunate circumstance that a fine collection of specimens by English writers is now available, published by Stainer and Bell, and edited by Dr. E. H. Fellowes. This edition is excellent and representative, and a special word of praise must here be given to Dr. Fellowes for the admirable and almost reverential way in which he has handled this music, especially on the controversial subject of the barring. Separate voice-parts were not barred during the Madrigalian era, and the omission has been made good as far as the changing metres allowed it, in an artistic and respectful manner.

MANDORA: A small pear-shaped, vaulted-backed, gut-stringed instrument of the Lute family. It is illustrated as early as the end of the Fourteenth Century, in a missal, and was probably used as far back as the Twelfth Century. The music of the period, of course, had no great compass, and consequently the short neck with which the instrument was provided was sufficient. By the Sixteenth Century it had become very popular in these islands and was much improved, the number of the strings being raised to five pairs. It was played with a plectrum and sometimes with the fingers. A book of tunes for the instrument is present in manuscript in the Advocates' Library at Edinburgh. The Mandora was used side by side with the larger lutes at this period, and sometimes a case would contain a pair—the Mandora being probably used for the melody and the larger lute for the accompaniment.

MASQUE: A form of entertainment introduced into England from Italy early in the reign of Henry VIII. In the country of its origin the Masque was an elaborate and often lavish spectacle that did much towards the development of stage-technique. The subjects chosen were generally allegorical or incidents from classic mythology, and there was often abundant opportunity for mechanical effects of the most amazing order. The costumes were usually very sumptuous and the scenery, besides being painted by the foremost artists of the day, was prepared regardless of expenditure. The most celebrated poets of the time provided the text, and the music was written by musicians whose names are still remembered, and who stand out in the history of music as important figures. The enormous expense of such productions, especially when we take into consideration the relative value of money in the Sixteenth and Seventeenth Centuries, was sufficient to prevent the Masque from becoming very popular on the public stage, and it was confined almost exclusively to the ball-rooms or private theatres of royalty and the most wealthy and influential of the nobility. A further reason for the great favour enjoyed by the Masque in high society and other cultured circles was that the music and dancing-loving aristocracy could take part in the performances themselves, and many cases are on record of kings, queens, and princes having played in Masques. All that has been said of the Masque so far applies to all the countries that used this form of entertainment.

In England the Masque appears to have been introduced by Henry VIII very early in his reign. We know that his relations with the Italian States were very intimate, and that Venetian embassies passed to and fro. It would not be difficult to visualise the alacrity with which the pleasure-loving Tudor would seize the opportunity of preparing such spectacles for his own edification, especially when the result was likely to be artistic in every way. But the Masques of Henry VIII differ very much in character from those of the Stuarts. In Hall's Chronicles we read of a kind of masked dance in which the king took part, and which the chronicler calls a "Mask, a thing not seen before in England"; but he makes no mention of a plot or of stage and scenery. In short, Henry's Masque appears to have been little more than a fancy-dress and masked dance, a weak imitation of the glories of the Italian Masque.

By the time that men like Ben Jonson, Shirley, Beaumont, and Chapman were writing the poems, and composers like the brothers Lawes, Alfonso Ferabosco, Matthew Locke, Christopher Gibbons, Lupo, and Campion were supplying the music, the Masque had become more like its Continental prototype. A few printed works illustrate the class of music used in England for the Masque: "The Description of a Masque presented before the Kinges Majestie at Whitehall on Twelfth Night last, in honour of the Lord Hayes and his Bride," 1607; "Ayres" by Alfonso Ferabosco, 1609; "The Masque of Flowers presented by the Gentlemen of Graies-Inne at the

Court of White Hall," 1613; and "Ayres Made by Severall Authors and sung in the Masque at the Marriage of the Right Honourable Robert Earle of Somerset and the Right Noble Lady Frances Howard," 1614. There can be no doubt that these Masques were the forerunners of the English opera.

The Lord Chamberlain's Records contain several entries relating to the Masques performed at Court, and one or two examples will suffice to show their nature. On May 20, 1627, a warrant was issued "to pay Andrew Miller for making fifteen long gowns for musicians, for the Queen's Masque performed at Christmas, 1626"; on January 19, 1633/4 a warrant was prepared "for payment of £16 to John Keely and John Laurence for two treble lutes, against his Majesty's Masque at Shrovetide, 1633"; and early in 1675 we have a large number of entries dealing with the famous Masque of that year, huge sums of money having been paid (or owed) for costumes, music, and instruments. As early as 1610 (Christmas) the "Rewards to the persons imployed in the Maske" amounted to quite respectable sums for that period. For example, "To Mr. Alfonso (doubtlessly Ferabosco), for making the songes £20; to Thomas Lupo for setting the dances to the Violins, £5; to the twelve musicians that were priests, that songe and played, £24," and so on.

No account of the Masque, however short, should be allowed to ignore *Comus* by Milton and Henry Lawes. Composed for performance at Ludlow Castle on the occasion of the Earl of Bridgewater's visit as Lord President of the Council in Wales and the Marches in 1634, the masque was a fine example of this class of work. It was published afterwards, and a modern reconstruction of the work by Sir Frederick Bridge and W. Barclay Squire is published by Novello.

MASS: The celebration of the Eucharist, and the music to which certain parts of the service are sung. At different periods the musical complexion of the Mass varied very considerably from a chanting in Plain-song to elaborate polyphonic compositions of the highest possible order. It was only natural that some composers, more concerned for the originality of their music than for its fitness to the text, should have so far abused their opportunities as to cause exception to be taken at the whole system of polyphonic writing for this service. It was only the fixing of certain rules and laws to govern the composition of Masses that prevented the devotional spirit being ignored, and the atmosphere which the Mass was to create, overlooked.

The first Masses were simply of chanted Plain-song, and even when the development of counterpoint enabled composers to elaborate their sacred work, the Plain-song was retained (as *Cantus Firmus*) and the various parts of the polyphony worked round it. Occasionally secular tunes of a popular character were utilised as thematic material, and the Mass named after the melody used. These works were naturally not written during periods worthy of imitation, and were only of an evanescent nature. Countless methods of setting the well-known texts were employed at different times, but after all had been tried, the tendency—directed as much by the higher artistic instincts of the best writers in the form as by the canons of Cardinals and Popes—was towards unity of treatment and fitness of materials. So many of the best examples of the Mass at different periods can now be seen in modern reprints, that it will not be necessary to quote them here.

The sections of the Mass to be treated musically are the *Kyrie*, *Gloria*, *Credo*, *Sanctus*, *Benedictus*, and *Agnus Dei*. These movements are interspersed with the remaining portions of the service, chanted or recited. The regulations imposed by Pope Pius X upon composers of Masses make very interesting reading, and must be studied by those who hope to have their music used. They are largely repetitions of older laws, and may be seen in Sir Richard R. Terry's *Catholic Church Music*.

MASTER-NOTE: 1. The note immediately below the key-note of the scale, to-day known as the Leading-note.

2. The name often given to the semibreve, probably because it was used as the standard of measurement in the Seventeenth Century. Notes larger than the semibreve were termed "Notes of Augmentation" and those which were smaller "Notes of Diminution," with the semibreve common to the two series. John Playford heads a chapter: "Of the Keeping of Time by the Measure of the Semibreve, or Master-Note."

MEAN: A term loosely applied in the Sixteenth and Seventeenth Centuries to any part, voice, instrument, or string, lying between the treble and the bass. Thus, the Alto and Tenor were Means, and Shakespeare uses the word punningly in *Love's Labour's Lost* (V, 2): ". . . nay, he can sing a mean most meanly. . . ." Cyril Tourneur, in *The Atheist's Tragedie* (1611), has the great musical truth: "But trebles and bases make Poore musick without means." While on this subject notice must be taken of the Counter-Tenor (*q.v.*), also a Mean. By analogy, the strings of the Lutes and Viols between the highest (treble) and lowest (bass), were named Means, the Small Mean being the second string counting downwards from the treble, and the Great Mean the third string. Playford even applies these two terms to the A and D strings of the modern violin. The treble string of the Lutes and Viols was often called the Minikin; but whether this was a further diminution of Small Mean is not clear, although it would be quite in keeping with the practice of the times.

MEASURE: In Elizabethan England a term used loosely to mean a dance. Later its application appears to have been restricted to the slower and more dignified forms. Sir John Davies (Orchestra, 1594) settles the question as to the character of the Measure in the lines:

> Yet all the feet wherein these measures go,
> Are only spondees, solemn, grave, and slow.

Shakespeare in *Much Ado about Nothing* (II, 1) shows that it signifies a movement "mannerly modest . . . full of state and antientry." I have not met with any dance-form called "A Measure" showing any peculiar characteristics, and can only suppose the name to have been applied generically to the slow and solemn dances which usually at Tudor and Stuart balls preceded the quicker measures such as, successively, the Galliard, the Coranto, and the Jig.

MENSURABLE MUSIC: Measured music as distinguished from the older *Cantus Planus*, or Plain-song, in which the only measure was that fixed by the rhythm of the text to which the music was set (*v.* PLAIN-SONG). This singing of notes of undetermined time-value answered well enough so long as the music was unisonal, or in octaves, fifths, or fourths, and all the parts moved uniformly. But the moment that more elaborate harmonisation was evolved, it must be obvious that some means of measuring the notes had to be devised. Exactly when this took place it is not possible to determine. To Franco of Cologne is sometimes given the honour of having fixed various signs and of having given them certain values. But even Franco himself writes of earlier authorities on this subject, and it must remain an open question as to who first used measured music, and when he flourished. It is quite possible that the idea was gradually developed, and there are signs that point in this direction. Judging from all accounts, it is not possible to place the use of Mensurable Music earlier than the opening of the Twelfth Century.

It must be plain that a complete consideration of this important and fascinating subject cannot find place or space in a work of this kind; but a fair idea of it may be gained if the articles on Breve, Large, Long, Mood, Time, Prolation, Alteration, and Proportion are first read. The Neumes (*q.v.*) used in Plain-song undoubtedly supplied the first notes, and once these had come into use and their utility proved, there was nothing in the way of further development. It would be absurd to suppose that measured music, *per se*, did not exist before the Twelfth Century, because people danced rhythmically, I suppose, from the earliest times in the history of mankind. But there was no system of making clear to the eye the relative duration of the various notes. It was probably the alternation of duple and triple rhythms in the dance that primarily suggested the Long of three *Tempora* and that of two—the Perfect and the Imperfect Moods.

Bearing in mind what has been said in the articles alluded to above, it will now be necessary to trace the connecting links in the historical chain. The earliest notes in use—that is, at the period when music begins to interest us—were the Long, the Breve, and the Semibreve. The first two had their two determined values; the Semibreve still remained indeterminate—*ultra mensuram*—and there could be any number of them, from two to a dozen, to the Breve or *Tempus* (Marchettus of Padua). Later on the Semibreve also came under the rules of Time (*Tempus*), and thence onward the basic principles of Mensurable Music, until the abolition of the Perfect and Imperfect Moods, remained unchanged.

The most noticeable feature in Mensurable Music was that the duration of a note was fixed in the first place by the signature which indicated the Mood or Time; in the second pl by its position in relation to the neighbouring notes. T principles of Alteration (*q.v.*) must be understood before t can be clear. For a Breve could endure for one or two be (*Tempora*), according to its position. But the rule of Alte tion only apply when not more than two Breves stand betw two Longs. When there are more than two, a great deal variation in the procedure must occur. In such a passage

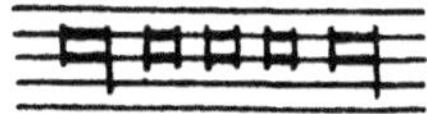

the requirements of the Perfect Mood are satisfied by int preting and grouping the notes thus:

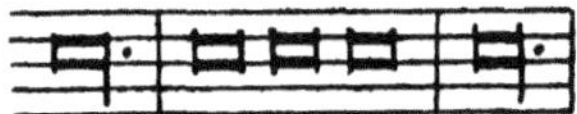

the two Longs can both be perfect, and the three Bre complete what we should call a similar measure. But su a succession of notes as the following:

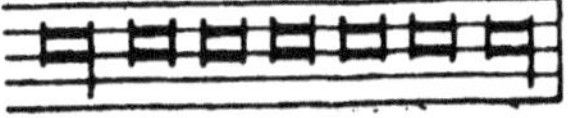

would have to be grouped thus:

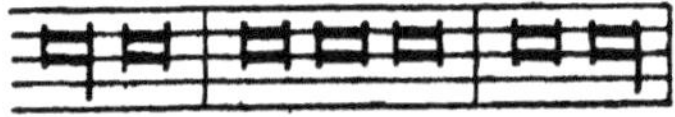

to keep the Mood perfect. Had there been six Breves inst of five in the last example, the last Breve would have b altered and the closing Long perfect, thus:

The necessity for the rules governing Alteration, natura only arose in the Perfect, or triple, Mood. The Point Perfection (*q.v.*) fulfilled the functions of the present-day c and converted any note in Imperfect Mood or *Tempus* int Perfect one. From what has been said above concern variable numbers of Breves between two Longs, it will be seen that the interpretation of the notes depended largely upon the rhythm required. But if *one* Breve fell between two Longs, either of these Longs could be made Imperfect by it. That is, the phrase :

could be performed as :

or as :

The ancients based the rhythmic performance of their music upon half a dozen "modes" corresponding with recognised metres. The first was Trochaic,

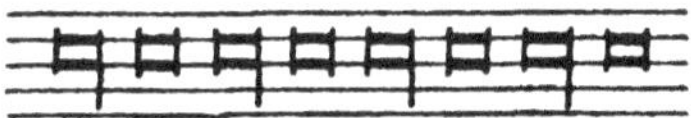

and it will be at once obvious that the Perfect Mood could not be maintained if the Long were counted, as it should be, as three Breves; for these three Breves added to the one which follows the Long, would produce a duple figure, not intended by the composer. The Long is therefore rendered Imperfect by the following Breve, and the phrase read :

instead of :

for it must never be forgotten that in the Perfect Mood the Long has the value of three Breves. In the second mode, Iambic, the same thing happens, and the Long is treated, because of the Breve which precedes it, as an Imperfect one :

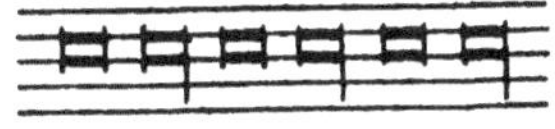

becomes

and not

The third (Dactylic) mode :

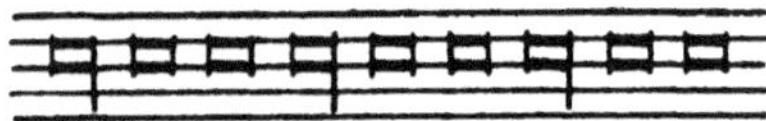

called Alteration into use, for the triple rhythm could only be maintained by doubling the value of the second Breve, and keeping the Longs perfect, thus :

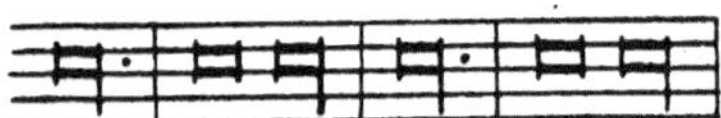

The fourth mode (Anapaestic) followed the same lines ; the second Breve of the rhythmic figure :

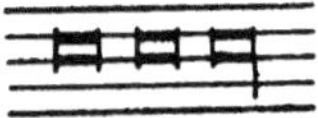

was altered to produce :

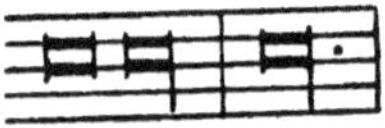

The fifth mode used only equal notes, and according to the accepted rule these were all Perfect.

Some indications concerning rests and time-signatures are given in other articles in this work, but as a rough guide to the latter it should be remembered that Perfect Time (triple) was shown by a circle, and Imperfect Time by a broken circle, semicircle, or capital C. A dot inside this mood-signature told that the Prolation (*q.v.*) was to be Perfect or Major, the absence of the dot indicating Imperfect or Minor Prolation. Other variations in the signature are dealt with in the article TIME (*Tempus*).

Another important branch of mensurable music is the study

of the change of rhythm effected by the use of black notes in place of white. This is alluded to in the article PROPORTION. But little more than an allusion is possible here, for it is a subject that requires a book to itself. The reader is referred to the articles in this volume mentioned above, in addition to that on Ligatures. Works dealing with the subject at greater length and in trustworthy manner are: Coussemaker, *Scriptores*; Volume I of the *Oxford History of Music* (Professor Wooldridge), and Heinrich Bellermann, *Die Mensural Noten und Taktzeichen des XV und XVI Jahrhunderts*, Berlin, 1858.

MI. *v.* ARETINIAN SYLLABLES *and* GAMUT.

MINEVEY: Most probably a corruption, due to faulty orthography or typography, from Minuey, a Seventeenth- and early Eighteenth-century spelling (on phonetic lines) of Minuet (*q.v.*). Such spellings as Minuvey and Minnua are to be met with. Nevertheless, it is a peculiar circumstance that Salter's *Genteel Companion for the Recorder* (1683) should use these spellings and also give a "French Minnuett." Undue importance should not be attached to this, for orthography was a very vague art in those days; and the most ordinary words are often spelled in the most fantastical manner.

MINIKIN. *v.* MEAN.

MINSTREL: Originally the Minstrel was most probably the assistant of the troubadour—and, as far as concerns us in this book, his accompanist. Though used to-day in a much wider sense, the word Minstrel appears to have been applied solely in the Middle Ages to such an instrumentalist. At all events the Minstrel was a trained musician and capable of performing important musical services when necessary. They even appear to have assisted at divine service, Rimbault quoting Rymer's *Foedera* in support of this. Certainly of French origin the Minstrel entered the musical scheme of England after the Norman conquest, and influencing the Saxon Gleemen, and perhaps also influenced by the latter, founded a national system of music that had as its chief form of expression the Ballad (*q.v.*). The instruments used by the Minstrel were probably the harp, crowd, rebec, citole, psaltery, and so on, according to period; and when employed in the royal service he fulfilled the functions of the later consort. Exactly what is meant by the term Minstrel when used by the later Tudors is not clear. It may merely have been a survival of the old name and applied to instrumentalists whose duty it was to accompany the singers, to play during banquets, and the like.

In the Wardrobe Accounts of Edward I we read: "To Minstrels and a Harper making their minstrelsy before the Prince between the Twelfth day of May and the Ninth day of June, 1300 . . . 3*s*." During the reign of Edward III the wages of the Minstrel amounted to 20*s*. a year. The records show a number of grants to Minstrels during the reign of Henry VI (from the year 1423 onwards). By the time of Henry VII the term seems to have been applied to instrumentalists generally, for records of that reign state that when the musician John Cliff went to France with the late king, he was accompanied by "seventeen Minstrels his companions." The term "Minstrelsy" would appear to have been applied exclusively to instrumental music.

MINUET: The English spelling of the French Menuet, a dance exceedingly popular in society and on the stage in the Eighteenth Century. Indeed, it was part of the social life of the period during which it was in vogue. It came to England from France soon after its appearance in the operas of Lully, and was fairly common in late Stuart publications. But in these it was given frankly as a new French dance. Playford's *Apollo's Banquet* (*ed.* 6, 1690) intimated on the title-page that the work included the "newest French dances now used at Court and in the Dancing-Schools," and among them were several Menuets. *Musick's Hand-Maide* (1678) also calls the form "the new Menuet." New it was to England, of course; but in France it had had a long period of development before it reached the proud position it occupied when it spread from its native country to these islands. Nearly all the music-books published after those already mentioned contain the dance.

It was during the reign of the last Stuart sovereign, and those of the first three Georges, that the Menuet received the greatest attention here, due, no doubt, to Court influence; for the Menuet was as popular at the Georgian Court as the Branles and Corants were in Stuart, and the Pavanes and Galliards in Elizabethan, England.

For the purpose of the dance a great deal of music was written during the period last mentioned; every royal birthday was greeted by the publication of an oblong volume containing a special Menuet for the occasion, and what the Court did was naturally copied by society. At Bath the Menuet was a regular and welcome feature, and Beau Nash's balls usually commenced with two hours of Menuet-dancing. In the spa's palmy days the Menuet was as popular in England as it was on the other side of the Channel; and to dance it well was a sign of gentility here as well as in France. And even Macaulay, in his History of England, has it that "Her authority was supreme in all matters of good breeding, from a duel to a Menuet."

The story of the Menuet is interesting and important. It rose from humble beginnings as a rustic Poitevin measure to be a dance which left more traces of its existence on musical form than perhaps any other. It played a part in the formation of its era's manners and beautified the best forms of musical composition, from the pianoforte-solo to the Symphony. How ancient it is would be almost impossible to decide; for it sprang from a dance that had been used for generations in various parts of France, and particularly in Poitou. It is most likely to be derived from a form of the Branle, and in its original form—rustic, lively, gay—it seemed to have been very unpromising material from which to evolve the stately measure of the Eighteenth Century. Lully was probably the first to use it in anything like the form that became so popular; certainly his Menuets were the first of any musical value. And the specimens with which Lully supplied the French stage were the models upon which the later examples were based. It is no exaggeration to say that from this date onwards almost every ball in Europe was opened by the "Queen of Dances," until the two revolutions (the French and the Waltz) dethroned it, and left it as a charming ingredient at the disposal of the Suite-builders.

Like most dances taken from a rustic environment, the Menuet became slower and more stately when adopted for use on the stage and in Society's ball-rooms. It enabled its performers to evolve the most graceful and artistic movements imaginable; its dignity preserved from weightiness by the charm and grace with which the dancers of the period endowed it. But it showed also the artificiality, the snobbery, the arrogance, and the affectation of the Eighteenth Century;—the little steps that gave the dance its name (*menu*, small) pictured the mincing gait of the affected dandy; and the humble curtsey of the lady heightened by its very humility her haughty self-complacency.

The commonest time-signature of the Menuet was 3/4, and the music was generally contained in two sections of four or eight measures, each repeated. Each section was divided from its successor by a marked *caesura.* The later forms of the dance, used as instrumental compositions only, were made up of a first Menuet followed by a second (usually in the relative minor and sometimes in the form of a Trio—*i.e.* in three-part harmony), and closed by a repetition of the major Menuet. In the Suite it took its place, as did all the *Intermezzi* or interpolated forms, between the Saraband and Jig.

It would be out of place to continue with the Menuet's further development, and the importance it assumed in Beethoven's hands; for these belong to the musical history of other countries. But the fact must not be ignored that the Menuet did not stop where the English musicians left it.

MIXED DIVISION: At a period when fine distinctions were drawn between Division, Descant, and Breaking the Ground (*q.v.*), a Mixed Division was one which combined the use of all three devices in one composition.

MODUS, MODE. *v.* MOOD.

MONOCHORD: An instrument consisting of a sound-box over which was stretched a single string, used for experimental purposes in musical physics. A movable bridge served to divide the string into any required proportionate parts, and the whole system of interval-ratios and many other musico-physical phenomena were discovered by its means. Its use dates back with certainty to the days of the ancient Greek physicists and probably to the scientific culture of the Nile. In the Middle Ages the Monochord was employed to determine the pitch for vocalists, and its influence on music generally has been a very powerful and far-reaching one. At first plucked with the finger or plectrum, and later played with a bow (the number of strings having also been increased), the Monochord in all probability first suggested the clavichord on the one hand, and the trumpet-marine and many other bowed instruments (*e.g.* the organistrum) on the other. Care should be exercised when dealing with the word, especially when spelled *Manichorde* with an *a*, and still more so when in the phrase "a pair of Monochords," for it is easy to confuse the true Monochord for experimental purposes with *Manichorde* and *Manicordo*, which are the French and Italian respectively for Clavichord.

MOOD: A term used in Mensurable Music to express the relative values of the Large (*Maxima*), the Long, and the Breve. The *Modus Major* dealt with the Large and the Long, was Perfect when the measure was triple, *i.e.* when each Large contained three Longs, and Imperfect when the measure was duple, *i.e.* when each Large contained two Longs. The use of the Great Mode is very rare. The signature was:

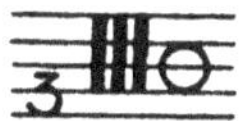

when Perfect, and when the Time (*Tempus*) (*q.v.*) was also Perfect. The broken circle: C (or C2) indicated the Imperfect Mood. A large amount of variation in the signature could occur, according to whether the Time was Perfect or Imperfect, and so on. In dealing with this subject in the amount of space that can be allowed it, there is great danger of committing sins of omission; and before the transcription of Medieval manuscripts is attempted, the reader is recommended to digest Heinrich Bellermann's *Die Mensuralnoten und Taktzeichen, etc.*, Berlin, 1858.

In the *Modus Minor* (Lesser Mood) the measurement was Perfect when each Long contained three Breves, and Imperfect when it was worth only two. The signature of the Minor Mode Perfect (when the Time was also Perfect) was:

and when the Time was Imperfect the same with a broken circle (C; which was the ancestor of the present-day signature for common time).

The complication of the system will be apparent when it is remembered that in a single composition the *Modus Major*

Perfectus could be used together with the *Modus Minor Imperfectus.* That is to say, every Large would contain three Longs, but every Long only two Breves. This is but one example of such "Moods." Thus in *Modus Major Perfectus* with Perfect Time, the Large would be equal to three Longs or nine Breves; in *Modus Major Perfectus* with Imperfect Time, it was equal to three Longs or six Breves. Similarly in *Modus Minor Perfectus* with Perfect Time, the Long was equal to three Breves or nine Semibreves, and in *Modus Minor Perfectus* with Imperfect Time, to three Breves or six Semibreves (*v. also* MENSURABLE MUSIC, TIME (*Tempus*), *and* PROLATION).

MORISCO. *v.* MORRIS DANCE.

MORRIS DANCE: A folk entertainment of high antiquity that varied in character according to period, from a solo dance and one for half a dozen men, to an elaborate spectacle or pageant with many characters and mummings. Its origin seems lost in the mists of the past, and several sources might with equal justice be suggested for it. Its features are such that it may be regarded as a survival of some ancient ritual; alternatively, it may be a descendant of a dance, already popular in France during the Sixteenth Century, the Morisco; thirdly, it may be a survival (in one of its forms at any rate) of one of those peculiar dances of armed men, pantomimic in nature and in vogue with even savage races; fourthly, it can be a simple folk-dance to which were added, from time to time, various trimmings in the form of ceremonial and historical or legendary happenings. Of all these possible origins, the only one from which we can trace the Morris Dance in any logical sequence, is the Morisco. Tabourot in his *Orchèsographie* (1588) says that in his youth (*i.e.* early in the Sixteenth Century) he saw the Morisco danced by boys with blackened faces, *etc.*; and this circumstance, added to the etymology of the name, would seem to point to a Moorish origin for the dance. Whether this Morisco, or the pantomimic dances bearing the same name in other parts of the Continent of Europe, had much in common with the Tudor Morris Dance is another matter; but the suggestion may quite easily have come from the Morisco, while the English talent for dancing and masking may have supplied the rest.

The date at which the form came to England can similarly

only be guessed at. Most writers suggest that the reign of Edward III was the period, and that John of Gaunt brought the dance from Spain. If we could fix upon the Spain of that era as the birthplace of the Morris Dance, then we could not deny it a Moorish origin. The dance is mentioned and alluded to frequently, but no clear idea of its nature can be formed until it had become thoroughly Anglicised, and ornamented with all the gaiety and imagination of the Tudor revellers. By the time of Henry VIII it had reached a state of popularity unequalled perhaps in any other amusement. Thence onwards it was elaborated and expanded, its original features having probably long been lost—the fate of the original characteristics in many of the ancient dances. The dancers alone soon ceased to satisfy the desire for pageantry, and gradually more and more figures were introduced into the game. There can be no doubt that from a simple dance with certain marked characteristics, whether of a semi-religious or military nature, it became a sort of allegorical masque, or spectacle with dancing. Whether these additional personages acted in dumb-show; whether they sang or spoke; whether they merely paraded; whether they danced; are questions that cannot be answered with any degree of certainty to-day. Whifflers (*q.v.*), hobby-horses, fools, kings, queens, squires, and such representative characters, as well as particular figures like Robin Hood, Maid Marian, Friar Tuck, and Little John, came and went as the Morris Dance passed through its kaleidoscopic career from century to century.

As far as can be ascertained, therefore, the Morris Dance became a combination of many forms; probably the serious, ritualistic, and exacting original dance was so confused and mixed with the May-day revellings and similar rejoicings, that no attempt was made to separate them. It was only when the added pageantry fell away that the Morris Dance emerged as a set dance, with varied figures, for six men who belonged to a very conservative body of experts. In this form the dance survives to-day in certain parts of England.

The fact that the Morris Dance was performed by men only would seem to point to its having had an origin far removed from the maypole spirit with its flirtation and kissing. The cake that was often carried at a sword's point might have been a burlesque or a survival of some ceremonial of deeper meaning.

Furthermore, the sword took part in too many of the ancient spectacles for it to be dismissed from the history of the Morris Dance without consideration. The more the question of this dance is studied the more fascinating it grows, and, at the same time, the more involved and entangled do the threads of its descent become.

Henry Machyn, citizen of London, tells us in his *Diary* (May 26, 1555) that there " was a goodly May-gam . . . with gyant and hobehorsses, with drumes and gonnes, and mores danse and with other mynsterelles " (at Saint Martin's-in-the-Fields). But by the time that Ben Jonson wrote, the Morris Dance had become very vague, and each locality seemed to have had its own traditions concerning its performance. " They should be Morris dancers by their jingle, but they have no napkins,"—" No, nor a hobby-horse,"—" Oh, he's often forgotten ; that's no rule ; but there is no Maid Marian nor Friar amongst them ; which is a surer mark. Nor a fool that I see." Bells seem to have been the inseparable adjuncts of the Morris dancer for a long time. In Greene's *Groatsworth of Witte*, 1617, we read : ". . . and wanted nothing but bels, to bee a Hobby horse in a Morrice " ; and in Fletcher's words : " My spurs jingle like a morris dancer." As late as 1772 a penny book gave evidence to the existence of a Morris Dance with a cleric, a beggar, and the Robin Hood quartette.

Shorn of its dispensable adjuncts the Morris Dance was an affair of gravity, not to be attempted in a flippant spirit. Physically, even, it was not easy of performance if it was to keep to tradition. Admission to the guild of professional Morris Dancers was not easy. The candidate had to submit to all the rules of the society, which was very conservative, and obtain his own costume, which was a matter governed by age-old traditions. His training was long and severe, and the result was a dancer who possessed the agility and knowledge of the form that were necessary to make of his performance the serious thing it was considered to be. The costume of the Morris Dancer consisted of a top-hat, white shirt, light breeches, strong boots, woollen stockings, a multitude of coloured and plaited ribbons and rosettes, and a number of bells fastened by a band below the knee.

The music of the true Morris Dance was supplied by the tabor and pipe, or the popular bagpipe. The latter instrument in connection with the dance is mentioned in a song dating from 1660: "Harke, Harke, I hear the dauncing, And a nimble Morris prancing; The bagpipe and the Morris bells." The falling into desuetude of the pipe and tabor, and, I suppose, the inability to procure a bagpiper readily in the South of Britain, caused the violin to take up the position of accompanying instrument and time-keeper.

It will be seen, therefore, that the Morris Dance at some periods in its history was an entertainment that helped to acquire for England the epithet of "merry"; at other times it was a careful, artistic, and canonical observance. There are still a few sets of Morris Dancers left in England, and men like Mr. Cecil J. Sharp are doing good work in reviving this form of old English art. His publications, *The Morris Book* (Novello, 1907) and others, dealing with various forms of the dance, are well worth reading by those interested in the revival (*v. also* SWORD DANCE).

MOTET: A term applied at different periods to compositions of varying character, but eventually used more exclusively to designate a work for sacred use, set to a Latin text generally (selected from the Psalms or other part of the Scriptures—sometimes even paraphrases on these), and treated in *a capella* style. Solo-Motets were not unknown, but the form in part-writing was and is by far the most common. In this use the Motet would date from the second half of the Fifteenth Century. Used to expand the Mass service, the Motet vanished as such in England at the change of the State-religion, and was replaced by the Anthem (in its "Full" form).

During the period of its greatest popularity the Motet was distinguished by the peculiarity that each voice-part was often given a different text, a feature that must obviously have pointed the way to vast changes in vocal writing, both dramatic and musical.

The form enjoyed a great vogue in Catholic England, and William Byrd's *Cantiones Sacrae*, as well as those of Thomas Tallis, both of which works contained what were really Motets, may be looked upon as typical of the work done in England with this form. They would suffer very little when compared with even the best of the continental examples. It has already been hinted that the Motet appeared in various forms in different stages of its long career, and it must be remembered that very early in its history it was a secular song. This must be borne in mind when Seventeenth-century secular compositions are met with bearing the title "Motet." Orlando Gibbons, for example, issued his *Madrigals and Mottets* in 1612, and such use of the word is not an isolated one at the period. The secular application of the term was not confined to England by any means, and it was probably used in that sense on the Continent before sacred Motets were ever written. Cotgrave's French-English Dictionary (1660) gives the French *Motet* as meaning "a verse in musick, or of a song, a poesie, a short lay"; while Florio's Italian-English Dictionary of 1598 (*A World of Words*), defines the Italian *Motteto* as "a dittie, a verse, a jigge, a short song, a wittie saying." And this last definition probably gives us the original meaning of the term (*cf.* French *Mot*, a word).

MUTATION. *v.* HEXACHORD SYSTEM.

NAKER: The Medieval kettledrum of Arabian origin, if the etymology of the name can be accepted as evidence. The earliest specimens appear to have been very small, so that a pair of them could be held by one hand and beaten with the other. They had convex bodies of wood or metal, and a single head of skin. As the increased resources of the West were applied to its construction the Naker grew in size and became a hemispherical shell of metal (generally copper) with a vellum head; the latter being tunable in the most highly developed specimens. The Naker is mentioned very early in our literature, having probably been brought from the East by returning Crusaders. The first traceable reference to its musical use is in the records relating to Edward I (beginning of the Fourteenth Century). In Tudor days the instrument was already known as the "Kettell drom" (1551). From this date onwards many references to the instrument are to be found in the State Papers, and it had become, by now, the accepted form of drum for mounted bands. It was used, as it is to-day, in pairs, one on either side of the horse's shoulders. In the symphony orchestra the descendants of the Naker, now known as *Timpani*, play an important and interesting part.

NEUMES: The signs used in the earliest days of writing music. Intended originally as aids to the memory in singing the chanted portions of divine service, a very complete code of such symbols was evolved, which passed through a long process of development until the modern system of notation emerged. Thus the *Punctum* (a grave accent), in its earliest form merely a dot, became the square note of Mensurable Music ; the acute accent (*Virga*), a nail-shaped sign like a dot with a tail, was developed to a shape that produced our tailed notes. Neumes in huge numbers were constructed by various combinations of these accents, and a complete study of this subject would need a considerable amount of space. A few examples must therefore suffice, some specimens of each form in different countries and periods being given.

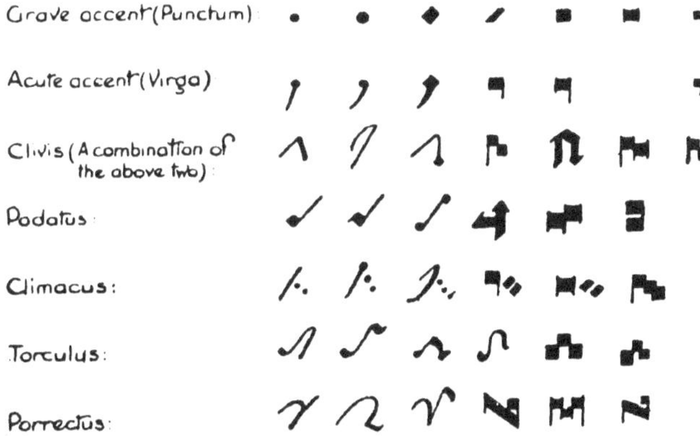

Many other combinations were evolved which were more or less complicated, some signs standing for quite elaborate groups of rising and falling notes. A study of manuscripts of known date is a great help to the understanding of the Neumes, and the best authorities for their interpretation are the *Scriptores* of Gerbert and Coussemaker, and the Benedictine *Paléographie Musicale* (Solesmes).

NOISE OF MUSIC : In Elizabethan and early Stuart England the word Noise was not always used, in a disparaging sense, to mean unpleasant sounds. In those days it frequently meant nothing worse than our word Sound, and Spenser refers to even a " heavenly noise." In Shakespeare's time a Noise of Music was a haphazard combination of instrumentalists not numerous enough to constitute a " band." In *II Henry IV* (II, 4) we have: "And see if thou cannot find Sneak's noise; Mistress Tearsheet would fain hear some music"; while Heywood (*Iron Age, Act* III) alludes to the same when he writes:

> Where's this great sword and buckler man of Greece?
> Wee shall have him in one of Sneakes noise,
> And come peaking into the Tents of the Greeks,
> With will you have any musicke Gentlemen?

Ben Jonson, in *The Tale of a Tub*, says: "Press all the noises of Finsbury in our name," a sentence that would be unintelligible without this interpretation. The *Diary* of Samuel Pepys and Dryden in the *Maiden Queen* both allude to a "Noise of Fiddlers," meaning a set or consort of these instruments. In the article on the Cornet it will be seen that "A Noise of Cornets" was also used. At a date anterior to these quotations the term was applied even to the voice, and we read of "a noise of singing children."

NOTATION: The system of signs and symbols by which the pitch and duration of musical sounds are made visible to the eye. The notation used in ancient times differed considerably in different periods, and for a very long time it was in a state of flux. Commencing with the Neumes (*q.v.*), or signs which indicated the rise or fall of the voice in Plain-song, the notation of music was developed as the rapidly increasing demands of harmony called for more exact means of writing down the sounds required. The Neumes did not stand for fixed notes or intervals, and their object was only to serve as an aid to the memory of singers who had learned the song from a teacher or by tradition. Differences of pitch were at first shown in a very rough-and-ready way by writing the Neume relatively higher or lower—dots or points being used later for this purpose. He must have been a genius who first thought of the brilliant though simple expedient of ruling a line to indicate one fixed note, and to write the signs representing higher or lower sounds above and below the line. This line was written in red ink, and all the signs placed upon it were of uniform pitch (F). Once the beginning had been made, the rest was easy. A second line was added above the existing one, coloured yellow, and bearing the signs of the sound a fifth above that on the red line. The note on the yellow line, therefore, was C. A black line between the two coloured ones was then added, and made to bear the note A. A fourth line above the yellow one completed the old stave, and, indeed, was sufficient for the ordinary range of music at the period. Later, however, when musicians desired to write all the parts of their polyphony on one stave, a greater number of lines was employed, and staves of from four to a score of lines were not infrequent.

The rise of polyphony made music capable of exact measurement a necessity; and with the advent of Mensurable Music a new epoch in the history of notation had begun. The change from the Neumes to the complete series of symbols used when Mensurable Music was at its prime was not effected suddenly, or even rapidly. For some time two notes had to suffice, a long one and a short. More complicated harmonisation compelled composers to give these notes fixed values. More notes of varying value were gradually added, a means of indicating the Mood or Time developed, and a system of grouping notes sung to one syllable of the text (Ligatures) was called into being (*v.* MENSURABLE MUSIC). The notes used were the semibreve, at first of indeterminate length (*i.e.* merely a short note), the breve, the long, and the large (or *Duplex Longa*), all of which see. The lozenge or diamond-shaped note followed, and was eventually displaced by the modern round note. The dividing of the music into sections of equal length, each containing regularly recurring accents—that is, the use of bar-lines—followed, and the notation of music settled in a form which, with only minor alterations, it still shows (*v.* BARRING, BREVE, CLIFF, LARGE, LIGATURE, LONG, MOOD, PROPORTION, *and* TIME (*Tempus*)).

NOTES OF AUGMENTATION: The semibreve, the breve, the long, and the large (*q.v.*) were known as Notes of Augmentation in the Seventeenth Century; that is, they were multiples of the semibreve, or Master-Note.

NOTES OF DIMINUTION: The minim, crotchet, quaver, and semiquaver were, conversely to the case of the Notes of Augmentation (*q.v.*), fractional parts of the semibreve (*v.* MASTER-NOTE).

OATEN PIPE. *v.* SHALM.

OCHETUS. *v.* HOCKET.

OLIPHANT: A horn made of ivory (Old English, *Olifaunt,*

Olifant, elephant), used for hunting and also for signalling in peace and war. It is of very great antiquity, the Victoria and Albert Museum (London) possessing very ancient specimens richly carved. It is mentioned in the story of Roland and Oliver (*temp.* Charlemagne).

ORGAN : A highly important keyboard wind-instrument, which had a tremendous influence upon the progress of musical art. It is obvious that a complete account of so vast a subject, especially in its modern aspect, cannot be given here ; but a summary of the principles underlying the use of the instrument in early times must not be omitted from such a work as

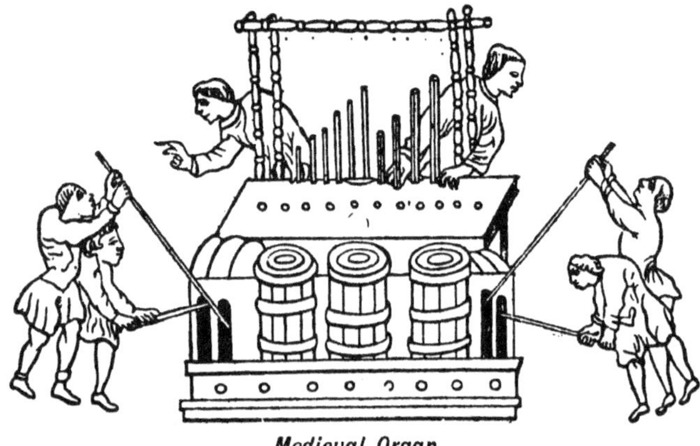

Medieval Organ

(Roughly sketched from an illustration in a MS. at Trinity College, Cambridge,—itself a crude copy of a drawing in a Netherlandish Psalter)

this. Fundamentally, the Organ was, and is, a collection of wind-instruments—one or more series of pipes made of various materials, and giving forth sounds by different means, such as fipple-heads, reeds, and so on. The pipes were made to speak by the action of wind admitted by the withdrawing of a slide in the older specimens, and by the depressing of a key in the more modern—which wind was supplied from bellows worked by hand or foot power, and, later, from mechanical " blowers."

The earliest references to Organs in England relate to an instrument belonging to the end of the Seventh Century. St. Aldhelm, Abbot of Malmesbury, describes the Organ of his period, and from his account we can form the opinion that the instrument was already of some size and furnished with a fairly large number of pipes. The Venerable Bede (beginning of the Eighth Century) also left some account of contemporary Organs, and from his writings we can gather that the tone they produced was full and pleasant, and that the notes spoke by "wooden tongues" admitting the wind to the required pipes by their withdrawal and silenced by their return. The entire compass of these Organs probably did not exceed an octave, and a complete chromatic scale was not used. These limitations, added to the difficulty of working the slides, made multiple Organs a necessity; that is to say, each organist could find hands enough to play one part only, and polyphony had to be produced by a different player for each part. This may account for the presence of the two or even three performers that we see pictured in some of the Medieval Organs. There appears to be no indication of a keyboard until the end of the Eleventh Century. With the introduction of these ready means of making a note sound by the action of a single finger, the playing of several parts simultaneously became much easier, and consequently the number of pipes was increased and the chromatic gaps filled in. But it was not until the Fifteenth Century that the Organ became fully chromatic, and at about the same time reed-pipes were added. The Psalter of Eadwin (Trinity College, Cambridge) contains an illustration showing such an early Organ as is described above, with two players and four blowers. A monk of the Tenth Century (one Wulstan) wrote of an Organ in Winchester Cathedral which required three players, a large number of blowers at the bellows, and which had as many as four hundred pipes. But it must not be supposed that this was really such a large Organ; it meant that the aggregate number of pipes was four hundred, but that they were operated by different musicians from different sets of slides; the instrument thus being really a combination of three distinct Organs. Once the keyboard had come into common use, and reed-pipes added, the scope of the instrument was considerably widened and the way made easy for further additions and improvements. The presence of two or three players at the Organs of the Middle Ages, as I have mentioned above, argues that each played his own part, and what these parts were in relation to one another a glance at the articles on Organum and Faux Bourdon will make clear (*v. also* REGAL, PORTATIVE, *and* POSITIVE).

ORGANISTRUM. *v.* HURDY GURDY.

ORGANUM: Probably the most ancient form of harmony, consisting, in the first instance, of two parts separating diatonically from the unison to the fourth and returning to the unison in the same way. At the time of Hucbald (Ninth Century) the Organum became a parallel sequence of fourths and later of fifths, and, frequently, the doubling of both parts in octaves. John Cotton (end of the Eleventh Century), after Guido d'Arezzo had instituted the crossing of parts, already developed the Organum to what became a true descant. Much on this subject is contained in the writings of the theoreticians included in Coussemaker's *Scriptores*, but a certain amount of confusion in nomenclature exists (*v. also* DIAPHONY).

ORPHERION: A plucked instrument handled as were the lutes, and popular very early in the Seventeenth Century. Mace (*Musick's Monument*, 1676) says that the "Auferions" had wire strings like the Pandora, and again like the latter instrument, had the strings in unison pairs. Their number varied from seven to nine pairs. A peculiar feature in the manner of stringing lay in the circumstance that the transverse bar which held the lower ends of the strings was affixed to the table in a slanting direction, and not at right angles to the centre-line as in the lutes. The slant ran upwards on the treble side, and had the effect of making the upper strings shorter than the lower ones. Since it was a fretted instrument, it followed that the frets had to be adjusted slantingly across the fingerboard to make up approximately for the slant. The advantage of this arrangement lay probably in the fact that the lengthened bass-strings gave greater resonance, and the shorter treble and means made for greater economy—not in the length of string used so much as in the reduced number of breakages. Still, with wire strings the latter could not have been a very important item.

In John Dowland's first and second books of "Songes and Ayres of foure parts with Tablature for the Lute. So made that all the partes together, or either of them severally may be sung to the Lute, Orpherion, *etc.*" (1600), the instrument is used for accompanying purposes. Three years later Thomas Robinson issued his "Schoole of Musicke: wherein is taught the Perfect Method of true fingering of the Lute, Pandora,

Orpherion . . . "; and in 1607 the instrument is once more mentioned in the title of Thomas Ford's *Musicke of Sundrie Kindes*.

PANDORA, PANDORE (*or BANDORE*)*:* A plucked instrument strung with wire (Mace) and used to supply a bass. Like the lutes, the Pandora had its strings mounted in unison pairs or ranks. The outline of the resonance-chamber was not a continuous curve, but was waved in three convex scallops on either side. It is quite possible that individual specimens may vary a good deal in outline. The instrument is mentioned as early as 1566 when George Gascoigne mentions it in the Euripidean tragedy *Jocasta* (in "the order of the dumme shewes and Musicke before every Acte"). Thomas Heywood, in the *Fair Maid of the Exchange* (1607), has: "What's her haire? faith to Bandora wiars, theres not the like simile. . . ." In 1603 Thomas Robinson names it on a title-page as an accompanying instrument, and in 1611 Thomas Morley published his "First Booke of Consort Lessons . . . for sixe instrumentes to play together: viz.: the Treble Lute, the Pandora, the Citterne, the Base-Violl, the Flute, and the Treble-Violl." If such a serious musician as Morley wrote for the instrument in such company, it must have been capable of producing very artistic effects. Samuel Pepys still alludes to it in 1662 when we find the entry: "Waked very early; and when it was time, did call up Will, and we rose, and musique (with a bandore for the base) did give me a levett" (October 15th).

PASPIE. *v.* PASPY.

PASPY: A dance descended from one of the forms of the Branle (*q.v.*) as the latter was used in Basse Bretagne, and known in France as the Passepied, from which the English name was (to some extent phonetically) derived. During a career of nearly two centuries the form became an exceedingly popular measure in practically all the art-loving countries of Europe.

The Paspy became known in England before the end of the Seventeenth Century, and Playford's *Apollo's Banquet* (1690) contains three examples. Thence onwards it was of comparatively frequent occurrence, became an integral part of the English musical scheme, and found writers in almost every musician of note, including Purcell. Early in the Eighteenth Century several French writers published collections of Harpsichord and Spinet music in England, and their work no doubt largely influenced the English composers of Paspies. But even in the Seventeenth-century purely English specimens the original form was not by any means strictly adhered to, and a good many liberties were taken with it. The research worker has to differentiate very carefully, when he is examining specimens of these ancient dances, between those examples written specifically for terpsichorean purposes and those composed purely as pieces of instrumental music. Tomlinson's treatise on the dance (1715) gives a specimen by a French dancing-master, in 6/8 time, with instructions how to dance it. This example is interesting since it is called "Passepied Round O"; which may, of course, have been the result of caprice, but which may, on the other hand, have been quite conceivably an indication that the Paspy was, in England, a round-dance, as it was originally in Bretagne at the period when it was known as a variety of the Branle.

In its original state the Passepied was a joyous dance high in favour with the seafaring population of Brittany; and the proximity of this part of France to Poitou may be an explanation for the great likeness that many authorities have found between the Paspy and the Menuet. Rousseau tells us that the older form was very like the Menuet, but quicker in *tempo*; and adds that another point of difference between the two forms was that the Passepied allowed of syncopation, while the Menuet did not. Compan and Brossard both bear out the musical philosopher in this opinion.

The character of this dance was light, merry, and full of gaiety; Niedt (*Handleitung zur Variation,* 1706) describes it as an exceedingly quick dance in which the feet were expected to exhibit exceptional agility, deriving the name from this circumstance. Mattheson says that the Passepied was never sung—a very peculiar distinction when we remember that almost without exception the old dances were accompanied by voices as well as instruments. As might be expected in a form that owed its origin to the Branle, the Passepied appears to have been written in a duple measure before it became the well-known triple dance of the Seventeenth Century. This peculiarity was not uncommon in the Sixteenth and early

Seventeenth Centuries, when many of the ancient dances had duple and triple forms. Tabourot (*Orchésographie,* 1588) mentions a duple variation of the Passepied. In the Seventeenth Century, however, the triple form became fixed, and it is to be found written generally in 3/8 or 3/4, the former being by far the most frequent measure. It was conventional for the form to commence on the up-beat, and another custom required it to be in the major. Later in its history the same methods were applied in its development as were used subsequently with the Menuet. The form it acquired when used as an instrumental piece was that of a major Passepied followed by one in the minor (in Trio form), the first Passepied being then repeated. In this shape it entered the stereotyped suite as one of the forms interpolated between the Saraband and Jig. It became further enlarged in the hands of some composers, and examples were written with as many as four sections, some of them repeated more than once. Grove says the Passepied concluded in the key of the third and fourth sections, which were in the minor ; but most of the specimens I have seen containing more than two sections have the first (major) portion repeated after the minor section has been played. The experience of F. L. Schubert must have been similar, for he says that the close should be major in any case. The use of so many sections in this form prepared the way for the Passepied with variations, and several examples in this shape are to be found in the works of the Eighteenth-century composers.

The history of the Passepied is quickly told. The original dance of the "round" nature was brought to Paris by itinerant musicians, and first danced in the streets of that city in 1587. Whether this was in the duple measure or not, we have no means of determining ; but I should be inclined to think that it was. Mersenne's *Harmonie Universelle* of 1636 gives two specimens of the *Passepied de Bretagne*, both being still duple. The change to the triple form must have taken place when the dance left the streets and became an artistic form in the court ballet of Louis XIV (1643/1715). Lully, Destouches, and Colasse, used it frequently in their operas, Marais wrote it in regular form, and Couperin affords an example of the Passepied with variations in the second *Ordre* of his Clavecin pieces (1713). By the time that Gluck wrote

(*Iphigénie en Aulide*, 1774), we find the phrase *mouvement de Passepied*, and this, as in the case of *Tempo di Menuetto* and *Tempo di Borea*, is a certain sign that the form had been converted to purely instrumental use. The Germans did not make much use of the form. Although already mentioned by Praetorius in 1612, we do not find many examples, and Bach, when he wrote his Passepieds, adhered to the original form only so far as it suited his purpose. In spite of this paucity of instrumental Passepieds in Germany, the form was much danced there ; and the only explanation I can offer is that the French dancing-masters who took the form to Germany used French music for their performances.

The various constructions, measures, and methods used at different periods in France in the writing of Passepieds, must be carefully studied if the reason for the variations in the English forms of that dance are to be understood. Its gay character and the merry agility of the movements required for it, made it a favourite in England ; and in this case, as in that of many another naturalised form, the original shapes and usages are all too often overlooked.

PASSAMEZZO : A Sixteenth-century Italian dance concerning which a considerable amount of doubt exists. If the only information obtainable were that of Arbeau (1588)—who says that when the musicians played the Pavane (*q.v.*) less heavily, it was called *Passe meze*—we should be justified in cataloguing the form as a variety of the Pavane. But we have sufficient evidence to prove that the two were distinct dances, although they have so often been confused. At the same time there can be little doubt that the Passamezzo was suggested primarily by the Pavane.

In Elizabethan England the form was a great favourite, although musically it may not have been treated as a distinct form in this country. In the English musical publications the name is usually to be found in association with another. Thus we find the term *Passamezzo Pavana* applied to a composition by William Byrd in the Fitzwilliam Virginal Book, and to another in the same manuscript by Peter Philips. It is possible that these were merely Pavanes written in a rather more florid style, and that they were movements upon which the Passamezzo could be danced. Each of the examples just quoted is followed by a *Galiarda Passamezzo*, which once more makes the meaning of the word, as it was used in England, uncertain. A consideration of the Italian uses of the name, however, may help to clear up this doubt. Thomas Robinson's Tablature *Schoole of Musicke* (1603) also contains a *Passemezo Galyard* and a *Passamezzo Paven*.

Whether Shakespeare actually used the term in *Twelfth Night* (V, 1), as quoted by many writers, must be left an open question owing to the varied readings given in different editions. The popular issues of the poet's works give the quotation as follows: "Then he's a rogue, and a passy-measures pavin." Theobald in his edition of 1733 (after "a faithful collation of all the printed copies") gives this version: "Then he's a rogue, and a past-measure *Painim*," which affords an entirely different reading. The reason for this would seem to be a difference between the first and second folios: in the one we find the word *Panyn* and in the other *Pauin*. The latter was the word most probably used by the poet, for by turning the first *n* in *Panyn* we should obtain *Pauyn*, the common English spelling of the dance-name. And a turned letter was by no means of infrequent occurrence. But whatever Sir Toby meant to say on the occasion in question, it is sufficient for our purpose to know that at the beginning of the Seventeenth Century (the time of the folios) the term Passymeasure was used to qualify Pavane, and it is of equal importance to us whether it originated with Shakespeare or one of his first editors. Suffice it to be established that the word was well enough known to have been used in a popular comedy.

The Passamezzo of Italy was of a simple and smoothly flowing nature; and though, according to all authorities, less slow than the Pavane, it was by no means a quick dance. The name, as it is given by Besarde in 1603, was *Pass'e Mezo*, and this, allowing for elision, was most probably derived from the Italian for "a step and a half," which was no doubt a feature of the dance. Such a derivation as the one from *Passer*, to walk, and *Mezzo*, middle—because the steps led the dancers across the centre of the room—is barbaric and cannot stand. Hawkins says that the Passamezzo was merely a diminutive of the Galliard; but he evidently came to that conclusion after seeing the term *Galiarda Passamezzo* in one of the Elizabethan manuscripts.

The antiquity of the form is considerable, for it can be traced back to the date of the early Pavanes. A collection of Italian forms published by the Gardano press in 1551 contains three "new" *Pass'e mezi*, which proves that older ones must have been extant. Besides this collection, the Gardano press issued another volume by Francesco Bendusi, which contains the dance. *Il Ballerino* (Venice, 1581) and *Nobiltà di Dame* (Venice, 1600) both include examples of the Passamezzo. Like nearly all the contemporary dance-forms, the Passamezzo was also sung.

In France the form was used as an Italian visitor, and in Germany also the examples printed show that the country of the Passamezzo's birth was not lost sight of, and a great many of the known specimens were written by Italians who published their works in Germany. In the Seventeenth Century the dance was probably less used for terpsichorean purposes, and its treatment in free form with many variations proves that it soon became an instrumental show-piece which gave the lutenists of the period some material for technical display.

The fact that the earliest known examples of the Passamezzo were published in Venice may account for its popularity there; and the same circumstance probably explains its being known in England so early, for the relations between this country and Venice were very cordial in the Tudor period.

PASSECAILLE: An instrumental form in triple measure derived from an ancient dance, and consisting of sets of variations on a ground-bass. In construction it was very like the Chaconne (*v.* CHACCON) and only in mood and spirit did it differ. In the late Seventeenth and early Eighteenth Centuries distinctions were observed between the two forms, the chief being that in the Chaconne the theme was supposed to be kept in the bass, while in the Passacaglio (to give the form its more common—Italian—name) it could be used in any part of the harmony. Further, it was decreed that the Passecaille should be in the minor and the Chaconne in the major, and specimens may be seen in which the minor sections are labelled *Passacaglia* or *Passacaglio*, and the major parts *Chaconne* or *Ciaconna*. These rules were soon broken, and both forms are to be found in major and minor.

Like the Chaconne, the Passecaille did not become very

popular in England. Receiving it from France, as the form of the name suggests, a few writers tried their hands at it and found it—like the Chaconne—too heavy for their style. A specimen may be seen in John Playford's *Musick's Delight on the Cithren* (1666), where it is called " Passingala," and another in *Apollo's Banquet* (1690). A third example is contained in Purcell's *King Arthur*.

As a dance the Passecaille in England did not differ much from the Chaconne. In Tomlinson's Treatise on the Dance (1735) we find the form called " our Chaconne."

PASSINGALIA. *v*. PASSECAILLE.

PASSYMEASURE. *v*. PASSAMEZZO.

PAVANE: An interesting and important dance-form of the Sixteenth Century. Written in duple measure, it was slow in tempo and dignified in character. Although it became so popular in England, the Pavane was only a naturalised alien. It had its origin in Italy and came hither *via* France. One of the earliest, and at the same time most accurate, accounts of the dance is that given by Tabourot in his *Orchèsographie* (1588). He says that the Pavane was slow, solemn, and dignified in movement; invested in a high degree of majesty. Its evolutions were sufficiently stately and grave to allow the gentleman to dance it "in his helm and sword—while you others, clad in your long robes, can also take part." No frivolity was allowed to detract from the solemnity of the dance at that period; the ladies were to perform their part in it " with an humble countenance and downcast eyes—glancing occasionally at their partners with virginal modesty." This character caused the Pavane to be much in demand, not only at court functions, but also at weddings and other religious and solemn festivals. It could be danced, said Tabourot, " by Kings, princes, and grave seigneurs with their grand mantles; and by Queens, princesses, and ladies with their long trains." If further proof of the manner of the Pavane's performance were needed, it would be forthcoming in the statement that the ladies' court-trains were carried throughout the evolutions by maids-of-honour.

In agreement with the custom of the period, the Pavane was sung as well as danced, and many beautiful examples have been preserved in the music-books of the time. The specimen given by Tabourot in his book—*Belle qui tiens ma vie*—is a splendid example of popular secular music at the time of the Great Armada.

Upon the Pavane's first introduction into England, its association with ceremonial functions was not so far forgotten as was a little later the case. Exactly when it was first imported is not quite clear; but the close relations between the English court and Italy—notably Venice—during the reign of Henry VIII, may account for its early appearance here. This is the only way in which we can explain the circumstance that the form was well enough known and liked for the king himself to have essayed an imitation. The Arundel Collection of royal manuscripts contains one of a number written by Henry VIII under the title of "King Henry's Pavyn." This specimen was transcribed and printed by John Stafford Smith in his *Musica Antiqua* (1812). Elizabethan examples are more frequent, and early Stuart specimens may be seen in *Parthenia* (1610), with an interesting Pavane by John Bull; in the works of John Dowland the lutenist (1605); in John Playford's *Court Ayres* (1655); and many other publications of the period.

As a dance the nature of the Pavane became modified by environment. Tabourot's sumptuously robed and cloaked figures made dignified motion imperative; and a long train, carried by servants, precluded in itself all careless and thoughtless movement. But when the form was borrowed by the masses and used on the village-green, the local spirit soon converted it into something more congenial to its own taste. Musically the Pavane fulfilled an important rôle, and many forms used later owe their existence to that dance. Thus one form of the Italian *Canzone* is descended from it, and one of its most beautiful developments was the *Largo* in the French Overture at the end of the Seventeenth Century.

A variation of the Pavane, known as the Spanish Pavane, was also very popular all over Europe, and particularly in England; but whether the differences extended beyond the terpsichorean aspect of the subject, I cannot say. I have not found any music specifically written for the Spanish Pavin with any characteristics differing markedly from those of the ordinary form. Literary mention of both varieties is frequent. Ford, in *The Lady's Trial* (1639), has as a stage direction

(II, 1): "Fulgoso whistles the Spanish Pavin," and Ben Jonson, in *Act* IV, *Scene* 2 of *The Alchemist*, says: "Your Spanish Pavin is the best dance." And if the existence of a popular tune of the era known as "The Spanish Pavin" accounted for Ford's direction, it would not do so for Jonson's use of the term.

The derivation of the name is simple. Pavane, for *Pavana*, *Paduana*, or *Padovana*, fixes upon Padua in Italy as the place where the dance first acquired popularity. The etymologists of the Eighteenth Century and their short-sighted imitators connected the word with the Latin *Pavo*, a Peacock, and in the dignity of the Pavane's movement found support for their crazy derivation, because "it was danced with singular motions of the feet so as to form a wheel, as is the habit of peacocks when in their pride" (Walther, *Lexicon*, 1732). This, of course, is sheer nonsense; the nobility of the dance and the similarity of its name to that of the peacock are accidental. One glance at the *a* in the centre of Pavane and another at the *o* in the root of *Pavo*, *Pavonis*, will suffice to cause the rejection of this barbarous etymology.

When danced in artistic circles the duple Pavane was invariably followed by the triple Galliard (*q.v.*), thus subscribing to the first principles of artistry, the demand for variety. Used together and almost inseparably until both became antiquated, the Pavane and the Galliard were followed by, and eventually made way for, a similarly contrasting pair of dances—one slow and the other quick—a pair of forms that under the names of Allemande and Courante were later to open the classic Suite.

PAVIN, PAVYN. *v.* PAVANE.

PERFECT OF THE LESS. *v.* MOOD.

PERFECT OF THE MORE. *v.* MOOD.

PINCHING NOTES or PINCHED NOTES: Harmonics on the Recorder and Flageolet, obtained by increased breath-pressure in blowing, the octave above the stopped note being produced. "To play these on the Recorder," says Humphrey Salter in *The Genteel Companion* (1683), "you must bend your left Thumb, and let it be half over the hole underneath the pipe, for that belongs to the upper line (*v.* DOT-WAY) where the pinch is made, and pinch the nail of your Thumb in the hole, then blow your Recorder a little stronger than you did when you played the other notes, and you shall find the Recorder sound eight notes higher." In playing the "Pincht Notes" the seventh hole had to be left unstopped (*v.* FLAGEOLET *and* RECORDER).

PLAGAL MODES. *v.* CHURCH MODES.

PLAIN BEAT. *v.* BEAT.

PLAIN FALL. *v.* FALL.

PLAIN-SONG: Broadly speaking, Plain-song was the unison unmeasured chant in use before the evolution of measured music. Later the meaning of the term was more narrowly applied, and used, often in its Latin form *Cantus planus*, to distinguish the unharmonised Gregorian chant from harmonised Mensurable Music. Its origin is to be sought in the earliest forms of religious worship, and there can be little doubt that in the Temple itself some such recitative was already used. Evidence of its employment in the Christian Church is available to prove its existence in the earliest centuries of the Christian era. Its character was modal, and its rhythm dictated by the scansion of the text. There seems to be no doubt that the more ancient Plain-song was less monotonous than the later, for everything points to the sense of the words having been carefully considered in the chant. But later "reformers" have all too well succeeded in stretching out the shorter notes of the recitative until a chant of almost equal notes resulted. By the end of the Sixteenth Century the monotony of the rhythm of Plain-song must have already been a characteristic feature, for in *Lingua* (before 1607, I, 1) we read: "The tedious plain-song grates my tender ears."

Plain-song still survives in the Church of England (High Church) and especially in the Roman Catholic service, where it remains to the present moment as an immensurable chant. Its English history began with the arrival of St. Augustine, and practised fairly true to tradition ever since, having been retained in part, even during the troublous times of religious flux in the Sixteenth Century.

The study of Plain-song is interesting and important from another, and often overlooked, point of view; namely, that of its influence upon the system of notation—many of the signs and symbols in present use having been directly borrowed from those employed in the Plain-song of very ancient times (*v.* NEUMES; *also the* Benedictine *Paléographie Musicale* of Solesmes).

PLATE: A name sometimes given to the fingerboard of the viol, Christopher Simpson (*Division-Violist*, 1659) speaking of the "Plate or Fingerboard."

POINT: A term used, alternately with Prick, to mean what is now known as a Dot. Playford speaks of a "Pointed Minim" as being equal to three crotchets, thus showing the word to have been synonymous with our dot. Various kinds of Point (*Punctum*) were known in Medieval and later music, and these will be found under their respective headings.

POINT OF ADDITION: A variant term for Point of Perfection (*q.v.*). Writers so far apart as Glareanus and John Playford use both these expressions to mean the same thing.

POINT OF ALTERATION. v. ALTERATION.

POINT OF AUGMENTATION: A dot which (like the same sign to-day) increased the value of a note by half its original worth. Used in connection with Mensurable Music, it would have the force of the Point of Perfection.

POINT OF DIVISION: In Mensurable Music, a dot placed between notes, or over them (where the present-day bar would be drawn and fulfilling the same functions in some cases), in order to make clear to the performer how the music was to be measured. It was of especial use in such places where doubt might enter into the interpretation of a note's value (*cf. also* ALTERATION). This dot was called the *Punctum Divisionis.* Glareanus (*Dodecachordon, Chap.* x) says that the Point of Division, under certain circumstances, caused Alteration: ". . . secunda perpetuo duplatur, non prima . . .," and then: ". . . id autem punctum divisionis saepius indicat." In all probability the modern bar is a descendant of the Point of Division.

POINT OF PERFECTION: In the old measured music a dot placed after a note in the Perfect Mood (*q.v.*), and used to render its measure once more perfect after its position in relation to other notes, had deprived it of its perfection. In such cases the force of the *Punctum Perfectionis* was the same as the present-day dot, for it converted a long containing two breves into one equal to three breves. Glareanus, in one of his musical examples (*Bk.* III, *Chap.* iv, *Dodecachordon*), shows that, in his mind, the Point of Perfection and the Point of Addition were practically the same.

POLIPHANT : A plucked instrument of which next to nothing is known. Playford attributes its invention to Daniel Farrant, a well-known violist of the period, and mentions it in *Musick's Recreation on the Viol, Lyraway* (1661) : " Daniel Farunt . . .

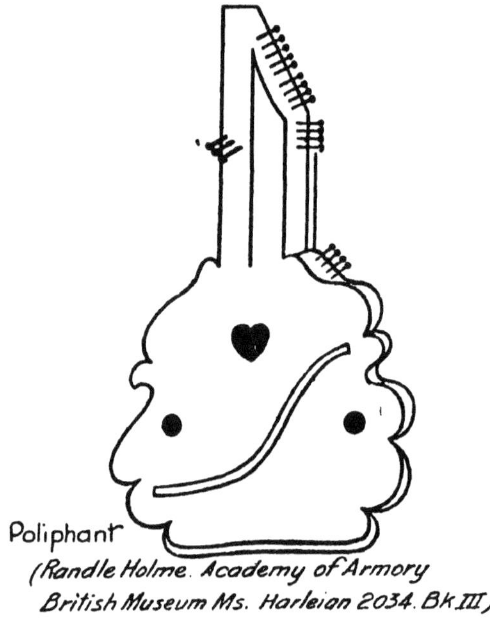

(Randle Holme. Academy of Armory British Museum Ms. Harleian 2034. Bk III)

was a person of much ingenuity for his several rare inventions of instruments, as the Poliphant and the Stump, which were strung with wire. . . ." Randle Holme, in his manuscript *Academy of Armory* (*Bk.* III, *Harleian MS.* 2034, British Museum), gives an account and a drawing of the instrument—the only trace of it that I have been able to find. Says Holme : " A poliphant of some called a poliphon. It is an hollow yet flat kind of Instrument, containing three dozen and five wire strings to be played upon." The sketch shows a shallow sound-box of fantastic shape, with a much scalloped outline, a bridge with a double curve, and three small sound-holes—two circular and one heart-shaped. Playford (*Introduction to the Skill of Musick*) had it from "an ancient musician" of Queen Elizabeth that her Majesty "did often recreate herself on an excellent Instrument called the Poliphant, not much unlike a Lute, but strung with wire." Unless Elizabeth played upon the Poliphant in the very last years of her life, I cannot see how her use of it and its invention by Farrant can be reconciled.

PORTATIVE : As its name implies, a small organ of a portable nature. Such instruments appear very early in the history of the organ, and it was only the increased size and weight caused by a greater number of pipes and manuals that brought the term Positive (*i.e.* immovable organ) into being. The Portative, is mentioned in the early metrical romances, and it must have been in common use in England before the Fifteenth Century. It should not be supposed, however, that the organ bearing this name was in any way an harmonium-like imitation of the larger instrument;—the Portative, however small it was, always had pipes and was generally blown by a second person at the bellows.

POSITIVE : A term once in use to designate an organ in a fixed position, to distinguish it from the smaller and lighter Portative (*q.v.*), which could be carried from place to place. Later on, the word was applied to one of the manuals of the Church organ to keep it distinct from the accompanying, or choir, organ. In spite of these two specific uses of the word, it was often employed loosely to any organ for chamber use that was too large to be called a Portative.

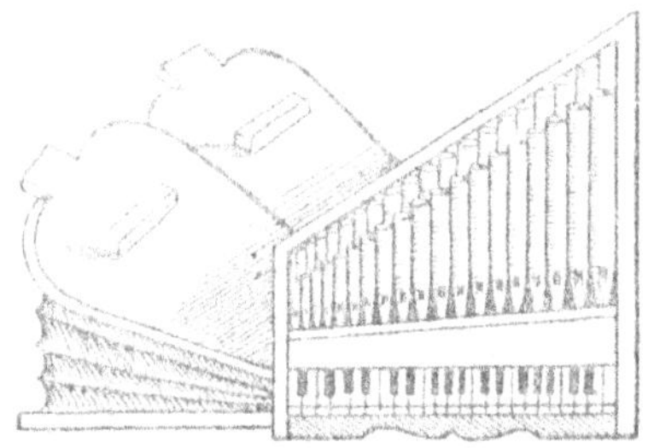

Positive
(Seb Virdung. Musica getutscht, etc. 1511

PRICK I : As a noun. In the Seventeenth Century the word Prick was frequently used in place of the more usual "Point" (*q.v.*).

PRICK II : As a verb. Tudor and Stuart music, when written down and not performed extempore, was said to be Pricked ; and a piece of vocal music thus written was a Prick-song. The State Papers of Henry VIII already contain a reference to this word when the payment of £20 " for a prick-songe boke " is authorised. Shakespeare refers to it in *Romeo and Juliet* (II, 4) : " He fights as you sing prick-song, keeps time, distance, and proportion. He rests his minim, one, two, three, in your bosom." John Playford, after the middle of the Seventeenth Century, still used the term, saying : " when any of the parts . . . shall come to be prick'd out."

The verb To Prick and the noun Pricker were applied almost exclusively to the writing of music and to the writers respectively, until the Eighteenth Century. Various amounts in payment for the " pricking " of music for the Chapel Royal and the King's Chamber-music are frequently mentioned in warrants preserved in the Record Office. Thus in 1668 (April 17), the authorisation to pay Louis Grabu a sum of money for music-writing included the item, " for the prickers dyett " ; in 1673 (May 23) the warrant included payment for the " prickers dyes " (ink) ; in 1675 (May 27) for " pricking the tunes in the Maske, and for paper, pens, and inke. . . £10 " ; in 1692 (June 24) Dr. Staggins, Master of the King's Musick, received £59 6*s.* for " Pricking severall compositions," stationery and the prickers' food being included ; and so on, until the joint reign of William and Mary, when we still find the word in the same use (June 22, 1698).

PRICK-SONG. *v.* PRICK II.

PROLATION : In Medieval music the term Prolation was used to designate the relation of the minim to the semibreve. It is not so ancient as Time (*Tempus*) or Mood, for it came into use only with the minim, which appeared early in the Fourteenth Century. Prolation was Major (sometimes called *Prolatio Perfecta*—on the Continent, at any rate) when the semibreve contained three minims, and Minor when it equalled two. The indication as to whether Prolation was Major or Minor was given by a dot in the centre of the circle or semicircle which showed the Time (*q.v.*). The number of minims that went to make up a rhythmic measure (for want of a better term in the absence of bars) varied, not only according to the nature of the

Prolation used, but also according to the Perfection or Imperfection of the *Tempus*. When Time was Imperfect, for instance, and Prolation Perfect, there were six minims to the breve (𝅜 = ◇ ◇ = 𝅗𝅥𝅗𝅥𝅗𝅥 𝅗𝅥𝅗𝅥𝅗𝅥) when Time and Prolation were Perfect the breve contained nine minims, owing to the fact that it was equal to three semibreves, each containing three minims. Similarly, six minims went to the breve when the Time was Perfect and the Prolation Minor ; and four when the Time and Prolation were both Imperfect. In Minor Prolation the values of the notes could be halved in value (or doubled in speed) when a line was drawn through the signature (*cf.* TIME). It by no means follows that every part in polyphonic music was given the same time-signature ; for it frequently happened that one part would be prefixed with ₵ and another with C, each part having to be read according to its own indication. In such cases the remarks made concerning the halving of the values apply. When all the parts showed the signature with the line, it indicated merely an increased *tempo*—not necessarily doubled speed.

PROPORTION: In ancient music the ratios by which a rhythmic measure was divided, serving the purpose, to a certain extent, of our modern time-signatures. It will be understood by those who have mastered the mysteries of Mood, *Tempus*, and Prolation (*q.v.*), that that which we call a triple measure to-day could be subdivided in duple time, that a duple measure could have duple subdivisions, and a triple one, triple. These alone give a considerable number of possible "Proportions," quite apart from intricate mixtures of rhythms. Furthermore, proportion fixed the relative rhythms of the various parts performing in harmony, when each part was perhaps read in a different, though harmonisable, proportion. An example of the latter is to be seen in Heyden's *De arte canendi*, in which the Discantus part is written with the *integer valor notarum* (*i.e.* the average or normal time-value of the breve, semibreve, minim, *etc.*—according to period), the Tenor in *Proportio tripla* (3/1, or 3 *in* 1), and the Bassus in Imperfect Time *Diminutum*, the whole giving in places what is really duple bass and treble parts to a triple tenor part. Combinations of various rhythms were thus quite common in Mensurable Music, and without this system of *proportiones*, no harmony could result, especially when we remember the absence of the bar. Fractions were the commonest means of indicating the Proportion, and no difficulty need be experienced in interpreting the works in which it occurs, if the correct time-values be given to each individual part. In the example of Heyden just mentioned, it simply meant counting three semibreves to the breve in the tenor, and two in the treble and bass. Changes of Proportion are quite frequent in the middle of a piece, and a certain amount of care is necessary to avoid overlooking them.

The subject of Proportion is a very large one, and includes the *Proportio Hemiola*, or the writing of, *e.g.*, semibreves black instead of white, thus giving them the value of three black semibreves to the breve; this would often occur in a piece with a duple time-signature, and meant a change to triple time, while the accompanying voices might still be going on in the duple. As soon as these blackened notes appeared in outline again, the original Mood or *Tempus* was restored. Care must be exercised not to read a "black minim" as a crotchet, for the black minim stands to the white minim in the ratio of two to three. The writing of minims as black notes was called *Hemiolia prolationis*. The *Proportio Sesquialtera* had varieties, as had nearly all of the others, the most frequent being a ratio of three to two. *Proportio Sesquitertia* was as four to three. Sebaldus Heyden, treating of this subject, stops here and says that he leaves the other Proportions out, because they are of no use to the practical musician, and are only to be regarded as mathematical conjuring-tricks. Nevertheless, a large number of compositions may be found containing the most extravagant time-ratios, such as 7/4, 9/5, 11/7, 13/9, 13/7, *etc.* (*Musice Practica*, Franchinus Gaforius). Unfortunately, a work of this size allows no space for a closer consideration of this highly fascinating subject.

PSALTERY: A stringed instrument played by plucking with the fingers or a plectrum. It is to be met with in a variety of shapes, the shallow sound-box being chiefly triangular, square, or oblong; or a modification of one of these forms produced by the cutting off of the corners and rounding the new edges concavely. The number of strings varied with the period, and the method of playing differed according to the skill of the performer and the fashion of the country. Illustrations of it most commonly show it played by being held upright with one hand, while the other plucks the strings; or resting flat on the knees of the seated performer, leaving both hands free to pluck and damp the strings. In an old metrical romance, for instance, we read: "Shee laid a sauter on hir knee, Ther on shee plaid full lovesomelye." Its antiquity can scarcely be determined. It was an instrument of simple construction and must have been discovered or evolved very early in history;—in fact, it may be an improvement on one of the biblical instruments, or, at all events of Asian origin.

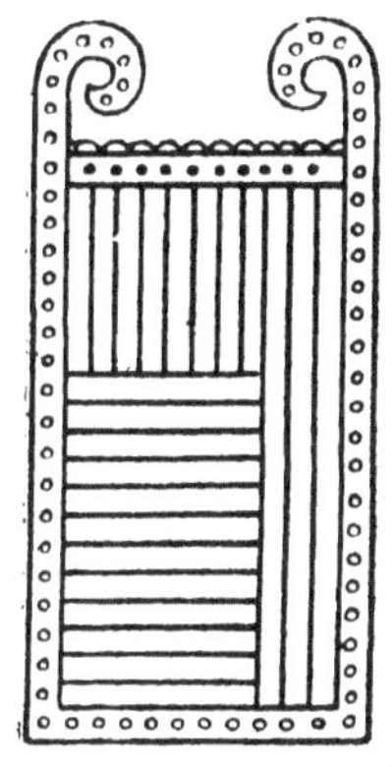

Psaltery (British Museum Ms. Tiberius C VI. fol 17b, Anglo-Saxon 11th Centy

The tone of the Psaltery must have been quite pleasant and Mersenne as late as the first half of the Seventeenth Century was very enthusiastic over its sweetness. But Mersenne must not be followed too closely with regard to the Psaltery, for he appears to have mixed it up with the Dulcimer (*q.v.*), and it may have been the latter instrument which pleased him so much. Still, there is every excuse for Mersenne's ambiguity, for psaltery and dulcimer were sufficiently alike to mislead any but a most careful observer. The two instruments differed

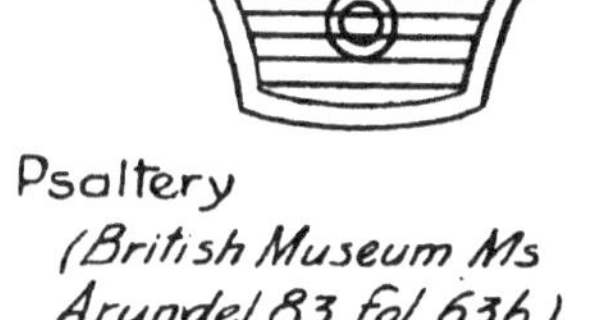

Psaltery (British Museum Ms Arundel 83. fol 63b)

in the method of playing and manner of stringing (*v.* DULCIMER).

The first literary mention of the Psaltery that I have been able to trace is that of Robert Mannyng, or Robert de Brunne (*c.* 1300), when he speaks of the "Sautre." At the famous Westminster festival of 1306, players on the Psaltery were active, and one of them, Gillotin or Gillot le Sautreur, was paid forty shillings for his services ; while a mark was bestowed on Janin le Sautreur. Chaucer frequently mentions the instrument :

> And al above ther lay a gay sautrye,
> On which he made a nightes melodye.
> (*Miller's Tale*, 3213/4).

and later on :

> He kist hir swete, and taketh his sautrye,
> And pleyeth faste, and maketh melodye.
> (*Id.* 3305/6).

The instrument is also mentioned in Gavin Douglas' *Palace of Honour* (1501). These citations could be multipied a hundredfold, for the Psaltery seems to have been in everyone's hands, and there is scarcely a writer of the Fourteenth and Fifteenth Centuries who does not name it.

Psaltery (British Museum MS. Add. 19352. fol. 188b. A.D. 1066)

It is clear that the Psaltery with its plucked strings, first with the fingers and then with the plectrum, was the humble forerunner of keyboard instruments like the Virginal, Spinet, and Harpsichord, in which the strings were brought into vibration by the keys causing plectra of some sort to twang them. And it was the growing popularity of these its successors in the Sixteenth Century that caused the decline of the Psaltery. Still, it persisted in small country communities, among people who could not afford the luxury of the then very expensive keyboard instrument, for quite a long time.

Illustrations of the Medieval Psaltery may be seen in several

British Museum manuscripts, such as *Additional* 35166 (late Thirteenth Century), *Tiber, C.* VI (Anglo-Saxon, Eleventh Century, ff. 16*b*, 17*b*), *Ar.* 157 (Early Thirteenth Century, *f.* 71*b*), *Additional* 19352 (1066, *f.* 188*b*), and others. The roof of Manchester Cathedral (1465) is ornamented with some fine carvings of angels playing instruments, one of them handling a Psaltery with quite a score of strings.

QUATRIBLE : A descant in fourths, as the Quinible was one in fifths (*v.* QUINIBLE).

QUINIBLE : An extemporised added part harmonised in fifths, obviously used in an era when consecutive fifths were not forbidden. It was of frequent occurrence, and, to our ears, of horrible effect. The treatise of Chilston (end of the Fourteenth Century) contains the rules that were applied to descanting in Quatrible and Quinible. He says that the Quatrible was to be sung by a child, which is obvious when we are told that it " begynnyth in a twilfth above " (the Plain-song). Cornish, in his *Treatise between Truth and Informacion,* still uses the word Quatrible in 1528.

Chaucer's use of the word shows at once how the term was employed, how common it must have been to stand inclusion in the *Canterbury Tales* without further explanation, and exactly what it meant to the ordinary layman :

In twenty manere coude he trippe and daunce
After the scole of Oxenforde tho,
And with his legges casten to and fro
And pleyen songes on a small rubible ;
Ther-to he song som-tyme a loud quinible.
(*Miller's Tale.*)

QUINTUS : In the part-writing of the period that had the Sixteenth Century as its centre, the Quintus was the fifth part in compositions of more than four parts. It was not an independent voice, and only duplicated one of the others. In some compositions it was a second treble, in others a second tenor, and so on. Frequently the range of the music contained in the Quintus part extended from one part to another, and it was thus sometimes called *Pars Vagans,* or " wandering part." When it is said that the Quintus was not an independent part, it must not be supposed that it actually duplicated another part note for note, but only that it was written in the pitch of one of the other parts.

QUIRE: The more truly English spelling of Choir, which is a pedantic variation influenced by more recent foreign fashions. The prayer-book still uses the spelling Quire. So also in Playford: "Then followeth the Apostles Creed, which is sung by the whole Quire." In *The Squyr of Lowe Degre* (*l.* 789) we meet with the form *Quere.* Shakespeare uses the older form of the word in *Henry VIII* (IV, 1), though this has been changed in modern reprints. Francis, Lord Bacon (*Essay of Masques and Triumphs,* has: "I understand it, that the song be in quire. . . ."

QUODLIBET: A musical joke much enjoyed in the Sixteenth, Seventeenth, and Eighteenth Centuries. It consisted originally in a number of musicians simultaneously singing or playing on instruments whatever melody occurred to them. Tunes sacred and secular, slow and fast, were blended together into a "harmony" that was strikingly original, if nothing else. Cleverly performed, the Quodlibet could give much pleasure to an adroit musician, and as a relaxation from the more formal occupation of writing and singing music conforming to very strict rules, it served some useful purpose. The incongruity of many of the combinations was oft-times highly amusing. Later on, the name was given to certain classes of written and properly harmonised music, but still constructed out of the interweaving of varied airs.

QUOTLIBET. v. QUODLIBET.

RACKET. v. CURTAL.

RAKING: Sweeping the finger across the strings in playing chords upon instruments of the lute species. At one time the entire chord was played by striking the finger across the strings from the bass upwards; but towards the end of the Seventeenth Century the "fashionable way of playing them," according to Thomas Mace (1676), was "only to hit the Bass with your Thumb, and Rake down all the other three letters, with your Forefinger, at the same time." By "letters" Mace means notes (*cf.* TABLATURE).

RANKS: The unison pairs of strings on the lute, cittern, and kindred instruments. The best teachers of the Seventeenth Century recommend that the two strings of each Rank be fairly close together, but that the Ranks themselves should be as far apart as could be conveniently managed, in order to facilitate play.

RANT : An ancient dance of doubtful origin. It is possible that the name was derived from the verb " to rant," to use violent or bombastic language, and thus may have referred to a dance of wild character and formless type. If this were so, it may be traced to the Old Dutch *Ranten*, to dote or rave (*cf.* Westphalian *Rantern*, to prate ; Provincial English, *Randy*, wild, or mad ; Low German, *Randen*, and Modern German, *Ranzen*). Such a derivation would make Rant related to *Ranz*, a very ancient dance-tune (*cf. Ranz des Vaches*). The Stainer and Barrett *Dictionary of Musical Terms* advances the theory that Rant is a corruption of Coranto ; but, although this may be etymologically possible, the rhythms of the two forms differ to such an extent that the idea cannot be entertained.

In Stuart publications we sometimes meet with pieces called Rant, the most frequent being John Jenkins's *Mitter Rant* (Playford's *Musick's Hand-maide*, 1678, and other contemporary publications). Two other popular airs of the period were the *Fleece Tavern Rant* and the *Peterborough Rant*, both by Jenkins. It is not outside of the bounds of possibility that the genial old Jenkins applied the name to these compositions himself, and that it never really attained to general acceptance. The use of the word in Mrs. Centlivre's comedy, *The Platonick Lady* (1707), may thus only be a play on words given into the mouth of the misunderstanding Mrs. Dowdy : " I'll lead you a Courant, Madam,"—" Ay, a Rant with all my Heart ; I dan't understand the Names, let en be a Dance, and 'tis well enough."

RAY or RAYE : A dance of which little or nothing more is known than can be gathered from the etymology of the name. Alexander Barclay (*Eclogues*, 1508) uses the word in the line : " I can daunce the raye, I can bothe pype and syng,"—and its derivation is from Middle Dutch *Rey* or *Reye*, " a round-dance " (Hexham's *Large Nether-dutch and English Dictionarie*, 1658). Chaucer (*House of Fame, l.* 1236) mentions it : " Pypers of the Duche tonge, To lerne . . . daunces, springes, Reyes. . . ." The Modern Dutch is *Rei*, which is most probably cognate with the German *Reihen* or *Reigen*. This would make of the form something like the Branle (*q.v.*), from which it would be, in such case, derived.

RE. *v.* ARETINIAN SYLLABLES *and* GAMUT.

REBECK : A bowed stringed instrument of great antiquity of Eastern origin, and introduced into Europe as early as the Eleventh Century, probably by the Crusaders. The name, derived as it is through the Old French *Rebec* (also spelled *Rebebe*), from the Arabic *Rebab*, *Rababa(t)* (M. Devic, *Dictionaire Etymologique de tous les mots d'origine Orientale*, in the supplement to Littré's Dictionary), already betrays the source of the instrument. It is sufficiently proven that the use of the bow comes from the East, and the Rebeck must be counted among the first of the bowed instruments in Europe. Its shape was generally that of an elongated pear with a vaulted back, and it was provided with a couple of small sound-holes, one on either side of the bridge. It had three strings attached to a tail-piece. The neck does not appear to have been distinct from the body, but was formed by the narrowing of the latter. Whether the Rubebe (Rubible, Ribible) was identical with the Rebeck, or a variation of it, is not clear ; but the name is evidently from the same source, and if any differences existed between the two forms, these must have been evolved before the instrument came to Europe, for both are named at the same period. As might be expected, the Rebeck came to us *via* Spain and France, unless, as I have already hinted, the returning Crusaders brought it with them directly from the hands of the Saracens.

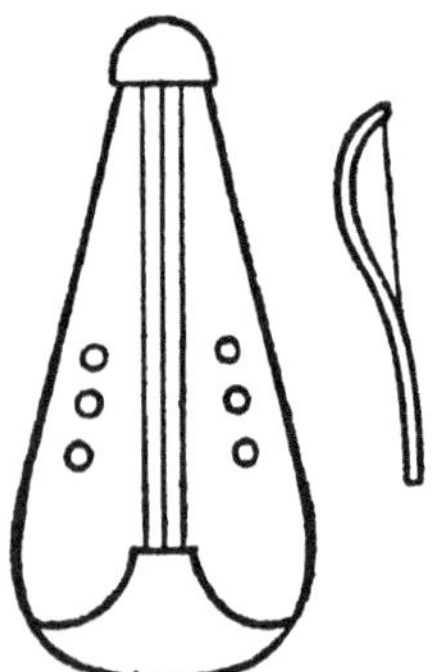

Drawings of the instrument are to be seen in British Museum manuscripts, *Tiber. C.* VI (Anglo-Saxon, Eleventh Century) ; *Ar.* 157 (Early Thirteenth Century), and many others, besides carvings in different cathedrals.

The Rebeck had a place in the royal bands of the Tudor sovereigns, and in Egerton Manuscript 2604 (British Museum, 1525/6) there are mentioned three "Rebikes." The Fifth Earl of Northumberland employed a large body of singers and instrumentalists, including a Rebeck. According to his

Household Book (1512) the wages of the player on the latter amounted to " xxxiij*s*. iiij*d*.," and on New Year's Day " in the mornynge, when they doo play at my Lorde's chambre doure," one pound was shared among the Tabret, Lute, and Rebeck, as a seasonal gift. The instrument is named as late as the time of James I, when a list of fees paid to musicians shows that rebeck-players were still employed (*Stowe MS.* 574, *f.* 16*b*; British Museum).

In ancient literature the Rebeck is mentioned so frequently that it is difficult to select characteristic quotations. It is referred to as the Ribible in the *Squyr of Lowe Degre* (*l.* 1071), and in Lydgate's *Reson and Sensualite* (*l.* 5581/2):

> Lutys, Rubibis, and Geterns,
> More for estatys than taverns.

Chaucer uses both forms of the name; Rebekke in *The Frere's Tale*, and Ribible in *The Cokes Tale* (*cf.* also quotation in article on Quinible). Stephen Hawes speaks of Rebeckes in 1506 (*Pastyme of Plesure*, *Chap.* 16), and Michael Drayton in *Eclogue* II (*The Shepherd's Garland*) says:

> He turn'd his rebec to a mournful note,
> And thereto sung this doleful elegy.

Milton, in *L'Allegro* (" and the jocund rebecks sound "), still finds use for the instrument, as he does again in his *Areopagitica*. Shakespeare, too, in *Romeo and Juliet* (V, 5) names one of his minstrels Hugh Rebeck.

REBIKE. *v.* REBECK.

RECORD: As a verb this term was a common one in Elizabethan England for the sense " to sing " or " to warble," and was especially used to mean the singing of birds, being thence applied to human music-making. A typical example of the literary use of the word is to be found in the Chorus to *Act* IV of *Pericles*: ". . . or when to the Lute She sung, and made the night-bird mute, That still records with moan. . . ." Another is given by Fletcher in Valentinian (II, 1, before 1618/9): " For you are fellows only know by note, As birds record their lessons." William Browne's use of the term shows that it was employed indifferently to human and feathered vocalists: " So while the nymph did earnestly contest,

Whether the birds or she recorded best" (*Britannia's Pastorals, Book* II, *Song* 4). An entry in the *Promptorium Parvulorum* of *c.* 1440 shows how early the term was used to mean the learning of exercises: "Recordyn lessonys, *Recordo, Repeto.*"

RECORDER: (English Flute, Common Flute, Fipple Flute, Flute Douce, Doucet, Doucette, *etc.*). A wind-instrument of the fipple-pipe, or whistle-headed family, very popular in England for more than three centuries. The essential features of the Recorder were a notch cut into the tube near the upper end, a plug inserted into the pipe at the notch which partly closed the former, and thumb-holes at the back of the instrument. The wind struck the lower edge of the notch and produced the whistle-like tone characteristic of the instrument. This principle is applied to all sound-producers of the whistle type, from the earliest instruments of Græco-Roman times to the modern organ pipe. The instruments of this class were all blown directly, thus being differentiated from the later *flauto traverso.* Their tone was soft and caused them to acquire the name of *Doucet* or *Flute Douce.* Bacon (*Sylva Sylvarum*, 1627) alludes to this when he says "recorders which goe with a gentle Breath," thus drawing a comparison between them and the "*Flutes* and *Fifes* which will not giue *Sound* by a Blast at the end, as Recorders doe, but are blowne at a Small Hole in the side." The distinction between the direct and the transverse flutes is thus made clear. Lydgate (early Fifteenth Century) already mentions the difference in tone between the Recorder and the other pipes when he says: "Lowde shallys and doucetes." Chaucer (*House of Fame, ll.* 1220/1) also uses the name "Doucet":

> That craftely begunne pype
> Bothe in doucet and in rede.

The Recorder was made in several sizes of different pitch, Praetorius mentioning as many as eight. Whether all these were ever used together is open to doubt, and I think that the ordinary quartet, consisting of Treble, Alto, Tenor, and Bass (as in the case of most other instruments), was the combination most usually employed for concerted music. Such a quartet is preserved in the Grosvenor Museum at Chester, and is believed to be the only complete set in original condition. Of these instruments, the Treble has a range up to the F above

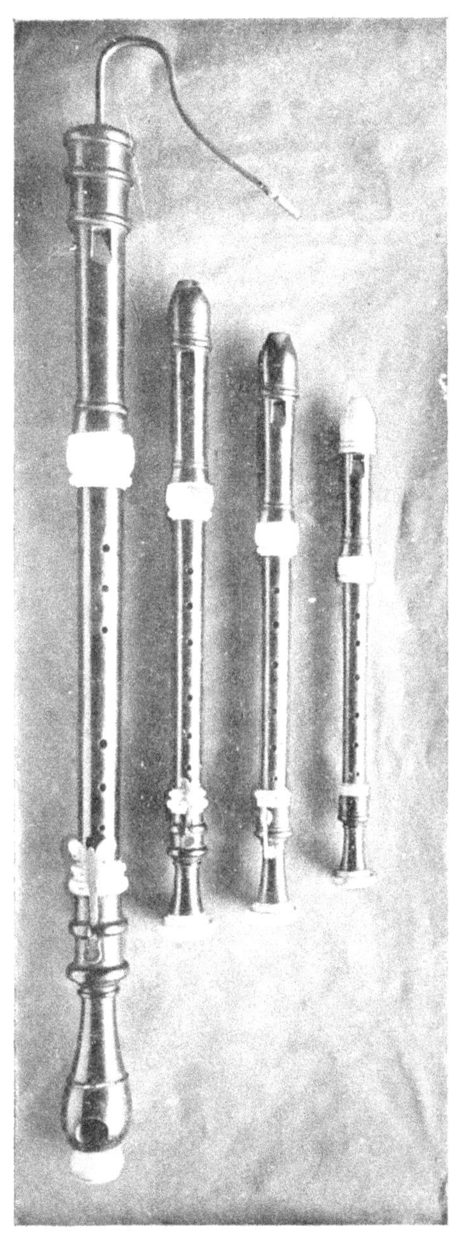

THE CHESTER RECORDERS

(Photograph by Professor R. Newstead, F.R.S., and lent by Dr. Joseph Cox Bridge, M.A., to both of whom grateful acknowledgment is made)

[*face p.* 188

the treble stave, and is pitched in F. The Alto is in the key of D, the Tenor in C, and the Bass in F, its range being down to the first D below the bass-stave. The Treble was thus an octave above the Bass, with the two means between them, a fourth and a fifth below the Treble respectively. Smaller Recorders were made which had a still more extended upward compass, and larger basses which descended lower. The increased size of the latter made some device necessary which would enable the player to reach the head of the instrument and still finger with ease. The difficulty was overcome by the use of a bent tube which carried the air from the player's lips to the top of the Bass-Recorder.

The makers of the early Recorders are unknown ; but from the Eighteenth Century, Bressan (who made the set at Chester) and Stanesby (father and son) may be mentioned. The last-named maker was probably the last of the famous English workmen, and later than this Recorders in sets were probably not made. The Bass fell into disuse first and was followed by the others in order ; but the instrument, in some form or other, persisted until very late, and the Nineteenth-century flageolets were really nothing but high-pitched Recorders. Their manipulation may vary somewhat from that of the Recorder, but they still possess the notch, the fipple, the direct blowing, and the thumb-hole at the back of the tube. Such flageolets were named " English Flutes " by those who made them, and under this name the early true Recorder often went. The fact that the Chester quartet is of so late a date renders it less valuable from the historical point of view, but specimens of earlier Recorders, though not in complete sets, may be seen in many museums ; a quartet in Nuremberg being complete except for a reproduced treble. These specimens date from the Sixteenth Century.

Recorders, like some other wood-wind instruments, were sometimes made double—*i.e.* with two pipes side by side, and intended to be used together ; one probably playing the melody while the other supplied the accompaniment. This use of double-pipes is very ancient and was already cultivated in Dynastic Egypt, as well as in Greece and Rome.

The English text-book for the instrument is " The Genteel Companion : Being exact Directions for the Recorder : With a collection of the Best and Newest Tunes and Grounds extant.

Carefully Composed and Gathered by Humphrey Salter, 1683." This book gives rules on fingering, cross-fingering, the production of harmonics ("Pinching Notes"), *etc.*, and the music is printed in a special kind of Tablature. It should be noticed that many writers speak of a hole in the instrument covered with skin as a characteristic feature. They probably derived their knowledge from an example in the Victoria and Albert Museum, which has such a hole. What this hole was intended for is not clear—perhaps it may have been accidental, or even experimental. Humphrey Salter describes his instrument fairly minutely, but says nothing of such skin-covered openings; moreover, the instrument in the museum is not Sixteenth Century, as is generally supposed, but Nineteenth Century.

Literary allusions to the instrument, and drawings of it, appear rather early in English history, the latter going farther back than the former. The University Library of Glasgow, and the Bodleian, Oxford, possess Psalters containing pictures of the Recorder, one dating from the Twelfth Century and the other from the Thirteenth. Early metrical romances, such as *The Squyr of Lowe Degre,* mention the instrument; and in the work alluded to it is given as "Recorde" (used as a noun). These early specimens cannot have been very perfect instruments; although the pictures represent them with a number of finger-holes the *Promptorium Parvulorum* (first half of the Fifteenth Century) gives a Recorder as a "lytyl pype, *canula,*" not a very happy definition. But the Latin writers usually referred to it as *Fistula Anglica* (English flute or whistle). The transverse flute was then already known as *Fistula Germanica.* A verse attributed to the reign of Henry VII, and once on the wall of the Leckingfield Manor-house (Yorkshire), is interesting as it draws attention to the technicalities of performance:

> The Recorder of his kind the mean doth desire;
> Manifold fingering and stops bringeth from him his notis clear;
> Whoso list to handle an instrument so good
> Must see in his many fingering that he keep time, stop, and mood.

The "manifold fingering" probably refers to cross-fingering, "pinching," *etc.* Towards the end of the Sixteenth Century, John Howes (*A Familiar and Friendly Discourse*) suggests that children should learn the Recorder in addition to other instruments ; and many other allusions to the instrument could be cited. Shakespeare alludes to the Recorder more than once ; the remarks passed by the Amazonian queen on Quince's performance immediately springs to mind : " Indeed he hath played on his prologue like a child on a Recorder ; a sound, but not in government " (*Midsummer Night's Dream*, V, 1). The scene in Hamlet, in which the instrument plays an important part, is too well known to need quotation. Milton still uses the word in *Paradise Lost*, and in a way that shows the instrument to have been kept distinct from the flute at the middle of the Seventeenth Century :

> . . . anon they move
> In perfect phalanx to the Dorian mood
> Of flutes and soft recorders ;

the softness of the tone being once more remarked. There is no reason for suspecting the accuracy of Milton's musical allusions, for he was an accomplished musician—as was his father—and at the house in Bread Street, London, the poet met the most celebrated musicians of the day—the whole of the Playford *coterie*. John Evelyn uses the term Flute douce in 1679 (November 20) : " There was also a *flute douce* now in much request for accompanying the voice."

The historical references to the Recorder are interesting, and afford a good idea of the uses to which the instrument was put. Henry VII employed players on the Recorders, and his bluff son, enthusiastic musician that he was, must have had a special liking for the instrument, judging by the number he had in his possession (list in *Harleian MS.* 1419, British Museum). On some of these he doubtlessly played himself, for we are told that he performed on the Recorder as well as on sundry other instruments. A very sumptuous set is described in the manuscript just mentioned : " Item. A case covered with crimeson vellat havinge locke and all other garnisshementes to the same of Silver gilte with viii Recorders of Iverie in the same case twoo bases garnisshed with silver and guilte," and a very costly set of Recorders this must have been. Among the other entries are : " Item. One case with vi recorders of Boxe in it " ; " Item. viii Recorders greate and small in a case covered with blacke leather and lined with clothe " ;

"Item. Twoo base recorders of waulnuttre one of them tipped with silver the same are butt redde woodde"; "Item. vi Recorders of Ivorie in a case of blacke vellat." There were over half a gross of Recorders in his collection. At the burial of Queen Elizabeth seven musicians for the Recorders drew allowances for mourning liveries; they were Alphonso Lanier, Robert Baker, and five members of the Bassano family (Lord Chamberlain's Records, 1603). Private music-lovers of that reign also used the instrument largely, if the case of Sir Thomas Kytson is to be taken as typical;—he left several specimens, seven of them in one box.

With the accession of the first Stuart, the Recorder became still more popular, and thence on to the end of the century we find them mentioned uninterruptedly in the State Papers. The list for July 15, 1628 (excusing musicians from paying subsidies), contains the names of six players on the Recorders. In 1635/6 there was a "warrant to pay £4 15*s.* to John Adson for a treble Cornet and a treble Recorder." The players on this instrument are alluded to again on November 12, 1663; and so it would be possible to go on quoting, but for the similarity of the entries. Four performers only are mentioned in the list of "Musicians in the Mask, 1674"; probably the basses had partially fallen into disuse by then, having been replaced by newer bass instruments. The records of the City of London show that the Recorder was used in the civic pageants round about 1675. In 1683, as we have seen, Salter's *Genteel Companion* was published, which shows that the popularity of the Recorder—in its treble and tenor forms, at any rate—was not yet on the wane. In 1683/4 (February 16), Henry Purcell was appointed keeper, *etc.*, of all the king's instruments, which included several Recorders. And when, in 1695 (November 30), "Dr. John Bull and Mr Bernard Smith" were appointed "in the place of Mr. Henry Purcell, deceased," Recorders were still in the collection. We cannot leave the century without seeing what Samuel Pepys has to say on the subject. On April 8, 1668, he writes: ". . . I to Drumbleby's, and there did talk a great deal about pipes; and did buy a recorder, which I do intend to learn to play on, the sound of it being, of all sounds in the world, most pleasing to me."

In the Eighteenth Century the references become fewer, but this does not argue that they had become obsolete yet;—in the early years of the century at all events. It is possible that the gradual changing of its name may have caused some allusions to it to be overlooked. It was often referred to simply as "Flute," and sometimes as "Common Flute," the *Traversa* being known as the "German Flute." Handel was very fond of the Recorder and made great use of it. He was always careful to make clear which family of instruments he intended should perform any particular passage; and in the Handel Society's issue of his scores, the distinction is clear between the *Flauto* (Recorder species) and the *Traversa,* occasionally *Flauto Traverso* (German Flute). The Bass Recorder, for which Handel also wrote parts—but called it the Bass Flute or the English Bass-Flute—was as good as obsolete, as far as common use went. It is curious that the good old title fell into disuse before 1700, and the noble family became known as "flutes" and "common flutes" at that period. Dr. Joseph C. Bridge (lecturing before the Musical Association on *The Chester Recorders*, Session 27, 1901) is of opinion that although the treble Recorders were still being manufactured as late as the middle of the Eighteenth Century, the bass had died out long before. He also said that since Malone, commenting on the *Hamlet* quotation on the Recorder, did not have the vaguest notion as to what sort of an instrument it was, we were forced to the conclusion that the big fipple-flutes were quite unknown by the middle of the Eighteenth Century, and that by the end of it the whole family was extinct (*v. also* DOTWAY, FLAGEOLET, *and* PINCHING-NOTES).

REEL: An ancient dance-form chiefly used in Scotland, where it was, and is, performed by two couples. It is not possible to fix upon its origin with any degree of certainty. The name could have been derived from a Scandinavian source (*cf.* Danish *Riel* or *Riil;* and Norwegian *Ril*), or from the Teutonic word (through Anglo-Saxon) meaning to turn rapidly. Even a Keltic origin could be suggested for the form. It consisted of the usual four or eight measures repeated, common to most dances, and the time-signature was generally 4/4, though specimens in 6/4 are to be met with. A variant used in Ireland differs chiefly in point of speed. The Reel, taken altogether, is of interest from the terpsichorean rather than from the musical point of view. In England some of the Sword-dances were closely akin to the Scotch Reels, except that the number of couples engaged was three. Skeat, quoting from Todd, gives : " Geilles Duncane did goe before them, playing this *reill* or daunce upon a small trump " (*News from Scotland*, 1591), and on the strength of this, several writers have supposed that the person mentioned performed the Reel as a solo-dance. Personally, I think the piece was merely played upon a small " trump " on the occasion in question, and not danced at all. The music of the Reel is generally a succession of equal quavers, with occasional semiquavers—but differing from the Strathspey (*q.v.*) in that it rarely has the dotted rhythm peculiar to the latter.

REGAL: A small portable organ sometimes with a single set of pipes and occasionally with a double set (" a pair of Regals ") ; producing its music by means of reed-pipes—chiefly of the beating type, set into vibration by air from bellows at the back of the instrument. Later on the Regal was supplied with further pipes of varying types, but the name was still applied to the newer instrument, which may be described briefly as a portable chamber-organ. Coming into use at about the middle of the Fifteenth Century, the Regal became very popular in England, and by the time that the more developed forms of the instrument were evolved in the first half of the next century it was in very common use. It was very artistic in construction and a good deal of ornamentation was frequently put into it. References to the Regal in the State Papers are fairly frequent and show that the instrument was used by the best musicians of the period. The Lord Chamberlain's Records for May 28, 1560, refer to a warrant to deliver " five yards of crimson velvet, to cover one payre of regalls, and one yarde of purple satten to line the same." A similar entry refers to " four pair of regalls and virginalls " and provides for the supply of crimson velvet for covering them, and for payment for " ornamenting the same with gold and silver lacquer." On June 10, 1673, Henry Purcell was admitted as " keeper, maker, mender, repayrer, and tuner of the regalls, *etc.*," and ten years later the instrument was still mentioned. In 1697 the celebrated Bernard Smith is given in Volume 487 of the Lord Chamberlain's Records as Organ maker and " tuner of the regalls." In 1699 the salary attached to this post was forty pounds per annum. Exactly what the use of the Regal was so late in the Seventeenth Century is not clear ; it is possible that the name was still attached to the formula of appointment, while the instrument no longer served. The environment, *par excellence*, for the Regal was in the music-room or great hall of the cultured classes in the Middle Ages.

RELISH I : Used as a verb, To Relish meant, in the Seventeenth Century, to embellish with graces or ornaments. The writer of *Lingua* (I, 1) gives the term this sense when he writes : " O, but the ground itself is naught, from whence Thou cans't not relish out a good division." Shakespeare, in *Two Gentlemen of Verona* (II, 1), has : ". . . to relish a love-song like a robin-redbreast."

RELISH II : As a noun the word was the name of a particular ornament that had a couple of variations in the Double Relish and the Sliding Relish. The nature of the grace will be understood from a couple of the commonest interpretations given to the term Double Relish in Playford's day :

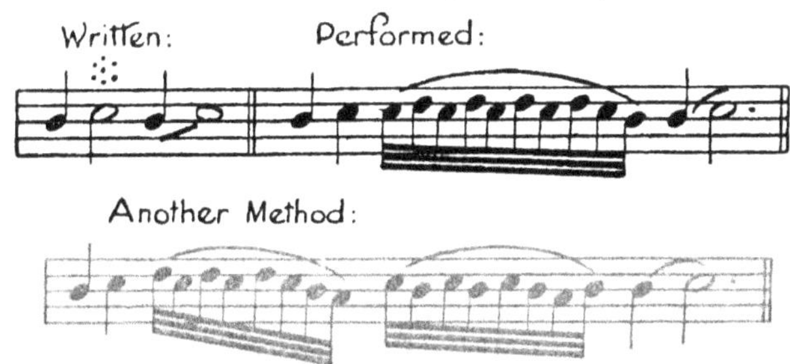

RIBIBLE. v. REBECK.

RIGADOON, or RIGODOON : A dance-form in duple time, not unlike the Bourrée (Bore), and being to the natives of Provence what the Bore was to those of Auvergne. Generally written in *alla breve*, with three or four repeated sections each of four measures, the form was lighter and quicker than the Bourrée ; it commenced on the last quarter of the bar and ended on the third. It was customary to write the third of the four sections a third lower than the others, in order to create a pleasing contrast in tone-colour, and to make of it a true Trio (*i.e.* in three parts). Some uncertainty exists concerning the derivation of the term, some authorities stating that the dance was named after its supposed inventor, one Rigaud. The popularity of the form in England caused more than one attempt to be made to find an origin for the name in this country, and the derivation from *Rig*, a frolic, trick, or wanton romp, has been suggested ; but where the rest of the word is to be sought these ingenious etymologists do not divulge.

Coming to England during the last quarter of the Seventeenth Century, the form was used by Henry Purcell, a specimen of whose "Riggadoon" was published by John Playford in *Musick's Hand-maide* (1689). Henry Playford's *Apollo's Banquet* (1690) contains two examples of the dance, one of them being in triple measure. Both of these last-named Rigaudons are included in the "newest tunes of dances," and the uncertainty of the measure seems to prove that it was not yet very well known in England. Mention of the form in the Eighteenth Century is generally confined to set-dances composed by French dancing-masters (*v.* Weaver's *Art of Dancing*, 1706 ; and Tomlinson's *Six Dances*, 1720).

In the country of its origin the Rigaudon was of a light and lively character, and, according to Richelet, "a joy and a pleasure to dance." It became exceedingly popular until, in 1664, the Parliament of Provence prohibited its use. Like most of the dance-forms that were taken from the village-green into the Court ball-room, the Rigaudon was changed considerably by its elevation. The spontaneous movements of the countryman gave place to a more settled and premeditated step which ultimately outlived the dance itself. Its use at Court in France extended from the reign of Louis XIII to the date at which the Revolution swallowed it up in the general ruin.

The Suite-writers used the Rigaudon extensively, and the examples they evolved were often of an elaborate nature, abounding in technical difficulties for the instruments to which they were assigned. Though already mentioned by Mersenne (*Harmonie Universelle*, 1636), we do not meet with the form in common use until we arrive at the time when Lully and his followers were writing for the opera of Louis XIV. During the latter part of the Seventeenth Century and the first half of the Eighteenth, the Rigaudon was of very frequent occurrence, only falling below the Menuet and Gavotte in point of numbers.

The use of the form in England cannot be considered as

universal as that of some of the earlier dances, such as the Pavane, Galliard, and Coranto ; and it was probably only the prevailing taste for French forms in art that popularised it at all in this country.

RISE. *v.* BEAT.

ROTE, ROTTA, ROTTE. *v.* CROWD.

ROUND : An exceedingly ancient form of English vocal composition, being a Canon in the unison or octave, but differing from the Canon chiefly in this respect. In the earliest days of its career the Round was a serious piece of writing, and although generally provided with secular words, some examples have an extra text of a sacred nature. This is the case in the most ancient specimen known, the old Round "Sumer is icumen in" (*Harleian MS.* 978; British Museum; early Thirteenth Century). Like its successors this Round exhibits the usual form of a serious Catch for four voices which enter one at a time at stated intervals, and supported by a two-part *Pes* or bass. The composer (given by William Chappell in *Popular Music of the Olden Time* as John Fornsete, a monk in the Abbey of Reading) added instructions for the performance of the Round to the music: "Hanc rotam cantare possunt quatuor socii. Paucioribus autem quam tribus aut saltem duobus non debet dici; praeter eos qui dicunt pedem. Canitur autem sic: Tacentibus ceteris, unus inchoat cum his qui tenent pedem. Et cum venerit ad primam notam post crucem (✠), inchoat alius; et sic de ceteris. Singuli vero repausent ad pausaciones scriptas, et non alibi, spatio unius longae notae."

That the Round was very popular at the period in which "Sumer is icumen in" was written, and common even earlier, is clear from the writings of Walter Mapes (a prelate of Oxford) of a date anterior to that of the Round just mentioned. Later the form became hopelessly entangled with the Catch, and often there was little to choose between them except, perhaps, in the decency of the words used—especially in the Seventeenth Century (*v.* CATCH).

The term Round was also applied to the round-dance, so called from the circumstance that it was performed in a circle (*cf.* the German *Reigen*). In this use it often appears as "Round O," *Apollo's Banquet* (Playford, 1690) containing four specimens so labelled.

ROUND-O. *v.* ROUND.

ROYAL MUSIC: The sovereigns of England have always entertained a body of singers and instrumentalists, generally known as "The King's Musick." From Saxon days, when perhaps a few Gleemen (*q.v.*) were employed, or Norman times when "Minstrels" took their place, to the late Seventeenth Century, when the king had a full staff of musicians (strings, wind, percussion, vocalists, and accompanists), a fully equipped Chapel, and often private chamber-musicians also—the King's Musick was a feature in the musical life of England, and the standard by which all other organisations were measured. Henry the Seventh's musicians included: Eighteen Gentlemen of the Chapel (among whom were organists, *etc.*), five sackbuts and shalms, several trumpeters, and minstrels (*q.v.*). Henry VIII was more ambitious, as became so able a musician, and if the list of instruments belonging to the king (*Harleian MS.* 1419; British Museum) counts for anything, enough performers were employed to provide excellent musical results. At the Coronation of Edward VI there were twenty Gentlemen of the Chapel, eighteen "Trumpettors," sixteen "Musicians" (among whom were several well-known violists), five flutes (probably Recorders), two "Vialls" (presumably Bass-Viols), a Harper, a "Bagge piper," four "Syngers," nine "Singinge men," "The King's Harper," and seven of the "King's Majesty's musicians" (private music). At the funeral of Queen Elizabeth there were in the royal service: seven "Violins" (Treble and Tenor Viols; *v.* article on the Viols), seven Recorders, seven Flutes, six Hautboys and Sackbuts, five "Lutes and others," twenty-two Trumpeters, and four "Drums and Fiffes." The number of performers on any particular instrument varies from year to year; but as a general rule is tended to increase as time went on.

In the reign of Charles I the "list of his Majesty's musicians" (in 1641) contained the names of "Master of the Musique" (Nicholas Lanier), eighteen "for the wind Instruments," thirteen "for the violins," twenty-three "for Lutes, Violls and Voices" (a list that contains such celebrated names as those of John Lanier, Nicholas Duvall, William and Henry Lawes, John Wilson, Diedrich Steffkins, Daniel Farrant, and John Mercure), one Harper, one Virginalist, one instrument-maker, and one "Organ keeper and tuner," not to mention one "musician extraordinary and stringer of the lutes." Charles the Second's musical establishment was very large, and a list of musicians "paid in the Treasury of the Chambers Office" in 1668, for example, shows fifteen violins at £46 10*s*. 10*d*. each per annum, seven more at £46 12*s*. 8*d*., and two at £58 14*s*. 2*d*.; three composers (including Matthew Locke at £46 10*s*. 10*d*.), three musicians "for the Wind Musick," and others. The private musicians of the king in that year numbered ten, in addition to Dr. Gibbons as Virginal-player, John Hingston as Organ-tuner and repairer, and Richard Hudson (succeeded by Brockwell) as Keeper of the King's Instruments. In addition to the usual consort, Charles II formed an exquisite band of twenty-four violins, modelled on the lines of the French *violons du roi*, such men as John Banister (the Elder) and Lewis Grabu directing them.

The duties of the royal musicians were not light. They were compelled, under threat of instant dismissal, to keep themselves in proper practice and were expected to rehearse punctually and regularly. Their services were required for coronations, royal funerals, marriages, and receptions in honour of foreign embassies; besides the usual work of performing at State balls, Masques, and assisting at special performances at the play-house patronised by the king. Music while the royal family was at dinner was probably supplied by the king's private chamber-musicians. There can be no doubt that the example set by the Court was followed by the nobility; and, as is to be expected, each grade of society imitated the one above it as far as their means would allow. The result of this was a very active cultivation of the musical art in England; and to a great extent the high standard of native music, especially under the later Tudors, was due to the encouragement, patronage, and personal example of the sovereign. Henry VIII sowed the seed of England's musical preeminence under Elizabeth, and, as far as his music was concerned at least, we might say with all due deference, *O, si sic omnes!*

RUBIBLE. *v.* REBECK.

RULES: In the Sixteenth and Seventeenth Centuries the lines upon which music was written were frequently termed Rules.

Playford speaks of a scale or Gam-ut (*q.v.*) "drawn upon fourteen Rules and their Spaces."

SACKBUT: The old English name for the Trombone. Like its improved successor, the Sackbut achieved absolutely true intonation by means of a sliding tube that lengthened and shortened the whole, thus producing the notes required. By modulating the distance of the slide the player could gauge the intonation with a niceness only obtainable on stringed instruments stopped by fingering. It is a peculiar circumstance that an instrument used in England so long under one name should decline in favour, to appear again under a new name—the Italian augmentative form, *Trombone.*

The story of the Sackbut resolves itself into nothing more than the early history of the Trombone in England. A mural painting by Dürer on a wall in the Town Hall of Nuremberg (end of the Fifteenth Century) will show how little antiquated the Sackbut looked. The error of supposing this instrument to have been a distinct type must be avoided. In France it was called the *Saquebute*, in Germany the *Busaun* or, as is still the case, *Posaune;* in Italy its name was always *Trombone* (*i.e.* great Tromba).

The development of the idea of a wind-instrument capable of altering its pitch by lengthening and shortening its tube must have begun very early. But the notion of a double tube sliding did not materialise until the single, straight tube had passed through a long period of experiment, during which it was first folded upon itself in a loop. This doubling of the tube would easily have suggested the idea of making joins so that one of the bends could be drawn out and back. This development must have been complete by the end of the Fourteenth Century, although the instrument was not introduced into England in its perfect form until the second half of the Fifteenth. At about this time it appears in the form shown in Dürer's picture. Additional Manuscript 7099 (British Museum) contains the item: "May 3, 1495. To foure Shakbusshes for their wages, £7." If four specimens were already used in the royal service before the end of the century, it is safe to assume that they were introduced somewhat earlier. The illustration of the Posaune (*Busaun*) in Virdung's work of 1511 shows an instrument differing very little from the modern form. Shortly before the date of that book, the manufacture of Sackbuts was taken up by the Neuschel family of Nuremberg, and Hans Neuschel, and his sons Hans and Georg (Jorg), were the acknowledged makers of first-class instruments of this category.

The country from which England received the Sackbut can probably be determined by a consideration of the etymology of the name. No useful purpose will be achieved in giving all the suggested derivations of the word, and I shall not waste space on speculation. There can be little doubt that the Sackbut came from one of the countries that used a kindred name for the instrument. These are France, Spain, and Portugal. Now, in the earliest English references we find the spelling *Shakbusshe* (*temp.* Henry VII, and the Lord Chamberlain's Records), and, not finding the final *t*, we must search the languages that likewise did not use this consonant. Such a procedure would rule France out, and cause us to turn to the Iberian Peninsula. In a list of Queen Isabella's instruments of music there are the entries : " One Sacabuche of silver in three pieces. . . . Another Sacabuche Grande of silver which has two pieces " (*c.* 1500). In Spanish the word *Sacabucha* was used, says Skeat, to designate a tube or pipe which serves as a pump (Spanish *Sacar*=to draw out, and *buche*=a maw or stomach). While agreeing with Skeat's etymology of the first half of the word, we must oppose the second half. A better derivation would be from the Spanish *Bucha*, evolved from the Latin *Buxus* (boxwood), from the pipes made of that material. And to strengthen this argument we have the Portuguese form *Sacabuxa.* The name of the instrument, then, if not the instrument itself, comes from Spain or Portugal, and though France and the Low Countries in all probability obtained the word from the same source, there is nothing to show how the final consonantal sound became changed to *t.* When dealing with imported terms at the end of the Fifteenth Century we must be guided more by the sound than by the appearance of a word. The spelling of foreign, and often of native, words was more frequently phonetic than not. The earliest uses of the word show the Spanish pronunciation more clearly than the French, and why the French form of the word was afterwards adopted is a mystery. We need not occupy space with a dissertation on derivations clearly founded on error, and thus we can ignore the identification of the name with the Chaldee

Sabeca (*via* Sambuke). But the mistake has led more than one otherwise trustworthy authority to speak of the Sackbut as a kind of stringed instrument.

The Sackbut is frequently mentioned in the literature of the Sixteenth and Seventeenth Centuries; in fact, so often do we find it that quotation will be unnecessary, since everyone will have come across at least one such reference in an early play or other work. Similarly, the Lord Chamberlain's Records contain entries relating to the appointment of players on the Sackbut, the purchase of instruments, and so on, from 1503 uninterruptedly until the end of the Seventeenth Century. During the last-named century the English players enjoyed a European reputation, and they were much sought after by foreign princes. During that period, too, the instrument must have been capable of excellent effects, and played as it was, through a mouthpiece more conical than cup-shaped, the tone must have been softer than we are accustomed to from its successor. The Sackbut was used in varying numbers in the royal band (ten players being maintained at one time) and in the Chapel Royal, to accompany the sacred music. During the reign of Henry VIII it was already used in Canterbury for a like purpose.

In the Eighteenth Century the Sackbut passed through a peculiar and unaccountable experience. Early in the century Robert Creyghton still mentions it with "its unfolded tubes of brass" (*Add.* 37074, *c.* 1727; British Museum), but whether it was still a popular instrument is very much open to doubt. It did not fall out of use entirely, for in conservative organisations such as the royal band it was still employed. But as an instrument in common use it was gone. So much so, that during the Handel festival of 1784 Dr. Burney had the greatest difficulty in securing performers on it, and was only helped out of his quandary by six players employed in the King's own band. On that occasion the instrument was used in the set, Tenor, Bass, and Double Sackbut (Contra-bass). When in the Nineteenth Century the Sackbut reappeared in England, it was with an Italian name, and as Trombone it has since been known.

SARABAND: A dance-form of great importance, which, after passing through an interesting and eventful career, finished as an indispensable movement in the classic Suite. Originally a slow and dignified dance, the Saraband was quickly relieved of its solemn characteristics when it came to England, and became a sort of Country-dance after the style of a Sir Roger de Coverley; and the music written for it was naturally also affected in the same manner and to the same degree. But before the change was completely wrought, it enjoyed considerable favour in a shape somewhat similar to its French form, to which we shall return later.

Charles II was particularly fond of the Saraband and it was consequently much used at his Court; nor was he above taking part in it himself. But the tendency was to make it an altogether lighter dance than it had been on the Continent, and it was this tendency that made it the popular form it became. Indeed, when a certain Italian named Francisco composed a Saraband while visiting England, it became such a prime favourite that the Chevalier de Grammont felt impelled to write: "It either charmed or annoyed everyone, for all the guitarists of the Court began to learn it . . . and a universal twanging followed." It is therefore not surprising to find all the composers of that reign busily engaged in creating new music for this dance. John Playford, in his *Musick's Handmaide* (1663), gives nine pieces suitable to the dance, some of them by William Lawes. The 1678 edition of the same work contains eight new Sarabands; while the second part, published in 1689, gives two more specimens by Dr. John Blow. Playford's *Musick's Delight on the Cithren* (1666) contains five Sarabands in Tablature on a four-line stave, two being by Matthew Locke, two by Dr. Charles Colman, and one by Simon Ives. *Apollo's Banquet* (1690) followed with another four examples. Playford's *Court Ayres* (1655) contains no fewer than fifty-three Sarabands, and this alone can give us a very good idea of the "universal twanging" of Sarabands that followed the first admission of the form into high society. The fact that the work just mentioned was published during the Interregnum makes no difference, for secular music suffered little, if at all, under the Commonwealth. The specimens given in these publications show how completely the Saraband in England had deviated from the path marked out for it in France.

Originating in the Middle Ages in Spain, the Saraband was a

form possessing strong Spanish characteristics with more than a tinge of orientalism. Whether it was a Moorish dance influenced by Spain, or a Spanish dance modified by the conquering Moors, need not detain us. A great many derivations for the name have been suggested, but the most likely seems to be that from the Spanish *Sarao*, a ball or meeting for dancing. Pineda's *Spanish Dictionary* (1740) gives *Sarao* as coming " from the Arabick," thus giving an Arabic name to a dance that was probably largely influenced, if not actually originated, by the race that occupied Spain.

The descriptions given by early Spanish writers force us to the conclusion that the Saraband must have been a dance deserving of very severe criticism. The historian Juan de Mariana (1536–1624), in his *Tratado contra los Juegos Publicos,* says : ". . . at this point mention need only be made that among the other inventions that these late years have produced, there is a dance and song so wanton in its words and so ugly in its movements, that it is enough to fire the most virtuous." On another occasion Mariana calls it " el pestifero baile de Zarabanda." The use of the word *baile* and not *danza* is significant, for on the authority of Gonzalez de Salas (middle of the Seventeenth Century), the *baile* was a dance in which the whole body was free to indulge in all sorts of movements, whereas *la danza* did not permit even the arms to assist, and in it the feet alone were allowed liberty of motion. The sinuous and suggestive movements of the body in the *baile* help to make more certain of the Moorish descent of the dance. Even Cervantes attacked it, and Guevara was of opinion that the shameful freedom of the Saraband was rapidly becoming " a disgrace to Spain." The result was that shortly before the close of the reign of Philip II (1598) its use was prohibited for a time.

In Spain at about this period the Saraband was generally danced solo by women, who accompanied themselves with song and castanets ; sometimes, in place of the latter, on the guitar ; and skilful performers were much sought after.

At the end of the Sixteenth Century the form crossed the Pyrenees into France. The cultured taste for art in France at this period soon gave the Saraband an aspect it had never presented in the country of its infancy. It was rapidly purified of its objectionable characteristics, and became one of the most popular dances that the Sixteenth and Seventeenth Centuries possessed. Becoming popular at a time when dances like the Pavane were high in favour, the Saraband was used in an exceedingly grave and stately manner. Its measure was triple, its construction the common one of two eight-measure sections repeated, and its rhythm—like that of the Chaconne—

usually :

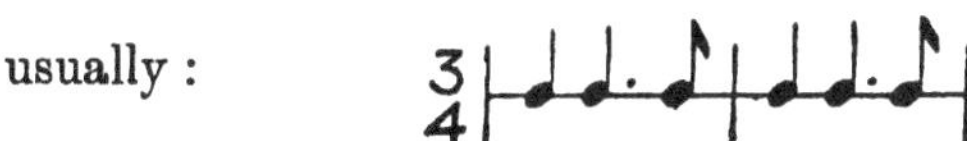

When the form had been accepted as a purely instrumental movement and its dance origin lost sight of, some composers wrote even extended Sarabands with variations. In the Suite it was placed between the Courante and the Jig, thus completing with the opening Allemande (Almain) the *Partita* of the classic period of Johann Sebastian Bach.

As a dance the Saraband was known in at least three forms. First, as the solo dance of an abandoned Spanish coquette; secondly, as a picturesque, stately, and ballet-like creation of the French opera and Court; and, thirdly, as the merry, light, and innocent Country-dance which it became in England.

SENNET: A military signal obviously different from the Flourish (*q.v.*). It is ordered in a great many Elizabethan stage-directions, and Shakespeare in common with his contemporaries often has "a Sennet sounded." The term is to be derived from the Latin *Signum* through Old French *Sinet, Senet, Segnet,* a little sign or signet, and hence a signal. Some authorities (*e.g.* Grove, Stainer, and Barrett, *etc.*) suggest an etymology from the word meaning seven, and suppose the Sennet to have been a signal of seven notes. Such a derivation cannot explain away such Old English spellings as Cygnet, Signet, and Signate.

SEQUENCE (*SEQUENTIA*)*:* A hymn dating from the Ninth Century and used to follow the Gradual (hence "Sequence"). In its original form it was a composition using for its text the vowel of *Alleluia,* a sort of jubilating rhapsody. Such pieces of music were termed, from their use, *Pro Sequentia;* and by a contraction of the abbreviated form *Pro sa,* they became known as *Prosa* or Prose. Pope Pius V, in the second half of the Sixteenth Century, abolished most of the Sequences, leaving only the few still in use.

SERPENT: A wood wind-instrument of bass pitch, played through a cup-shaped mouthpiece. It was thus akin to the Cornet (*q.v.*) and acted as the bass to that category of instruments. Made of two pieces of shaped wood and covered with leather, the long (eight feet) tube was rendered capable of being managed by three U-shaped curves, the instrument ending at the bell-end in a bend of a half-circle. This sinuous curving of the body gave the Serpent its name. The tube opened gradually from a little over half an inch at the mouthpiece adapter to about four inches at the bell. The hemispherical mouthpiece was made of various materials—in the early specimens generally of ivory—and was connected with the body-tube by a brass fitting. The length of the instrument was divided by six finger-holes, arranged in two groups of three, not very far apart, but at a great distance from the mouthpiece and bell respectively. The series of notes that could be produced varied enormously with the period and the dexterity of the player. So also did the compass, all other things being equal. The range extended from just over two octaves (de Felice, *Encyclopédie*, 1772) to four octaves (Lichtenthal, *Dizionario della Musica*), but the latter referred, of course, to the late specimens of the instrument and quite exceptional performers. Keys were added to the instrument in the Eighteenth Century, and when it was admitted into the English military bands it was often made of metal. Concerning its tone, the critics of the Serpent differed as much as they did touching the tone of the Cornet. Judging by all the evidence, I should imagine that the tone, like the technique, depended upon the player; for overblowing easily rendered it rough and harsh. Treated very carefully the Serpent was capable of tonal effects that were very useful for certain purposes. Used in small country churches (especially in France, where it was known as *Serpent d'Eglise*) it supported the choristers' music in place of the absent organ. In England, too, it was often used for a similar purpose, and it persisted until the end of the Eighteenth Century—in remote communities even as late as the Nineteenth. Composers of note used it occasionally, Wagner and Mendelssohn, among others, writing parts for it in isolated works. The active life of the Serpent extended from the end of the Sixteenth Century to the first half of the Nineteenth, when it was superseded by the bass-tuba.

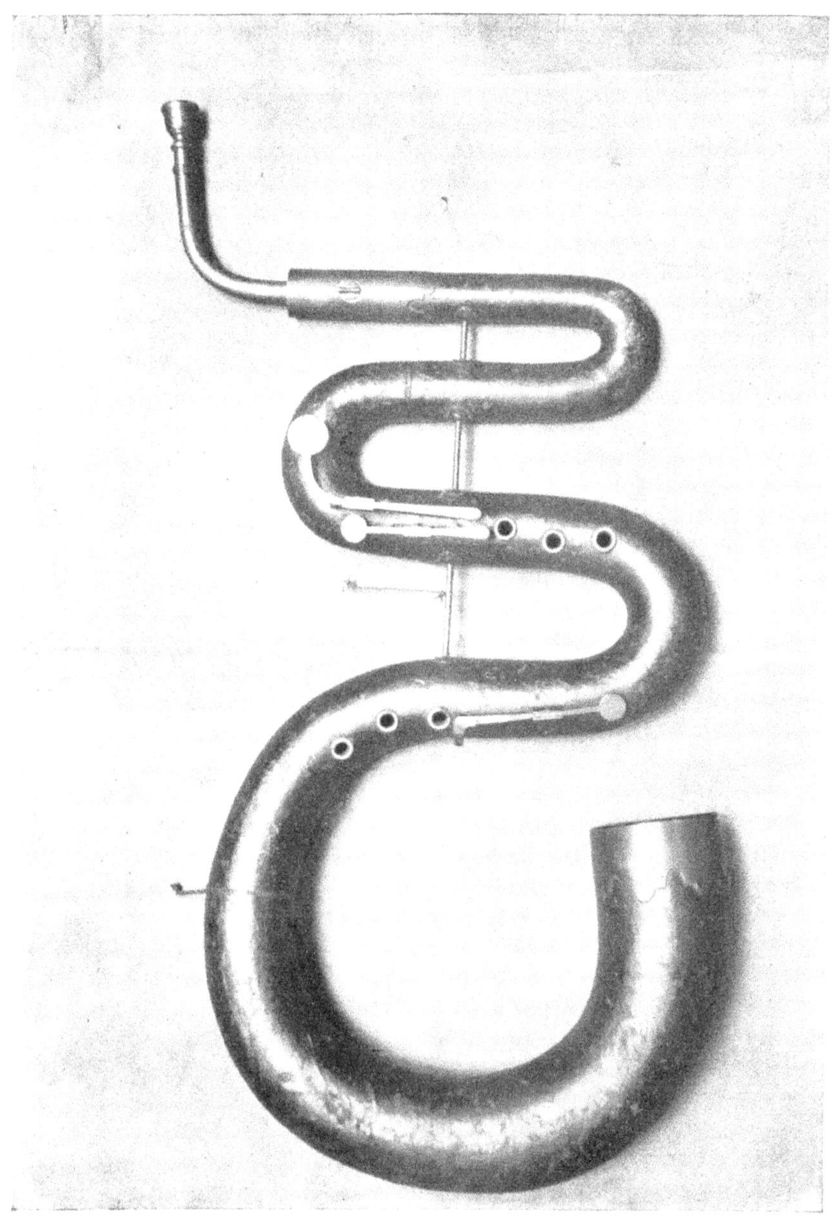

SERPENT
By Gerock Wolf, London
(*Victoria and Albert Museum*)

[*face p.* 206

SESQUIALTERA. *v.* PROPORTION.

SET or SETT : The old English name for Suite ; a succession of short pieces strung together, and connected only by their character, and sometimes by their key. A consideration of the history of the Set would run on practically the same lines as a dissertation on the Suite or Partita, of which it was the English counterpart.

SHAKE : The word Shake was used in the Seventeenth Century as we employ the term Trill to-day. The " Shaked Grace " differed from the " Smooth Grace " in that a trill or rapid repetition of a pair of notes formed part of it. The " Close Shake " is rather difficult to understand in an age that knows no frets on the bowed instruments ; but Playford's description, together with the ingenious way in which he illustrates it, should make its nature clear. " The Close Shake is when you stop with your first finger on the first fret and shake with your second finger as close as you can." Trilling with a finger as close as possible to another would produce very little difference in pitch in the case of a fretted instrument, for it must not be forgotten that the finger has to be advanced to the next fret to produce a note a semitone higher. Playford illustrates this as follows :

where the varying elevation of the A shows that although there is an audible effect from the action of the trilling finger, the difference in pitch is not as great as a semitone. The modern violinist produces what is probably equal, musically, to the " Close Shake " when he employs *Vibrato.*

An Open Shake is " when you stop with your first finger on the first fret and shake with your third finger on the third fret " (Playford), thus producing a trill the two notes of which were a whole tone apart. Simpson (1659) adds that wider than two frets, or a whole tone, " we never shake."

SHAKED BEAT. *v.* BEAT.

SHAKED CADENT. *v.* CADENT.

SHAKED ELEVATION. *v.* ELEVATION.

SHALM or SHAWM: An ancient wood-wind instrument of conical bore, played with a double reed, and made in a variety of pitches from treble to bass (*v.* BOMBARD). It was provided with a number of finger-holes, which produced a useful range of about ten notes. Later, when the instrument became developed, the position of the reed was altered, the finger-holes were supplied with keys, and the bore of the tube reduced considerably (*v.* HAUTBOY).

The name of the instrument was derived from the Old French *Chalemie* (also *Chalemelle*), " a little pipe made of a reed or of a wheaten or oaten straw " (Cotgrave, 1660), which in its turn was borrowed from the Latin *Calamus*, a reed (under Greek influence). The French word *Chalumeau* came after the English Shalm was in use, and thus was not the ancestor of the latter. In Germany the instrument was called *Schalmey* (Modern German, *Schalmei*), Praetorius (*Syntagma Musicum*, 1619) giving illustrations of the whole family, from Discant Schalmey to the Bass-Pommer. The " oaten pipe," referred to so often by the Sixteenth-century writers, was most probably a primitive Shalm, especially when we remember Cotgrave's definition.

The name, in the spelling Shalmye, is found in Chaucer's *House of Fame* (*l.* 1218) : " That maden loude menstralcyes In cornemuse and Shalmyes " ; and in Gower's *Confessio Amantis* (end of Fourteenth Century ; *Lib.* 8 ; *l.* 2483) : " With Cornemuse and Schallemele." One of the inscriptions on the walls of the Lekingfield Manor-house (copy in the British Museum ; *Royal* 18 D. II) says that " A shawme makethe a swete sounde," *etc.* (*temp.* Henry VII). During the reign of Henry VIII the instrument attained to Court use, and in the *Privy Purse Expenses* of that sovereign there is the entry : ". . . paied to phillip of the pryvay chambre for a shalme xxvj*s.* viij*d.*" (February 25, 1530). Sir Thomas Elyot, in the *Castel of Helthe* (1533), recommends the playing of Shalms for the reason that he gives when approving of the Sackbut, for they " requyre moche wynde " and are thus beneficial to the " entrayles whiche be undernethe the mydreffe."

The exact meaning of the qualifying " still " or " styll " in the phrase " Styll Shalmes," as we find it in the Lord Chamberlain's Records (*e.g.* for a coronation, apparently that of Henry VIII, 1509, and in other places), is not quite clear. The same list also includes the names of musicians for the "Sakbudds and Shalmes of the Privee Chambre," and we are forced to the conclusion that between Shalms and Still Shalms some difference must have existed. Some authors suggest that the word "still" referred to pensioned musicians, but I prefer to connect the adjective with the same one used with the *Zinken* (Cornets) on the Continent, where "Stille Zinken" meant softer toned Cornets (*Cornetto Muto*), the difference being due to an alteration in the fitting of the mouthpiece. It is quite possible that some similar procedure made of the ordinary Shalm a "Still Shalm." In the Henry VIII entry just alluded to, the first musician mentioned is termed the "Marshall." Now, in the early history of the Waits (*q.v.*) the word *Marshall* was often applied to the leader or conductor of such a band of municipal musicians. If this has any bearing upon the subject under consideration, it will prove that the "still shalms" were the instruments known as Waits and played by musicians bearing the same name (*v.* WAITS).

SHALMEY, SHALMOY. *v.* SHALM.

SHARP: To-day the adverb is used to indicate that the pitch of a note is too high for perfect intonation, while the noun is the name of the symbol used to raise the pitch of a note by a semitone. In these uses the word replaces John Playford's *B Mi Cliff* (*v.* CLIFF.) But in Playford's day the expression "sharp" was employed more commonly to indicate a major interval, chord, tuning, or key. Thus we meet, and can explain, such phrases as "Sharp Third" (a major third), and "Harpway Sharp," an accordance by which the strings of the Bass-Viol were tuned to the notes of a major chord (*v. also* HARPWAY).

SHAWM. *v.* SHALM.

SIGNED CLIFFS: The name given in the Seventeenth Century to the Treble, Tenor, and Bass Clefs, because "they are always set at the beginning of the Lines on which is prickt the Song or Lesson" (Playford). Christopher Simpson calls them the three "Signal Cliffs" (*Principles of Practical Music,* 1665).

SINK-A-PACE. *v.* GALLIARD.

SLIDE : An ornament, obsolete as such in England, which consisted of a rapid series of notes connecting two successive notes of a composition diatonically. Its motion was either ascending or descending, according to the position of the second note, and it differed very little from the Elevation (*q.v.*) :

Written: Performed: Written: Performed:

In some of the older Virginal-Books an oblique line cutting the stem of a note showed that a Slide was intended. In such case, and, indeed, in all other cases also, the note written or printed was the last note of the ornament. This Grace, though its name has fallen into desuetude, is still used, being written out as Grace-notes.

SLIDING RELISH. *v.* RELISH.

SLUR : A word still in use to designate the sign for *legato* performance, but employed in the days of the Lutes to a succession of notes that could be played in an ascending direction upon any one string. In Lute-playing only the first note of the Slur was struck, the remaining fingers falling successively, and merely suggesting, by the rising ring of the string's vibration, the effect of elevation. The result of such manipulation was a kind of upward glide, which connected the first (struck) note of the Slur with the next struck note by a sort of faint *glissando.* A certain amount of virtuosity was necessary to perform this delicate embellishment really well, and it was used probably only in the most artistic of solo work.

SNAP, or *SCOTCH SNAP :* A peculiar rhythmic figure, not unknown in Seventeenth- and Eighteenth-century Italy, that characterises a good deal of Scottish music, particularly the Strathspeys. It consisted of the reverse form of a very common figure in dance-music (dotted-quaver, semiquaver) :

the short note taking the accent.

SOB, SOBB : A term employed by the lutenist to name an effect produced by reducing the finger-pressure on the strings immediately after the latter had been struck. Mace (*Musick's Monument*, 1676) describes the procedure as follows : " Cause them (the strings) to sobb, by slacking your stopping hand so soon as they are struck ; yet not to unstop them, but only so much as may dead the sound on a sudden. This gives great pleasure in such cases." The peculiar vibration of the Lute-strings produced many charming and delicate effects, such as the Slur (*q.v.*) and the Sob, difficult to understand to-day without practical examples.

SOL. *v.* ARETINIAN SYLLABLES *and* GAMUT.

SOLFAING. *v.* SOLMISATION.

SOLMISATION : The practice of singing to a series of syllables (*v.* ARETINIAN SYLLABLES), adapted by Guido d'Arezzo to fit his Hexachords in the same manner as the earlier Greek system of nomenclature applied to the tetrachords. The Eleventh-century monk realised the difficulty of teaching pupils the mysteries of his scale-series, mutations, *etc.*, without some ready means of memorising the sequence of the syllables and the notes they represented. To this end he evolved the hymn to St. John, mentioned in the article ARETINIAN SYLLABLES, and arranged them in such a way that the *Ut* of the verse was sung to a C, the *Re* to a D, the *Mi* to an E, the *Fa* to an F, the *Sol* to a G, and the *La* to an A. The series of notes which he named by these means constituted the " Natural Hexachord." When a melody happened to overlap, in either direction, the limits of a single hexachord, mutation had to be resorted to (*v.* HEXACHORD SYSTEM).

In England the term Solfaing (not to be confounded with the modern Tonic Sol-fa System) was often employed in place of Solmisation. John Dowland, in his translation of the *Micrologus* of Ornithoparcus (1609), used the verb " to solfa," and also the expression " The Rules of Solfaing." A similar use of the word as applied to " Lessons " or exercises is to be seen in the book-title : " In Nomines and other Solfainge Songes."

SPANISH VIAL. *v.* GITTERN.

SPINET : A keyboard instrument closely resembling the Virginal (*q.v.*) in its action, but differing from it in shape. While the true Virginal was in a rectangular case, the Spinet was in the form of a harp laid horizontally. The keyboard ran obliquely when compared with the central line. Sometimes the outward form of the case was five-sided—the longest side being generally the back and the next in point of length the keyboard front; the remaining three short sides connected these two; one on the left-hand side, and two on the right. In some instruments the side containing the keyboard was the longest. The name of the instrument is thought by some to have been derived from that of its supposed inventor, one Joannes Spinetus of Venice (*c.* 1503); but the more likely derivation would seem to be from *Spina*, a thorn or point, referring, of course, to the quill plectrum. Only by accepting the latter origin for the word can I reconcile such spellings as Espinette, which we meet with (*inter alia*) in the *Diary* of Samuel Pepys. Beyond the difference in shape, practically all that was said of the Virginal applies here also; except that, perhaps, the Spinet outlived the other.

The Spinet certainly dates from the reign of Henry VIII, in its English use at any rate, for *Harleian MS.* 1419, containing a list of the king's instruments, includes: "Two faire paire of newe long virginals made harpe fashion, of cipres and keis of Ivorie." But during the second half of the Seventeenth Century the Spinet rose to a point of popularity in England that entirely eclipsed its earlier vogue. The most famous makers were John Hitchcock, Stephen Keen, and Charles Haward (Hayward ?). Spinets autographed by Hitchcock are to be found between 1664 and 1703. Keene worked as late as 1719. The last-named builder is advertised by Playford as follows: "Mr. Stephen Keene, maker of Harpsycons and Virginals, dwelleth now in Threadneedle Street at the sign of the Virginal, who maketh them exactly good, both for sound and substance." Examples of Spinets made by Thomas Hitchcock (late Seventeenth Century and early Eighteenth), and by Johannes Player (*c.* 1700), are to be seen in the Victoria and Albert Museum (London). Pepys had a peculiar name for the instrument, for on June 14, 1661, he enters: "I sent to my house, by my Lord's order, his Shipp and triangle Virginal"; but the use of the word "triangle" shows clearly that the instrument meant was a Spinet. But on April 4, 1668, Pepys writes: "To White Hall. Took Aldgate Street in my way,

SPINET
By John Player, *ca.* 1700
(*Victoria and Albert Museum*)

[*face p.* 212

and there called upon one Hayward, that makes Virginalls, and there did like of a little espinette, and will have him finish them for me; for I had a mind to a small harpsichon, but this takes up less room." On July 13, 1668, he adds: ". . . I to buy my espinette, which I did now agree for. . . ." Two days later: "at noon is brought home the espinette I bought the other day of Haward; cost me £5."

Some of the foreign Spinets were very elaborate. One by Hans Ruckers of Antwerp had a smaller instrument, tuned an octave higher, placed on the left-hand side of the larger keyboard; this was a survival of the practice resorted to in the earlier Virginals, and which accounts for the expression "a pair of virginals." A beautiful example of Italian work is preserved in the Victoria and Albert Museum, by Annibale dei Rossi of Milan, dated 1577, and decorated with nearly two thousand precious and semi-precious stones. This specimen has a compass of four octaves and a semitone.

SPRINGER: An ornament in common use during the Seventeenth Century, and given by Playford as follows:

Christopher Simpson said that the Springer made "the Sound of a note more acute, by Clapping down another Finger just at the expiring of it."

STAY. *v.* HOLD.

STILL SHALM. *v.* SHALM.

STING: An embellishment in lute-playing, of similar effect to the left-hand Vibrato of the violinist. No modern phraseology could describe this effect so well as that used by Thomas Mace (*Musick's Monument*, 1676). After saying that the grace was not "modish in these days," he continues: "First strike your note, and as soon as it is struck, hold your finger (but not too hard) stopt upon the place (letting your thumb loose) and wave your hand . . . downwards and upwards, several times, from the nut to the bridge; by which motion, your finger will draw, or stretch the string a little upwards and downwards, so, as to make the sound seem to swell with pritty unexpected humour, and gives much contentment upon cases." This effect is, of course, perfectly easy to understand; the waving motion of the hand rolled the tip of the stopping finger backwards and forwards in such manner as alternately to sharpen and flatten the note very slightly. This produced the faint "beat" responsible for the tremulous note.

STRATHSPEY: A dance peculiar to Scotland, not unlike the Reel, except that it is slower. A feature of the form is its dotted rhythm in duple time. Although it was probably danced earlier, named specimens of the Strathspey are not found before the Eighteenth Century. Writers of that period were not always careful to keep this form and the Reel distinct, and we must conclude from this circumstance that with slight modifications the same music could be made to serve for both dances. The music written specifically for the Strathspey, however, shows a frequent use of a characteristically Scottish rhythmic figure of a very short note, taking the accent, preceding a longer one:

and known as the "Scotch Snap."

STUMP: Beyond the fact that this was an instrument strung with wire, and that Daniel Farrant was its inventor, nothing is known of it. The only reference to it that I have been able to trace is the one made by Playford in 1661 (*v.* POLIPHANT).

SWORD DANCE: A very ancient dance that bears a close resemblance in many respects to the Morris Dance, though there is sufficient to separate them. It is true that sword-bearers were common adjuncts to the Morris, but the mumming that was added to the latter keeps it distinct from the true Sword-dance. The Morris (*q.v.*) seems to have been a later development, and was subject to many influences at different periods; yet the possibility is present that—in one of its aspects at any rate—it may be descended from the Sword-dance. Still, the fact remains that such dances as the *Danse des Bouffons* and the *Matacins*, both using sword and shield, were mentioned by Tabourot at the same time as he speaks of the Morisco; so that an equal possibility remains that the Sword-dance may have been derived from one of these. But whatever its origin, it is undoubtedly of great antiquity, and may have had its beginnings in some primitive war-dance. It is quite likely that the wooden staves used by the Morris dancers in the South may have been borrowed from the swords of the dancers in the North of England.

The character of the Sword-dance was that of a serious and complicated performance; its movements were exceedingly intricate, and they called for great physical activity and a quick brain. It was invariably danced by men only, and in some some parts of the country it is still cultivated. Mr. Cecil J. Sharp, who is responsible for *The Morris Book*, also collected music and steps for the Sword-dance (Novello), and his researches bear all the signs of authority.

TABERET. *v.* TABOR.

TABLATURE: A system of musical notation in which letters, figures, and other signs took the place of the usual method of writing notes. As far as England is concerned the system was employed chiefly for the music of Lutes, Viols, Citterns, and other fretted instruments, and for wind-instruments like the

1. Lute Tablature etc.
(Robt Dowland. A Musical Banquet, 1610)

2 Viol Tablature etc.
(John Playford Musick's Recreation on the Viol, Lyra-way, 1661).

Recorder and Flageolet. On the Continent of Europe Tablatures were even used for the keyboard instruments, but this never became popular in England. For the other instruments mentioned, however, this method of writing was very largely used, especially towards the end of the Sixteenth Century and the first half of the Seventeenth.

Commencing with the "letter" Tablature for the lutes, the system was in principle very simple. A stave of lines as numerous as the strings of the instrument carried letters of the alphabet corresponding to the frets on the fingerboard. The letter *a* on the second line, for example, meant the first fret on the second string; an *e* on the fourth line represented the fifth fret on the fourth string, and so on. The times values of the notes were given by the note-tails used in ordinary notation, placed over the stave of Tablature. Music for the Cittern or Gittern was written on a four-line stave, one for each string (or, rather, pair of strings). In like manner, the Tablatures for the Viols were written on six or seven-line staves, according to the stringing of the instrument. Since each fret on all these instruments was at the distance of a semitone from its neighbour, it follows that on the same line of the stave, *a* and *b* were a semitone apart, *a* and *c* a whole tone asunder, and so on. Such a system, of course, was possible only so long as the instruments were fretted. In the case of wind-instruments, figures sometimes replaced the letters, each number applying to one of the finger-holes. A different method was applied for the Recorder and Flageolet, for which the "Dot-way" system (*q.v.*) was used. The different Tablatures varied slightly in different countries and periods, but none are really difficult to decipher.

TABOR: A drum varying in size and method of handling according to the period. The word itself is of great antiquity, and occurs in our literature very early. Derived from the Spanish *Atambor* (the initial *A* of which betrays a Moorish origin) the word—and presumably the instrument also—passed through Old French and Middle French *Tambour*, to the English of the Thirteenth Century (*Tabour*). In this form the word is to be found in *Havelock the Dane* (*Ed.* Skeat; *l.* 2329): "The gleumen on the tabour dinge"; in Stephen Hawes' *Pastyme of Pleasure* (1506; *Chap.* xvi); and in Shakespeare's *Winter's Tale* (IV, 4): "O, Master, if you did but hear the pedlar at the door, you would never dance again after a tabor and pipe." At about the date of the last-named play, the *u* of the French word was dropped. As "Taborn" the instrument is mentioned in *Octavian Imperator* (Fourteenth Century; *ll.* 67/8): "Ther mygth men here menstralsye, Trompys, Taborns, and cornettys crye." The diminutive form "Tabourine" (not to be confounded with *Tambourine*) was also frequent, and may have had something in common with the long, narrow, Provençal drum called *Tambourin.*

Shakespeare uses this word in *Antony and Cleopatra* (Act IV): "Trumpeters, With brazen din, blast you the city's ear, Make mingle with our ratling tabourines." The variant *Tabouret* was contracted to the familiar biblical *Tabret.* The player on the Tabor was called a *Taborer*, or *Tabrere;* in the latter spelling Spenser used it in the *Shepherd's Calendar* (May 23, 1579): "A lusty tabrere That to the many a hornpipe played."

The Tabor in its commonest form was small and light, but covered at both ends with skin. It was attached to the left wrist or thumb of the player by a loop, and beaten with a single stick held in the right hand, while the fingers of the left hand played on the pipe (*v.* TABOR-PIPE). Larger Tabors were carried obliquely on the left side, suspended from a belt and played by beating with two sticks on the uppermost head.

TABORINE. *v.* TABOR.

TABOR-PIPE: A small instrument of the whistle or fipple-flute type, with two finger-holes in front, and a third for the thumb at the back of the pipe. As its name implies, it was almost inseparable from its companion, the Tabor or hand-drum; and together they supplied the music for the rustic dances of old England. The bore of the pipe was a cylindrical one, and on account of its evenness a rich supply of harmonics was procurable. With the assistance of these the range of the pipe covered an octave and three notes, though not completely chromatic. The Tabor-pipe was manipulated by the left hand only, leaving the right free for beating the drum.

TABRERE. *v.* TABOR.

TABRET. *v.* TABOR.

TANGENT: The brass pin or stud which was the characteristic feature of the Clavichord (*q.v.*). It was about an inch in height, broadened at the head, and tapering to the point at which it was fixed into the end of the key farthest from the player's hand. The depression of the key caused the Tangent to rise and strike the string stretched above it. This method of playing did not cause the whole length of the string to vibrate in a way that would produce one tone, but divided it into two portions, one much larger than the other. Both of these parts vibrated, but the unwanted section was damped by means of a strip of cloth interlaced between the strings. Now, since the tangent formed, at one and the same time, the bridge and the hammer, it follows that sounds of only a certain strength (or lack of strength) could be obtained; for the moment that the strings were struck too forcibly, the pitch of the note was raised. The tone however, such as it was, proved to be of a very sweet quality, and on that account the instrument played by Tangents persisted in favour for a long time. More than one Tangent could be used for each string, the pitch of the note depending upon the position of the Tangent (*v.* CLAVICHORD).

TENOR STRING: The fifth string of the Viol, counting downward from the treble. This string was in the ordinary accordance tuned to G, and hence was often named the Gamut-string.

THEORBO: A large lute, sometimes used as the Tenor instrument in a consort of lutes (when the Arch-lute was also used), and sometimes as the Bass. It differed from the ordinary lute in that it had extra bass-strings at the side of the fingerboard (not over it), which were plucked with the thumb to provide a bass. They were tuned from a peg-box situated at the side of the ordinary one, or, as in many examples, from pegs in a second head placed above the other as an extension. These extra strings were only used unstopped. In appearance the Theorbo was a very complicated instrument, and we can very well understand how it came about that when Inigo Jones brought an example to England, the authorities at Dover mistook it for a Popish infernal machine, and sent the bearer of it to the "council table" for trial. The strings passing over the fingerboard were mounted in unison pairs as usual, and the Theorbo was possibly even more popular in England as an accompanying instrument to the voice than was the ordinary lute. This system of using extra bass-strings was a very ancient one and can be seen in use in many of the very early plucked instruments. Thomas Mace (*Musick's Monument*, 1676) says that "the Theorbo is no other than that which we call'd the old English lute," and that it was originally so called. He adds that as many as twenty-four strings were used on the instrument and that he personally—"truly on my Theorboes I put twenty-six strings."

The Lord Chamberlain's Records abound in references to the

Theorbo, but a selection of them will suffice to show how common it was. On June 6, 1629, a warrant was issued to pay £20 to John Coggeshall for a year's supply of strings for "his Majesty's lutes and theorba," a like sum being paid on other occasions. In 1632 the sum of £15 was paid to Mr. Roberts for a "theorba," and in 1633 a similar sum was given to Nicholas Lanier for another example. In the list of musicians for 1660 John Jenkins appears as a musician on the Theorbo in the place of John Coggeshall, and John Lylly in succession to John Kelleye. Captain Henry Cooke, Master of the Children of the Chapel Royal, taught the choristers to play on the lute, theorbo, and other instruments, and in 1667 received £110 for the work—a sum which included strings, "fire for the musicke roome," and other extras. Entries referring to payments for such service are frequent. In 1673 Pelham Humphrey, the new Master of the Children, received £6 each for two Theorboes supplied for use in the schoolroom, cheaper instruments being thus employed for teaching purposes. In 1679 the cost of a Theorbo for professional use was £14, but in 1662 Henry Cooke received £20 for one, no doubt a fine specimen, richly ornamented and possibly old—for twenty pounds was a large sum of money at the middle of the Seventeenth Century. The instrument was used well into the Eighteenth Century, and only the improvement in the keyboard instruments caused its decline.

THOROUGH-BASS: A bass-part written continuously throughout a composition, and on that account also called Through-Bass (Italian, *Basso Continuo;* German, *General-Bass*). It was indicated by one or more figures placed under the bass notes of a harmony, each figure referring to a note of the chord required; this provided the basis of the accompaniment, and the intelligent use of the system required the ready brain of a really well-schooled musician. It appeared first in Italy at about the commencement of the Seventeenth, or perhaps the very last few years of the Sixteenth, Century, There seems to be little reason for supposing that this method of indicating the bass was the invention of any one person; it would appear rather to have been called forth by the necessity for some such means of writing a support for the monodies then becoming popular. The enthusiastic *coterie* of musicians and noblemen who made of Florence so important a musical centre at that period provided in their works the earliest examples of Thorough-Bass. In England it was taught in the last quarter of the Seventeenth Century, although, of course, isolated compositions printed earlier already show it—used probably in imitation of foreign examples.

THREE IN ONE or THREE TO ONE. *v.* PROPORTION.

THUMP: A form of composition of which little seems to be known; possibly only a variant of Dump (*q.v.*). It was mentioned in Thomas Ford's *Musick of Sundrie Kindes*, 1607: "A Pill to Purge Melancholie; M. Richard Martin's Thumpe."

TIE: In addition to the usual sense of this term—that of connecting two notes of the same denomination over an intervening bar—there was applied an older one which gave it the force of the present-day "slur," or sign of the *legato.* "The second sort of Tye," says Playford, "is, when two or more notes are to be sung to one syllable, or two notes or more to be plaid with once drawing the bow on the Viol or Violin"; a sentence which shows the old meaning in the first half and the modern sense in the second.

TIMBREL: An ancient tambourine; a shallow hoop of wood covered on one side only with skin, and having a varying number of metal "jingles" in the wooden frame. In the *Promptorium Parvulorum* (first half of the Fifteenth Century) the form *Tymbyr* occurs, and is defined as "a lytyl tabowre, *Timpanillum.*" "Tymbres" are mentioned in *Kyng Alisaunder* (Weber's *Metrical Romances*). Gower, in *Confessio Amantis* (*ll.* 1843/4) has:

Timbrel
(From a small drawing in British Museum Ms. Harleian 6563, ca. 1330)

> Wher as sche passeth be the strete
> Ther was ful many a tymber bete.

a spelling that with French influence would explain the name for a performer on this instrument (*Timbestre; Romaunt de la Rose, l.* 769). Timbrelle and Tymbrelle are clearly derivatives from Timbre or Tymbyr, and examples of the use of the word, and its more modern descendant, Timbrel, will be too common to need quoting.

A performer on the Timbrel is clearly shown among the figures in the "Minstrels' Gallery" of Exeter Cathedral (Fourteenth Century), and a drawing in *Harleian MS.* 6563 (British Museum), dating from the early years of the Fourteenth Century, shows the Medieval form of the instrument very well. The specimen illustrated has four jingles, and a straight line drawn across the parchment would suggest a catgut "snare," still used on the modern side-drum.

TIME (*TEMPUS*)*:* In Medieval music the quantitative relationship between the Breve and the Semibreve, the term being also used to designate the Breve itself as a unit of measurement. In Perfect Time (*Tempus Perfectum*) the breve equalled three semibreves, and was thus the contents of what we should call one measure in triple time. In Imperfect Time the breve contained only two semibreves. The signatures were a circle for the Perfect, and a broken circle or a semicircle (later the capital C) for the Imperfect. A line drawn through these signs halved the values of all the notes. Reversing the semicircle thus : Ɔ halved the values likewise, and a line through this sign further reduced the duration of the notes to a similar extent. A passage with the prefix : Ɔ̸ was thus four times as fast, and one with the signature : Ɔ twice as fast, as one marked with the simple : C. Fractions were sometimes used to reduce the values of the notes in the same way, as $C\frac{2}{1}$, $C\frac{6}{3}$, *etc.* The indication C2 is also frequently to be met with (*see also* MENSURABLE MUSIC, MOOD (*Modus*), *and* PROLATION).

TOY : A light and trifling composition, frequently mentioned in late Sixteenth- and Seventeenth-century literature. It seems to have possessed no particular features that could make of it an accepted form, and Mace's description of it (1676) probably fits it exactly : "Toys or Jiggs, are light squibbish things, only fit for Fantastical and Easie light-hearted people ; and are in any sort of time." There are three specimens of the Toy in the Fitzwilliam Virginal Book and another in Benjamin

Cosyn's Virginal Book (beginning of the Seventeenth Century). In *Musicke of Sundrie Kindes* by Thomas Ford (1607) there is a trifle called, " A Snatch and Away ; Sir John Paulet's toy," and this use of the word is typical of many.

TRIPLA (*PROPORTIO TRIPLA*)*:* The indication of triplicity in Mensurable Music. Sometimes it merely meant the same as Perfect Time or Mood, in which three notes of any value went to one immediately above it in the series (three breves to the long, and so on). Frequently the Tripla time (shown by a figure 3 above or below the stave) indicated the same as our modern triplet sign, and it was used when such a triple figure occurred in the body of a composition. In the Seventeenth Century the term was used simply to show triple time as distinct from duple. Some writers understood a quicker tempo to accompany the demand for Tripla ; *i.e.* a rhythm of threes in the time of twos.

TRIPLEX : An old term for triple time (*v.* TRIPLA). Shakespeare uses it in *Twelfth Night* (V. 1) : " the triplex, Sir, is a good tripping measure." The word was also employed to designate the third part in polyphonic music.

TRIPLUM. *v.* CANTUS.

TROPES : Interpolated pieces of vocal music used to extend the dimensions of the sacred service music, out of which grew the Sequences (*q.v.*). They became expanded as time went on, and eventually were given their own texts. The period during which the Tropes found favour lay between the Ninth and Sixteenth Centuries, after which they gradually fell out of use leaving only the few Sequences still in divine service.

The term was also applied to the closing *formulae* of the lesser doxology attached to the Introit. Each of the Church Modes originally had its own Trope, but later on a greater number for each mode was used.

TRUMPET MARINE : A very ancient stringed instrument played with the bow, and most probably evolved from the still more ancient Monochord. It must be remarked at the outset that the instrument came to England fairly late in its career, and when it did arrive was looked upon more as a curiosity than as a musical instrument calculated to give pleasure to a society already accustomed to far better things. Nevertheless, it was much used for the scientific observation of musico-physical phenomena, and thus deserves some consideration. There are not many references to it in our older literature, but such as there are require explanation. Moreover, the accounts given of it are usually so incomplete and full of error, that something on the subject may be of service. Samuel Pepys, writing in his *Diary* under date October 24, 1667, says: ". . . we in to see a Frenchman, at the house, where my wife's father last lodged, one Monsieur Prin, play on the trump-marine, which he do beyond belief; and the truth is, it do so far outdo a trumpet as nothing more, and he do play anything very true, and it is most admirable and at first was a mystery to me that I should hear a whole concert of chords together at the end of a pause, but he showed me that it was only when the last notes were fifths or thirds one to another, and then their sounds like an Echo did last so as they seemed to sound all together. The instrument is open at the end, I discovered; but he would not let me look into it, but I was mighty pleased with it, and he did take great pains to shew me all he could do on it, which was very much; and would make an excellent concert, two or three of them, better than trumpets can ever do, because of their want of compass." Pepys's mystification would not have been so great at the vibration of the natural harmonics had he but been able to satisfy his curiosity by peering inside the instrument and seeing the sympathetic strings there. But before going into the history of the instrument it will be interesting to notice that a concert, such as the diarist thought advisable, was actually advertised. In the *London Gazette* for February 1–4, 1674/5 (No. 961), was the announcement: "A Rare Concert of four Trumpets Marine, never heard of before in *England*. If any persons desire to come and hear it, they may repair to the *Fleece Tavern* near *St. James's*, about two of the Clock in the afternoon every day in the week, except Sunday. Every concert shall continue one hour, and so to begin again. The best places are one shilling, the other sixpence."

Although the Trumpet Marine was an amusing novelty when it was first introduced into England, it had passed through more than five centuries of usefulness. A representation of the instrument on the coping-stone over the door of the Abbey of Vezelay dates from the Twelfth Century; it is mentioned in a Fifteenth-century manuscript of Froissard; and when printed books became fairly common, accounts of it multiplied. Virdung gives an account and an illustration of it in 1511, and Agricola, in his *Musica Instrumentalis Deudsch* (1545), prints amusing metrical hints on its handling, and suggests that letters be painted on the fingerboard to assist the performer in finding the positions of the notes. The *Dodecachordon* of Glareanus (1547) gives a very full description.

It would be very unsafe to give to any particular country the credit for having invented or evolved the Trumpet Marine; but judging by the popularity it enjoyed in Germany very early in history, it would not be too speculative to look for its place of origin in that country. From the Thirteenth Century to the Sixteenth it was in great favour there—in the hands of the masses as well as in the study of the physicist. By the third quarter of the Eighteenth Century it had penetrated into every corner of Europe—and yet, to-day, it seems as little known as if it had belonged to the antiquity of Ancient Assyria.

In physical respects the Trumpet Marine, or Tromba Marina, as it was more generally known on the continent of Europe, consisted of a long, narrow, triangular box running in a gradual taper from its open base to the head or peg-holder. Perhaps the best description of it would be that it was constructed of three long (often six or seven feet) boards each in the shape of an isosceles triangle, so put together that the open end showed an equilateral triangle. It was, in the first stage of its career, provided with a single string which passed over a bridge that was one of the characteristic features of the instrument. This bridge, or shoe, as the old Germans called it, was curved in shape, one of its feet resting firmly on that side of the box which formed the belly, while the other foot, very slightly shorter, lightly touched the table. The result of this unequal pressure was to cause the vibrating string to set up a rattling between the short foot and the belly, and give the tone of the Trumpet Marine the peculiar buzzing quality that was its particular feature. Sometimes a morsel of ivory, glass, or metal was fixed to the loose foot of the bridge, the vibration of which, enhanced by a piece of glass let into the belly under the foot and against which it rattled, still further increased the buzzing effect. The tone that resulted was, according to many writers, so like that of a trumpet that no further search after the origin of the first half of the name need be attempted. The string was put into vibration with a short bow applied near the bridge. In operation, the instrument rested against the shoulder of the standing performer, its wide end on the ground. The string, which was of the thickness of a 'cello D-string, was stopped lightly with the thumb, and only harmonics were used. This being the case, it produced only the series of notes peculiar to the natural trumpet.

The fact that the instrument was particularly adapted to the production of overtones caused it to be developed, and further strings of varying length and differing tuning were added. These extra strings were not played with the bow, but merely used to vibrate in response to some note produced on the bowed string. Glareanus mentions a two-stringed Trumpet Marine. Praetorius gives the information that the first added string was half the length of the bowed string, thus producing the octave; but this, of course, was unnecessary, since modification by means of the tuning peg could easily have secured an octave without undue consideration for the length of the string. Praetorius (*Theatrum Instrumentorum*, 1620) gives an illustration of a four-stringed specimen, each string of different length. This particular picture shows the construction of the instrument very well. In Germany the term Tromba Marina seems to have been reserved for the older monochord form, and a variant—Trumscheidt—was used for the three- and four-stringed specimens (*v.* Valentin Trichter, *Curiöses . . . Exercitien Lexicon*, 1742). The sympathetic strings that interested Pepys so much were often placed inside the soundbox, and thus produced very peculiar effects from no apparent cause. Vidal speaks of such an example in the Conservatoire of Paris, and another with forty-two sympathetic strings is in the Victoria and Albert Museum, London. The present writer remembers having seen a very fine collection of these quaint instruments in the museum of Dr. D. F. Scheurleer at The Hague.

The tone produced by the Trumpet Marine varied with the skill of the performer, and judging by the widely different opinions expressed by many writers, one is forced to the conclusion that the skill of the performers varied too. The combination of the floating tone produced by harmonics with the rattling of the loose foot of the bridge must have been very original, and need not have been at all unpleasant. When Paganini removed three strings from his violin, and played harmonics, he merely converted his instrument into a small Trumpet Marine in effect; for the tension of the single string (G) depressed one side of the bridge only, leaving the other foot fairly loose and capable of independent vibration. Who knows how far the peculiar effects produced by the great violinist were due to such physical causes?

A great many improvements were introduced, but the present-day importance of the instrument will not merit more details being given under this head. The uses to which the Trumpet Marine was put were many and varied. Its social status fluctuated in different centuries, and those to whom it appealed ranged from the wandering vagabond to the ducal minstrel. In 1619 Praetorius said that "the minstrels carried it about the streets"—yet at the same time it was being used in the laboratories of the serious students of acoustics. One of the most dignified of its uses was to fill a part in the musical service of the nunneries. In this environment it probably took the place of the inaccessible wind-instruments, and it was employed in complete sets of three or four. In the hands of a careful player—one whose hand on the bow was not too heavy—the tone must have been eminently suited to accompany the vocal *ensemble.* Personally, I see no reason why they should have been less musical than, say, the Bass Cornets. In France the Trumpet Marine became very popular, and in 1666 no fewer than six performers on it were on the lists of the French king's musical establishment. Yet more amazing is it to find that as late as 1767 there were still references to it in the French State Papers. Its use in England was, as we have seen, only very slight from the musical point of view—although learned societies made a good deal of it for acoustical research.

TRUMP-MARINE. *v.* TRUMPET MARINE.

TUCK. *v.* TUCKET.

TUCKET: A military call stated by Francis Markham (1622) to have been "a signal for marching used by cavalry." This shows clearly how closely Shakespeare could keep to facts when he introduced technical details: "Then let the trumpet sound the tucket-sonance and the note to mount" (*Henry V,*

IV, 2). The derivation of the term would be through Old Northern French *Touket*, and Old French *Touchet*, a blow, from a Teutonic source (*cf.* German, *Tusch*, a flourish of brass). The *Tucket* may, originally, have been a drum-signal, as the Teutonic word from which it had its name had the sense of "to touch" or "to beat," and especially so since the noun Tuck meant a drum-beat (*cf.* the Italian *Toccata*, touched; *i.e.* music touched or struck on a keyboard, as distinct from *Sonata*, sounded, and *Cantata*, sung).

TUT: In lute-playing the Tut was the sudden deadening of a note just played, by damping the vibration of the string with the next finger.

TYMBYR. *v.* TIMBREL.

UT. *v.* ARETINIAN SYLLABLES *and* GAMUT.

VIAL, VIALL. *v.* VIOLS.

VIOLS: A family of bowed stringed instruments that became exceedingly popular in England. Indeed, they became so acclimatised in this country, that their foreign origin, at one period at any rate, was almost lost sight of. The influence they exercised on the history of English instrumental music was very great, and in this class of composition the English use of the Viols even affected continental art. In its commonest form the Viol was used in three sizes and pitches—Treble, Tenor, and Bass—and combined as mentioned in the article CHEST OF VIOLS. The instruments of this family are distinguished from those of the modern violin species by having a flat back, sloping shoulders, C-shaped sound-holes, a tail-piece fixed on a notched pin, and generally six strings. Their tone was soft and sympathetic, eminently suited to the music of the period, and especially well-fitted to be an accompaniment for voices—a use in which the Viols might be profitably revived to-day. The Treble-Viol was the first of the family to disappear before the irresistible invasion of the Violin. Its six strings were tuned in fourths with an interpolated third, as follows:

showing a tremendous range when compared with the modern violin. Possibly the gravity of the bass-string used on the body-size of the Treble-Viol was too great; and this circumstance, added to the greater facility with which the violin could be handled, conspired to hasten the demise of the treble.

The Tenor-Viol was tuned a fifth below the Treble:

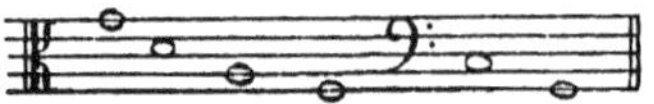

It was, as John Playford says, "an excellent inward part (*q.v.*) and much used in Consort (*q.v.*), especially in Fantasies and Ayres of three, four, five, and six parts." To ensure proper resonance for strings of such gravity, the size of the sound-box (body) had to be proportionately greater than that of the modern viola; and a specimen of the instrument in my possession is in its original condition. This is a very rare state of affairs, since vandal modernisers have been all too busy cutting down the depth of the ribs of the old Tenor-Viols in order to make them as easy of manipulation as the viola. The result of such cutting down was to reduce the air-contents of the body and thus entirely destroy the balance between string-weight and body-resonance. My example is labelled: "William Turner, at ye hande and Crowne in gravelle Lane nere Aldgate London, 1652," and thus dates from the period of the instrument's greatest popularity. The marks of the old catgut frets can still be seen impressed in the varnish of the neck. It was the custom to apply frets to all the instruments of the Viol family, even when they were not used Lyraway (*q.v.*), Playford observing that it was "a most sure and easie way for the first entring of Scholars, and after, to cut them off when they become perfect in the knowledge of all the several notes." Certain it is that the difficult divisions of Christopher Simpson could not be played easily with frets in the way of free movement for the left hand.

The Bass-Viol, or Viola-da-Gamba (leg-viol), because it was played between the legs of the performer, was used in three different sizes according to the particular purpose for which it was required. These were known as the Consort-Viol, the Division-Viol, and the Lyra-Viol (see these three headings). The tuning of the Consort-Viol was like that of the Treble-Viol, but an octave lower. The Lyra-Viol, of course, was tuned to

TENOR VIOL, by William Turner, London, 1652
In the author's possession
Size: Back, 16½in.; Greatest Breadth, 9in.; Length over all, 28½in.; Finger-board, 10¾in.; Ribs, 2¾in Left Sound-hole, 2⅞in.; Right Sound-hole, 2¾in.

[face p. 228

the chord indicated in each piece of music written for it and played from Tablature (*v.* LYRAWAY).

Each string of the Viol had its own name, counting from the highest downwards, as follows: Treble, Small Mean, Great Mean, Counter-Tenor, Tenor, and Bass.

The uses to which the Viols were put in England were of great interest and importance. Chronologically the predecessors, and later on for a time the contemporaries, of the violin family, though historically and structurally they had less to do with their successors, the Viols—in all probability introduced into England from the Netherlands—enjoyed a vogue here unequalled in any other country. Nowhere in Europe were the Viols clung to so tenaciously, and nowhere were they given up in favour of the violins with greater reluctance. The English performers brought their virtuosity to a very high pitch, and many foreign students came to England to perfect themselves in the art of Viol-playing. For this purpose Maugars came from France, Paul Kress, David Adams, Vogelsang, August Kuehnel, and others, came from Germany. At this period the technique of the English gambists exceeded that possessed by those of any other country, and the music written here often asks for great dexterity. Most of the musical publications at the beginning of the Seventeenth Century were arranged so that the Madrigals and Ayres which they contained could be performed equally well on the Viols. The decline of the Madrigal and the rise of technique soon made the composition of special music for the instruments of the Viol family an absolute necessity. At first the old vocal music sufficed and it was used for some time; but the advent of the craze for Divisions (*q.v.*), and the successive development of the In Nomine and the Fancy (*q.v.*), provided music to meet the popular demand. So rapid was this development of purely instrumental music that scarcely a single generation separated the time when the violist was compelled to play a well-known song if he wished to have a solo, from the period at which elaborate suites and fantasias were being written on an almost wholesale scale, specifically for each and every member of the Viol family, and for all of them in consort. Anthony Holborne, only four years before James I ascended the throne, issued a typical specimen of the former class of composition—music that could be played on wind-instruments, stringed-instruments, or sung. Giovanni Coperario (*né* John Cooper), Alphonso Ferabosco III, and their numerous contemporaries, were writing true Viol music, intended for this one purpose only, under the very next sovereign.

The State Papers preserved in the Record Office and a few public and private collections of manuscripts afford all the information necessary to give us a good idea of the instrument's English history. In 1526 the list of the royal musicians of Henry VIII contained fifteen trumpets, three lutes, three rebecks, three taborets, a harp, two viols, four drumslades, a fife, and ten sackbuts; but whether these instruments were ever used in combination is very open to doubt. The moral to be drawn from this list lies in the fact that only two viols appear in a list containing a great amount of percussion and brass. And even these two viols were played by foreigners—two Flemings named Hans Hossenet and Hans Highorne—at a salary of "xxxiii*s*. iiij*d*. paide monethly" each (*Egerton MS.* 2604; 17 Henry VIII). Only six years later mention is made of "three of the Viols," a remark that would point to the probability that there were more than three of them by then. The new names are now Italian. During the reign of Henry VIII a constant stream of embassies passed between England and Italy—and particularly Venice—and it is not at all surprising that many Italian musicians should be preferred to positions in the royal music. Henry had a very highly developed taste in the art, and his discrimination was well known. Therefore he rarely allowed a good player to enter any other service once he had formed a good opinion of the foreigner's performance. The Audit Office accounts for 1540 state that "Alberto da Venitia, Vincenzo da Venizia, Alexander, Ambroso, and Romano da Milano, and Joan Maria da Cremona" were appointed as "Vialls" during the king's pleasure at a wage of twelve pence per day. Henry's collection of viols was of very respectable size and quality (*v. Harleian MS.* 1419A). Exactly when English players first appear in the royal band cannot be fixed with certainty; but the first native name I have come across in the State Papers is that of Thomas Kentt "lately admitted to the Vialles in place of greate Hans deceased" (1549; Lord Chamberlain's Records). In 1554 (December 23) Thomas Browne was engaged as one of the

"Vyalls." In 1555 the word "Violon" is used, and we find it frequently during the reign of Mary Tudor and Elizabeth. These entries have caused many authorities to come to the conclusion that the modern violin was used in England thus early in the Tudor era. I shall return to this point later; for the moment let it suffice that I consider the term "Violin" to have been applied to the smaller Viols—Treble and Tenor—thus giving the Italian diminutive termination its proper sense, while the word "Viol" was employed for the larger, or bass, viol.

The accession of Queen Elizabeth and the general elevation of the musical plane in England had their effect upon the viols. Their use became more extended, and the excellence of the composers of the period settled the artistic future of the instrument. At Court the Italian performers were still employed, but English names began to become more and more frequent. The entries in the State Papers of that period provide a good deal of very interesting information of every kind. Thus, *Additional MS.* 5750 (British Museum) tells us that a "sett of Vyalls" cost the Queen "the some of 15 poundes" It is also instructive to note that the Italian players, who have hitherto been described as "Vials" or "Violons," appear in 1559 as "Violetts." There can be no doubt that the same Viols were meant in each case, and that "Violet" was used as a diminutive for Viol just as was "Violon." The prices paid by Elizabeth for a set of Viols seems to have been a usual one, for the "Account Book" of Trinity College, Cambridge, for 1595 gives the item: "xiii*li* for a sett of Vialles." The cost of "viall strings and mending ye College Instruments" was twelve shillings. Sir Thomas Kytson, of Hengrave Hall, paid 20*s*. for "a treble violin" in 1592, and when he died he left "six violenns." I have no doubt that Treble and Tenor Viols were meant in each case.

Towards the end of Elizabeth's reign the way in which the Viols were used is very interesting to note. Besides the work of 1599 already alluded to (*Pavans, Galliards, Almains, and other Short Aeirs both Grave and light, in five parts, for Viols, Violins, and other musical Winde Instruments*) Anthony Holborne published a *Cittharn Schoole* in 1597, which contains, among other compositions, twenty-three pieces for the Cittern in Tablature, with an accompaniment in ordinary notation for the Bass-Viol, and two for the Cittern accompanied by Treble, Tenor, and Bass Viols. In this case also, I am of opinion that Holborne meant Treble and Tenor Viols when he spoke of "violins" on his title-page. Another work which shows a typical use of the Bass-Viol as an accompanying instrument, is John Dowland's *Second Booke of Songs or Ayres . . . with Tablature for the Lute or Orpherian, with the Violl de Gamba* (1600). At the end of the last Tudor reign a new figure of great importance in the history of the Viols rose above the musical horizon in the person of Alfonso Ferabosco II (born *c.* 1580). He was "an excellent composer for instrumental Musick" (Anthony Wood), and was one of the first to write music Lyraway (*q.v.*). His importance lies in the circumstance that he, more than any other one musician, laid the foundations for that English school of Gambists and writers for the instrument which, according to Maugars (one of its most celebrated foreign pupils), surpassed all others in the world.

The question of the use of the modern violin in Tudor times is interesting and worthy of being cleared up. Carl Engel thinks that violins were used together with viols, lutes, *etc.*, from the time of Elizabeth onwards; the Rev. F. W. Galpin says: "Violins, as distinct from Viols, had already been included in the King's music; and at the time of Henry the Eighth's death they were played by six Italians from Venice, Milan, and Cremona. . . ." These two quotations are representative of many; and it may be well to consider a few pieces of evidence in opposition to these statements. For true violins to have been firmly established as orchestral instruments by the middle of the Sixteenth Century, would have made it necessary for the very earliest specimens to have been introduced. It is, I think, fairly well established that no instrument of the modern violin-family was made before the middle of the Sixteenth Century. It is, of course, quite possible, chronologically, for early examples to have been brought to England, especially when we remember how active was the correspondence between this country and Italy during the reign of Henry VIII. But to expect at least six violins to be accepted as an integral part of Henry's orchestra so early in the career of the new instrument is, I think, rather too much. When authenticated cases of their importation are recorded, the fact is especially noted as something unusual. On March 14, 1637/8 a "Treble Violin bought . . . for his Majesty's service" was paid for with the sum of twelve pounds (Lord Chamberlain's Records of that date), and on January 31 of the same year a similar amount was paid for "a Cremona Violin to play to the Organ." Here, clearly, treble viols are not meant, and this reference is probably the first in which the celebrated products of Cremona are mentioned. These entries occur more than eight decades later than the first mention of "Violins" in the State Papers. Had violins been used in England for so long a time, we should certainly not have had to wait until the mid-Stuart period for famous English performers on it to appear; especially when we remember the state of technical excellence shown by the native violists. How can the fact be explained away that we have to wait until Playford's *Introduction to the Skill of Musick* appeared before we find a picture of the true violin? The confusion, I suggest, was caused by the musicians of Tudor England modifying the Italian diminutive *Violino* for the purpose of naming the "small viol." The Italians themselves used the word *Violino* when referring to true Viols. An Italian chap-book of *c.* 1550 has on its title-page a picture of an old viol and the name *La Violina, etc.* The circumstance that the early players on the Viols at the court of Henry VIII were Italians, would help to explain the use of the Italian term. Furthermore, before the Restoration the violin was considered to be a far more inferior instrument, socially, than the Viol. Anthony Wood tells us that the gentlemen who attended music parties played on Viols, "for they esteemed a violin to be an instrument only belonging to a common fiddler, and could not endure that it should come among them, for feare of making their meetings to be vaine and fiddling." This being so, would so artistic a pair of sovereigns as Henry VIII and Elizabeth have employed them in their bands? It was necessary for a Charles II with his French tastes to make this innovation, and his imitation of the French king's band of violins was really the first sanction given the newer instrument. And even then many of the more orthodox among the older musicians complained bitterly at the change.

To return to the history of the Viols. The succession of the house of Stuart marked the beginning of the greatest period for the Viols in England. They came more and more into favour, even usurping the place hitherto held by the lutes. Composers and publishers encouraged the fashion by issuing ever-increasing quantities of music for the Viols. It was part of everyone's education to learn at least one of the instruments of the family, and to play on it at sight (Peacham, *Compleat Gentleman*). The literary works of the Seventeenth Century abound with references to chance visitors being asked to take up a Viol and " bear a part " in the consort. This explains the ubiquity of the Chest of Viols (*q.v.*). The manner in which the playwrights of the era helped themselves to the instruments proves how common they were. In *Twelfth Night* (I, 3) Shakespeare gives the sentence, " he plays o' the Viol-de-Gamboys " to prove the culture of one of his characters ; and in *Pericles* (I, 1) we have :

> You are a fair viol and your sense the strings,
> Who, finger'd to make man his lawful music,
> Would draw heaven down and all the gods, to hearken.

In George Chapman's comedy *Monsieur d'Olive* (*Act* III, 1606) a dandy of the period says : " Here shall stand my Court Cupbord, with its furniture of Plate : Heere shall runne a Winde Instrument : Heere shall hang my base viall : Heere my Theorbo : and heere will I hang myselfe." Middleton, in *A Trick to Catch the Old One* (1608), says : " She now remains in London to learn fashions, practise music ; the voice between her lips, and the viol between her legs, she'll be a fit consort very speedily "—a reference that shows how early the ladies played the Gamba in Stuart England. With this evidence of the instrument's popularity it will not be necessary to draw on the State Papers for further proofs. Suffice it to say that the *Calendar of State Papers* contains countless entries concerning the appointment of violists, their work, and their instruments.

During the Commonwealth the Viols suffered no neglect, in spite of the historians who would have us think of this as a mirthless and songless period. The Puritan wife of the Puritan soldier, Colonel Hutchinson, said of her husband that " he had a great love to music, and often diverted himself with a viol on which he played masterly." Of course, there were a few fanatics who thought that because the puritanical decree went forth against the ornate Cathedral music, all music should be banned. The notorious Solomon Eagles, who became a Quaker in 1660, burned his Viols and music. But the action of a few men like Eagles did not prevent music being cultivated very largely during the Commonwealth, though more space cannot be spared for a history of the music of those famous eleven years than suffices to draw attention to the musical publications that appeared. In 1653 East's *Fantasies for Viols* were issued. Roger L'Estrange's description of a private concert attended by Cromwell will be enough to show that the Protector did not ban music secularly, and since it includes references to the Viols it is worth quoting once more: "Being in St. *James* his *Parke*, I heard an Organ Touched in a little Low Room of one Mr. Hinckson's (John Hingston). I went in, and found a Private Company of some five or six Persons. They desired me to take up a Viole, and bear a Part. . . By and By (without the least colour of a *Design* or *Expectation*) in comes *Cromwell*. He found us playing and (as I remember) so he left us."

With the accession of Charles II the violin became a more serious competitor of the Viol. The formation of the select band of violins, already mentioned, gave the *coup-de-grâce* to the Treble and Tenor Viols, at any rate. The increasing number of the violinists required for the royal music and that of the nobility, offered a new incentive to musicians to take up the newer instrument. With artists like Davis Mell to imitate and teachers like John Banister (the Elder) to learn from, a school of violinists arose in England that compared very favourably with the Viol-players of two or three generations earlier. The Bass-Viol alone persisted in public favour, and it was a full century more before the Gamba could be said to have become antiquated. Samuel Pepys gives a few pieces of interesting information in his *Diary* concerning the Bass-Viol of his time. In 1663 he went to his Viol-maker in Bishopsgate Street, London: "his name is Wise, who is a pretty fellow at it." He paid three pounds for his instrument,—"besides the carving which I paid this day 10*s*. for to the carvers." The diarist also makes frequent mention of ladies playing the Gamba. On February 19, 1663/4, Mrs. Jaggard played ". . . but so well as I did not think any woman in England could and but few Maisters." The Bass-Viol was also used in the Chapel Royal, and at the concerts of Thomas Britton, the musical coalman, the Gamba was extensively used.

Although it is not intended to make of this work one of biography, it is necessary to mention two men who played a very important part in the later history of the Bass-Viol. Each was representative of a certain class of composer and performer : the one appealing to the serious musician, and the other—though himself a great musician—to the more popular taste : one of them Christopher Simpson, and the other John Jenkins. The former by his sound musicianship and amazing technique said what was probably the last word in the development of viol-music. He published a good deal of educational music, the chief being his *Compendium* (1665, 1667, and seven later editions, the last appearing near the end of the Eighteenth Century), and his *Division-Violist* (first edition, 1659), a purely technical work on the Viol and its handling in Divisions. Jenkins was typical of the " old-fashioned school," and though not so profoundly learned as Simpson, secured the affectionate regard of all his contemporaries by his geniality, originality, and charm.

The Bass-Viol, the last of a great and noble race, died none too easily. Thomas Mace, in the last quarter of the Seventeenth Century, did his utmost to defend the older instrument against the " scolding violins," but it was too late. A few good players still remained, and a post was open for a violist in the Chapel Royal until the middle of the Eighteenth Century ; but the glory had departed, and the place of the Gamba was taken by the bass of the violin family.

VIOL DE GAMBOYS. *v.* VIOLS.

VIOLET, VIOLLETT : Undoubtedly derived from the Italian *Violetta,* a Small Viol. Although the meaning of the term is quite clear, it is not always easy to know exactly what instrument is referred to when the word was used in the Seventeenth Century. In its earliest uses this diminutive of *Viola* was certainly applied to a high-pitched treble-viol ; later it named the small French violins, possibly also the Kits. It is to be found occasionally as a designation for the Viola d'Amore, but this last-named instrument was far too little used here to require special treatment at this place. Why he should have done so is not clear, but Leopold Mozart referred to the Viole d'Amour as the English Violet.

VIRGINAL: A keyboard instrument in a rectangular case, popular, roughly speaking, from about 1500 to 1700. The defects in the methods of tone-production in the Clavichord (*q.v.*) caused a different system of string-vibration to be developed; and undoubtedly taking the plectrum-plucked Psaltery as a model, the experimenters of the early Fifteenth Century replaced the tangents of the Clavichord with small quill points so mounted that they twanged the strings that were stretched above them. These quills were inserted into strips of wood known as Jacks, which in their turn stood perpendicularly at the end of the balanced keys. On the latter being depressed, the Jack was raised carrying the quill with it, until the plectrum was forced past the string, which was thus set in vibration. In the descent of the Jack a small hinged and sprung portion at its head turned aside to allow the quill to return without again twanging the string; and a piece of cloth at the top of the Jack damped the tone as soon as the key reached its position of rest. This method of producing vibration in the keyboard-instrument family was employed in several of its members which differed from the Virginal chiefly in size, shape, and efficiency. Crow-quills were the commonest plectra used, though strips of hard leather, whalebone, or metal were used at different periods. The compass of the Virginal also varied at different times, and one or two typical specimens will be referred to later. In the Seventeenth Century a second, smaller, Virginal was added to the larger one, and placed on the top of the case, as was sometimes done in the case of the Clavichord. This auxiliary instrument was tuned an octave higher than the other and was used together with it, thus most probably explaining the expression "a pair of Virginals." Later the added octave strings were placed in the case under the ordinary strings. These latter, again profiting by the development of the Clavichord, were often bichord or trichord. In the Harpsichord, of course, the octave strings were a permanent feature. One specimen of double Virginal known to the writer had a compass of four octaves on each of the two keyboards, ranging from the second C below middle C to the second octave above. The auxiliary keyboard, which was detachable, operated strings tuned an octave higher.

It would be interesting, from an antiquarian point of view, if it could be definitely proved that the inscriptions on the walls of the Leckingfield (Yorkshire) Manor-house dated from the reign of Henry VII. If this were decided—though there is no good reason for doubting it even now—then we possess in England the first reference to the Virginal. The verse in question reads :

> A slac strynge in a Virginall soundithe not aright,
> It doth abide no wrestinge it is so loose and light ;
> The sound-borde crasede, forsith the instrumente,
> Throw misgovernance, to make notes which was not his intent.

Henry VIII himself played on the Virginal, besides employing professional performers. *Egerton MS.* 2604 (British Museum) records payment to "a Virginal player" (*c.* 1525), the musician probably being John Heywood, or Haywood, who appears in the State Papers for 1520, first as a singer, and later as virginalist. He was still active under Mary Tudor when he, Antony Chaunter, and Robert Bowman are entered together as "Players on the Virginals" with a salary of £92 11*s.* 8*d.*, presumably between them. In the book containing Henry the Eighth's Privy Purse Expenses (N. H. Nicholas, 1827) is the entry for April, 1530 : "Item the vj daye paied to William Lewes for ii payer of Virginalls in one coffer with iiii stoppes, brought to Grenewiche iii*li.* And for ij Virginalls in one coffer brought to the More iii*li.* And for a little payer of Virginalls brought to the More xx*s.*" There can be no doubt that the word Virginal had by now become very loosely applied to other instruments with keyboards. The fact that these entries refer to "pairs" of Virginals need not, as we have seen, prove that anything but Virginals were meant ; but the "iiij stoppes" are more difficult to explain away. We can only suppose that some such device as was used in the later Harpsichords was employed in these instruments. A warrant in the Lord Chamberlain's Records of April 10, 1558, is very interesting reading, for it deals with the handing over of "as much grene velvett as will suffice for the covering of one pair of Virginals and as much grene satten as shall serve to lyne the same, with passamayne lace of silver for the garnishing and edginge of the same. And that ye paie unto the said John Grene as well for two cases of tymber covered with lether and lyned, th' one being for the aforesaid Virgynalls."

During the reign of Elizabeth the Virginal probably enjoyed its greatest vogue in England. The Queen herself—and, indeed, every lady of education—played on the instrument, and several contemporary pieces of evidence point to the fact that excellence in performance was keenly sought after. Elizabeth, in an interview with Sir James Melville, the envoy from Scotland in 1564, was anxious to know if Mary Stuart " or sche, played best. In that I gaif hir the prayse." But the Scot's private opinion was that Elizabeth played passably for a queen, but that she performed only when she " was solitary to shun melancholy." The Virginal supposed to have been Queen Elizabeth's was an Italian instrument of about 1570. It contained fifty Jacks and quills, and had a range of four octaves and a semitone, from B to C. When in use at its own period, this Virginal had the lowest string tuned down to G (a common procedure in those days). The instrument is now in the Victoria and Albert Museum. In the case of a German Virginal of *c.* 1600 (also in the same collection) the compass was three octaves and a tone (from G to A), the highest G-sharp being omitted—another common practice.

The State Papers of Elizabeth's reign contain many interesting references showing that the instrument was a regular feature in the official music-making. The Lord Chamberlain's accounts for Michaelmas, 1582, for example, authorise a warrant for giving crimson velvet for covering and lining the queen's keyboard instruments, and orders payment for covering four pairs of Regals and Virginals with velvet and embellishing them with silver and gold lacquer. In 1593 entries of a like nature are to be found. In that year a list " of all in the offices in England with their fees " is given, and includes " Players on the virginalles 3, fee to every of them, £50." In 1595/6 the payment is ordered for " fourteen yards of carnation velvet and eight yards of wrought velvet black and ash colour, employed and spent in covering of our Virginals, and for twelve yards of grene velvet to cover a greate instrument, all being garnished with lace of gold and silver and silke riben and sewing silke to them " (Lord Chamberlain's Records, *Vol.* 797).

At the turn of the century the Virginal was a frequent piece of furniture in the barber's establishment, and "barber's virginal" was synonymous with whatever was common property, a distinction which it shared with the Cittern (*q.v.*).

If the word Virginal was loosely applied during the reign of Henry VIII, it was still more so during those of the Stuart kings. It is, I think, beyond doubt that many of the instruments alluded to in this era were Spinets or Harpsichords, though England seemed to cling affectionately to the older names. At the same time there were such instruments as true Virginals still in use, side by side with the Harpsichord; for as late as the reign of Charles II (1663) we find the two instruments named together in an entry in the Lord Chamberlain's Records. In 1664 Captain Cooke, Master of the Children of the Chapel Royal, received £78 "for teaching of the children of the Chappell . . . and for strings for violins, lutes, and virginals. . . ." In 1665/6 Giles Tomkins was engaged as "musician in ordinary to his Majesty for the Virginalls in the place of Richard Deering, deceased." Another familiar name appears in the entry for January 7, 1667/8, when Christopher Preston was appointed musician for the Virginal "and private musique without fee in the place of Dr. Christopher Gibbons, to come in ordinary with fee after the decease of the said Dr. Gibbons. . . ." The latter celebrated musician received £46 per annum as virginalist, and made Preston wait until 1676 for his post. John Blow was appointed as a performer on the Virginal in 1668/9, while Henry Purcell was given the post of keeper of the king's instruments in 1683/4—his charges including Virginals. It will be seen that some of the most famous names in Seventeenth-century English music are to be found connected with this instrument. Before leaving the official records we must note that in 1696/7 (William and Mary) Dr. John Blow is mentioned again as a virginalist, and in 1699 as one of the "tuners of the regalls, organs, virginalls, etc."

In the Seventeenth Century the Virginal no doubt occupied the position, in the domestic life of England, of the pianoforte of to-day. At the same time it must not be forgotten that it could be far more easily dispensed with in those days than could the pianoforte at the present day. The practice of accompanying the voice with the lute had not yet died out, and the popularity of the viols was still great. Towards the end of the century, when lutes and viols had gone the way of the "good old times," the instruments of the violin family were employed in other directions, leaving the keyboard instruments as the means of accompaniment. At the period of the Great Fire of London there must have been a Virginal or similar instrument in almost every house. Pepys, describing the conflagration in his *Diary*, writes under date September 2, 1666: "... River full of lighters and boats taking in goods.... and only I observed that hardly one lighter or boat in three that had the goods of a house in, but there was a pair of virginalls in it" (*see also* SPINET, HARPSICHORD, JACK, *and* WREST).

VOLTE : An ancient dance-form that originated as a variety of the Galliard (*q.v.*) and became very popular in England. So great a favourite did this dance become in the days of Elizabeth that the Queen herself fell a victim to its attractions and danced it frequently. Mary Stuart was also a lover of the form, but, although she showed surprising agility in its performance, she "did not dance so high as her royal cousin of England" (Melville). The "height" of her dancing referred to the fact that in this successor of the Galliard the cavalier turned his partner (whence the name) and assisted her to leap high in the air; and the excellence of the dancer was gauged by the height of the leap. Such wild springing, of course, made of the Volte a butt for the censure of moralists, and a vigorous campaign was waged against it both in Germany and France. Sermons were preached and pamphlets written condemning the form, and the Volte did not survive very long on the Continent. Whether its early abandonment there was caused by the outcry of the puritans or by the too exacting nature of its steps, cannot be determined with certainty. The feature which caused the condemnation of the Volte on the Continent remained one of its chief characteristics in the merry England of the last of the Tudors. Shakespeare speaks of it in *Henry V* (III, 5).

> They bid us to the English dancing schools,
> And teach lavoltas high and swift corantos.

Robert Greene's play, *The Honorable History of Friar Bacon and Friar Bungay* (first acted in 1591), contains the lines:

> Like Thetis shalt thou wanton on the waves,
> And draw the dolphins to thy lovely eyes,
> To dance lavoltas in the purple streams.

Ben Jonson has it that "Ixion is turned dancer and leads lavaltoes"—a line which shows that the dance lived up to its name (*i.e.* turning dance). These quotations, too, show the different forms that the name had in England; its curious appearance being accounted for by the fact that the French definite article was retained as part of the name.

The popularity of the Volte continued in England until Stuart times, for we are told that James I and his queen were excellent in these "feats of capering." But although the dance may have survived later, there is not much music for it to be found in the works of the later Stuart writers. The examples which have made us familiar with this form in England are nearly all to be found in the Elizabethan books, and after the middle of James the First's reign the Volte was of rare occurrence in native music. The Fitzwilliam Virginal Book contains it (William Byrd); the works of Thomas Morley also include the "lavolto"; and seven specimens may be seen in Robert Dowland's *Varietie of Lute Lessons* (1610). Remembering the frequent use made of the word by the writers of the period, the comparative paucity of Voltes in the musical publications may occasion some surprise. But it may be that the dance did not absolutely need special music, and that it could be executed to Galliard-music of sufficient spirit, just as the Canary could have been danced to Jig-tunes.

Arbeau (*Orchésographie,* 1588) would be the best authority on the Volte in its original form, and he states that its measure and rhythm were identical with those of the Galliard, and that it was very much favoured by the Provençals. Mersenne's *Harmonie Universelle,* 1636, contains specimens of the dance as it was written in France, and Besard's *Thesaurus Harmonicus,* published in Cologne (1603), give no fewer than thirty-four examples. In Germany it was mentioned by Praetorius in 1612, and Fuhrmann's *Testudo Gallo-Germanica* (1615) has eleven Voltes.

It will be seen that even the German publications containing the form were influenced by French fashions, and there can be no doubt that the dance came to England also direct from France.

WAIT, WAYTE, or WAYGHTE: An instrument dating from the Middle Ages and used by the watchmen who waited at the gates of castles and cities. It no doubt derived its name from that of the watchman himself (*v.* WAITS) and it is mentioned very early in the State Papers. The Wait was a Shalm (*q.v.*): either that instrument itself or some slight variation in pitch, size, or (and) tone-quality. The term was used quite late, and even in the Chapel Royal a place was found for the instrument it designated; the Cheque-Book of that institution describing Dr. John Wilson as a "Musician for the Waytes" in 1641. Rimbault is in error when he says that the name was never used in the singular number. It is so used, for in *Egerton MS.* 2604 (British Museum) "a waite" is mentioned, as also in a Statute of the Thirteenth Century. The players upon this primitive oboe were often called Waitmen.

WAITS: Originally the watchmen who kept the gates of a city or castle, and who announced the hour of the night on a pipe of the Shalm type. The name is to be derived from the same source as "Watch" (Middle English, *Waitan;* Anglo-Saxon, *Wacan; cf.* German, *Wacht*), and an early meaning applied to the verb "to wait" was "to watch." These night-watchmen date from very early times—certainly from the Thirteenth Century. During the reign of Edward IV (1461/83) there was "A Wayte that nightely from Mychelmas to Shreve Thorsdaye, pipe the watche within this Courte fowere tymes; in the somer nightes iii tymes, and makete Bon Gayte at every chamber, doore, and office. . . ."

Although in the Middle Ages only playing some sort of signal on their pipes, the Waits later on became more ambitious musically, and performed all the popular melodies of their own period. In the Fifteenth and still more so in the Sixteenth Century, they were looked upon as proficient and well-organised musicians, having become, in effect, municipal bandsmen. They drew their salaries from the towns' coffers, and assisted musically at all civic gatherings. They were never to be confounded with the itinerant begging musicians, and to prevent all risk of losing the respect that the dignity of their calling merited, the Waits were early formed into conservative guilds. Apprenticeship was common, and no one was admitted into their profession without acquitting himself well in very searching tests.

It will not be necessary to make long quotations from the

records dealing with the Waits and their duties. A few representative entries will be sufficient to show that they were an accepted feature in the social life of the cities. In the Privy Purse Expenses of Henry VIII are noted two payments to the "Waytes at Caunterbury" (1532) in reward for playing during the King's progress through the Cathedral city. When Edward VI passed through the City of London, on one occasion, the Waits were stationed at St. Peter's Church in Cheapside (where now the plane-tree flourishes). At about the same period there are references to the Waits doing duty for the Mayor and Sheriffs. In the reign of Elizabeth there is an entry respecting the retirement of one Jeffrey Foster, a City Wait, and the relinquishment of his chain of office. When the Queen traversed Cheapside in 1558 she was greeted by "the Waytes of the Citie which did give a pleasant noyse with their instruments as the Queen's Majesty did pass by" (and in reference to this use of the word Noise, see the article NOISE OF MUSIC). It must be clear from these documents (relating to the activities of the Court of Common Council) that the Waits enjoyed a certain status of which they were very proud. One entry in particular shows that they were actually employed as are many military bands to-day: "1642. Ordered that the City Waits shall cease to play at the Royal Exchange on the Sundays as heretofore hath been accustomed, but shall perform the said service every holiday hereafter at and for the time accustomed"—the civil disorders of that year probably causing the curtailment. As late as 1802 the City Waits numbered eight.

There are likewise many indications that the Waits assisted in Church services and processions, as choristers as well as in the capacity of instrumentalists. The *Diary* of the London citizen Machyn (printed by the Camden Society) contains many references to such employment. For example, when speaking of the Parish Clerks' procession on May 27, 1555, he says: ". . . ther was a goodly Masse be hard, . . . and the whettes playing round Chepe and so to Ledynhall"; and already in 1554, "the 25th day of Juin anodur Masse kept at the Grey-frers for the sextons of London and after precessyons with the whetes plahyng, and clarkes syngyng thrug Chepe-syd. . . ."

Naturally, the Waits of the City of London were kept in

such state as was in keeping with the dignity and magnificence of the first city in the kingdom. They were richly liveried and their "Chains of Office" were wrought of silver. So highly esteemed were the Waits at the end of Elizabeth's reign that Thomas Morley, dedicating his *Consort Lessons* to the Lord Mayor, says: ". . . as the ancient custom hath been to retain excellent and expert musicians to adorn your Honour's famous feasts and solemn meetings, to these your Lordship's Waits I recommend the same to your servants' careful and skilful handling." It is highly probable, however, that by the Sixteenth Century the Waits had entirely ceased to be what they originally were—*i.e.* night-watchmen who piped the hour —and had become, as was the custom all over the continent of Europe, the town band. What applies to the Waits of London can be repeated, *mutatis mutandis*, in the case of other towns and cities. The period during which the Waits really flourished was from the beginning of the Sixteenth to the end of the Seventeenth Century. In some towns they lingered on in reduced numbers and limited use, until the police took their place as watchmen, and military bands fulfilled their musical function.

At the time during which the Waits performed as organised bodies of musicians they were part of the life of the city, and the allusions in contemporary literature to their music show how great a part they played in the entertainment of our ancestors. Whetstone's translated play of *Promos and Cassandra* (used by Shakespeare in *Measure for Measure*) mentions them in 1578: "Erect a stage that the Waits in sight may stand." From a play of James Shirley it appears that the Waits could be hired for private merrymakings: ". . . keep our Wedding at my own house at Croydon. We will have the City Waits down with us" (*v. also* WAIT).

WHIFFLER: The player on a kind of pipe (Whiffle), who led the way in a procession as an usher. The instrument probably received its name from the puff of wind, or whiff, required to produce its music, and the pipe named its player. The fact that the Whiffler led a procession soon extended the meaning of the term, and it became applied to any herald who preceded a notability, whether he actually played on the Whiffle or not. Shakespeare uses the word in the Chorus to *Act* V of *Henry V* in a metaphorical sense : ". . . the deep-mouthed sea, Which like a mighty whiffler 'fore the king, Seems to prepare his way." In one of Bishop Hales's sermons we meet with it again when he says : " . . . if there do but an earthly prince come over, what pressing there is to see him ! So as there is need of ushers and whifflers, to stave off the multitude." In the *Diary* of Henry Machyn (Camden Society) we read of a procession in the City of London in which there were twenty-eight " wyfflers in velvet cotes and chaynes of gold with white staves in their hands." The Whiffler was an indispensable figure in that essentially English diversion, the Morris Dance (*q.v.*).

WHITTLE : A colloquial term for the Tabor-pipe (*q.v.*). Tabor and Pipe were often called " Whittle and Dub," but whence Whittle is to be derived is not clear. The only suggestion I can offer is that it was connected in the mind of the Sixteenth-century merrymaker with the small pipe known as the Whiffle (*v.* WHIFFLER).

WREST : To wrest, when used in connection with music, meant to tune the strings, particularly of the keyboard instruments ; the verb having been evolved from the mechanical action of the tuning-key on the pins or pegs which held the strings. The Middle English *Wresten*, from the Anglo-Saxon *Wraestan*, signified " to turn or twist forcibly," and this perfectly described the movement used in tuning. At the turn of the Fifteenth Century we read an interesting reference to the word :

> The Clavicorde hath a tunely kynde,
> As the wyre is wrested hye or lowe.
>
> . . . .
>
> Any instrument mystunyd shall hurt a trew song,
> Yet blame not the Clavycorde the wrester doth wrong.

Here we find the noun which was derived from the verb. Another reference of about the same era reads :

> Who pleythe on the harp he should play trew ;
> Who syngeth a song, let his voice be tunable ;
> Who wrestythe the clavychorde, mystuning eschew.

The satirical Skelton, in his *Colin Clout*, shows that the word was used in connection with the harp as well as the keyboard instruments :

> My penne now will I sharpe,
> And wrest up my harpe,
> With sharpe twynkyng trebelles.

Shakespeare has a figurative use for the word in *Troilus and Cressida* (III, 3):

> . . . but this Antenor,
> I know, is such a wrest in their affairs,
> That their negotiations all must slack,
> Wanting his manage. . . .

The employment of the word "slack" in a breath with "wrest" explains the force of the metaphor.

Although To Wrest and Wrester have given place to the more modern though not more happy, To Tune and Tuner, the word has not entirely fallen into disuse; it survives in the language of the present-day pianoforte manufacturer, who still speaks of the Wrest-plank and Wrest-pins.

www.ingramcontent.com/pod-product-compliance
Lightning Source LLC
LaVergne TN
LVHW010607100826
845148LV00014B/2881

* 9 7 8 1 6 3 3 9 1 5 4 4 2 *